PRAISE FOR *WHEN A FRIEND*

Everyone can relate to the pain of a fractured friendship. Dealing with the resulting hurt, confusion, and bitterness in a godly way (without too much obsessing) is a topic that is long overdue, and Elizabeth tackles it with grace, vulnerability, wisdom, and even humor. Through relatable narratives and biblical application, she helps us navigate what it looks like to follow Jesus' example and embrace God's expectations for our relationships.

JENN SCHULTZ, author of *She's Not Your Enemy*

Is friendship difficult for you? If so, Elizabeth Thompson is the friend you need to take you by the hand to guide you through navigating these vital, yet complicated relationships. In her book *When a Friendship Falls Apart*, Elizabeth vulnerably shares her own stories as well as biblical stories to help you know you aren't alone in your companionship struggle. This book is your go-to when a friendship falls apart to give you the practical steps needed to heal, forgive, and maybe even let go.

RACHAEL ADAMS, author of *A Little Goes a Long Way: 52 Days to a Significant Life* and host of the *Love Offering* podcast

Elizabeth Laing Thompson writes with the kind of gentle vulnerability, humble understanding, and deep wisdom that could only belong to a woman who's *been there*. She can relate, and she repeatedly points her reader to her Jesus, who can relate too. Unfortunately, none of us will escape broken friendships this side of heaven. Fortunately, we have books like this one. *When a Friendship Falls Apart* is a book every one of us needs on our shelf.

HANNAH C. HALL, bestselling author

Elizabeth is such a wise and talented communicator. She's both relatable and thought-provoking. I'm so grateful for her insight into the challenging seasons so many of us face in life!

STEPHANIE MAY WILSON, author and host of the *Girls Night* podcast

Phew! We've all been there, haven't we? Left with the shattered pieces of the brokenness we experience this side of eternity. Elizabeth's words matter deeply for any friend (that's all of us!) walking through a tough season. Her wisdom comes from a deep well of biblical truth—the only and necessary place for us to ground ourselves when attempting to walk through a friendship that falls apart. A MUST-read for the Christ follower seeking healing and forgiveness!

REBECCA GEORGE, author of *Do the Thing: Gospel-Centered Goals, Gumption, and Grace for the Go-Getter Girl* and host of the *Radical Radiance* podcast

Elizabeth has experienced all the feels about friendship and eloquently writes about the feelings you may not even know you have had, whether you've experienced a dramatic blowup or a slow fade in friendships. As I read this book, I felt better about my losses as I cried and laughed along with Elizabeth's personal stories and creative retellings of familiar Bible stories. Whatever your friendship situation is now, you'll find affirmation and guidance for moving forward from a caring author who truly understands.

SARAH GERINGER, Christian blogger, speaker, podcaster, creative coach, and author of six books, including *Transforming Your Thought Life: Christian Meditation in Focus*

Elizabeth Laing Thompson offers us a deep well of compassion and advice in these pages. *When a Friendship Falls Apart* is a must-read for anyone attempting to navigate the complicated path of friendship with grace and hope. Thompson offers wise counsel for our broken friendships as she answers our questions about how God would have us respond when a break occurs and reminds us that he doesn't expect us to do it all alone.

CARRIE STEPHENS, author of *Holy Guacamole* and *Jesus, Love, and Tacos*

when a friendship falls apart

when a
friendship
falls apart

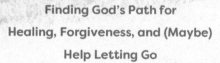

Finding God's Path for
Healing, Forgiveness, and (Maybe)
Help Letting Go

Elizabeth Laing Thompson

TYNDALE
MOMENTUM®

A Tyndale nonfiction imprint

Visit Tyndale online at tyndale.com.

Visit Tyndale Momentum online at tyndalemomentum.com.

Visit Elizabeth Laing Thompson online at lizzylife.com.

Tyndale, Tyndale's quill logo, *Tyndale Momentum*, and the Tyndale Momentum logo are registered trademarks of Tyndale House Ministries. Tyndale Momentum is a nonfiction imprint of Tyndale House Publishers, Carol Stream, Illinois.

When a Friendship Falls Apart: Finding God's Path for Healing, Forgiveness, and (Maybe) Help Letting Go

Designed by Ron Kaufmann

Edited by Deborah King

Published in association with The Bindery Agency, www.TheBinderyAgency.com.

Library of Congress Cataloging-in-Publication Data

A catalog record for this book is available from the Library of Congress.

ISBN 978-1-4964-6312-8

Printed in the United States of America

29	28	27	26	25	24	23
7	6	5	4	3	2	1

With endless gratitude to God, the most faithful friend

My God and I go in the fields together;
We walk and talk as good friends should and do.
"MY GOD AND I," BY AUSTRIS AUGUST WIHTOL

CONTENTS

AUTHOR'S NOTE

The personal stories in this book are drawn from some difficult moments in my life and in others' lives. A number of people entrusted me with their painful friendship memories and gave me permission to pass those stories on to you—I am humbled and honored by the gift of their honesty. I have changed names and identifying details in some of the stories I share (both my own experiences and others'), while doing my best to faithfully preserve the true spirit of the actual conversations and events. I pray our stories, even with all the mess and complexity and nuance and confusion they contain, will help you to feel seen and understood— less alone—as you seek healing in your own story.

FOUR BROKEN THINGS

Let's imagine we're sitting in a café, you and I. I've got my half-caff mocha; you've got your favorite drink too. We've been friends for a while, close enough that truth flows unedited.

You take a shaky breath and share about a broken friendship. A flood of feelings pours out: hurt, bewilderment, shock, disappointment, insecurity, anger, self-doubt, shame, betrayal, bitterness.

"There's this . . . hole," you say, teary-eyed and warbly voiced. "This place where she used to be." You clench a fist in front of your heart. "Sometimes I feel like—like I lost part of myself along with the friendship. And everywhere I go, everything I do, it's . . . haunted. Tainted."

I pass you a tissue, understanding. "Because you used to go to all those places together, do all those things together," I say, feeling your heaviness in my own chest. "And now, those places—and the memories you have there—feel . . . polluted. Like even the happy memories now have a shadow on them."

"Exactly." You trace a finger around the rim of your mug. "And . . . I mean, I'm telling you about this today, but the truth is, there's hardly anyone I can talk to about it. She knows my other friends, and I don't want to gossip or make her look bad or pressure people to take sides, and it's just so private and . . ."

"Complicated," I finish.

You take another sip. "I don't know how to process this. How to resolve it. Part of me is hurt, and furious—like, what's *wrong* with her, and how could she act like this? I don't get it!—but then . . . I question myself, and I know I made mistakes too, and I feel sick—stomach-churning sick—when I think about it, you know?"

"I do know. I know that feeling way better than I wish I did." Tears prick my eyes, but I don't swipe them away because you know I'm a sympathy crier, and you don't mind.

And you say, "What do you think? Can this friendship be saved? *Should* it be saved? And how do I even start working through all of this? I don't want to be stuck in this place, mourning this friendship—and missing this friend—forever."

I let out a long breath, thinking and praying. After a few moments I say, "I'm honored you value my opinion. I can't tell you what's best, but . . . I have an idea. You know how, when people asked Jesus for advice, he often told them parables, stories that helped them think for themselves and find truths about God?"

You nod, lifting your mug to your lips.

A sly smile pulls one side of my mouth. "Well, I know you'll be shocked to hear that I'm not Jesus—"

You snicker mid-sip, inhaling a little liquid into your lungs.

When you finish coughing, I say, "So as long as we're both clear that I'm not Jesus, in the spirit of his parables, can I tell you some stories—true stories from my own life, about four broken things—that might point you toward some answers?"

"Sure."

I begin.

THE MUG

The Wound That Keeps Haunting

I burrowed deep into my friend's armchair, cradling a mug of hot tea. Drawing the mug up close to my face, I blew on the steam; it curled away in graceful wisps.

The next few seconds boiled over in a wild blur:

An ominous *sh-crunch* sound.

Tea sloshing, then flying.

My skin zinging, then burning. Still burning.

I leaped to my feet with a screech, holding the mug's handle in one bleeding hand; balancing the half-empty, broken mug in the other; desperate not to spill the rest of the tea. My skin was still screaming.

I dropped the handle, and with my free hand, clawed at my soaked and scalding clothing.

"What—oh—oh, no, let me—here—give me the mug." My bewildered friend scrambled to help, trying to grasp what had just happened—one second I'd been curled into her chair, the next I was shrieking and jumping up, soaked in tea. She took the broken mug so I could use both hands to pull the hot clothes away from my skin.

When at last the tea cooled and the pain subsided, we shared a shaky laugh. My skin was red but not blistered; my thumb was cut, but the wound was not deep.

My loyal friend tossed the traitorous mug and its handle forcefully into her trash bin, as if to exact revenge. "I will never buy a mug from that pottery place again!" she vowed.

By the next morning, my skin was no longer flushed, and my thumb hardly needed a bandage. On the outside, you'd never know I'd been burned, but on the inside, something had changed. I shuffled, bleary-eyed, into the kitchen, set an empty mug on the counter, and poured myself a cup of coffee—coffee, blessed coffee, heaven's gift to weary souls—but as I stretched out a hand to pick up the mug, I hesitated. Hands tingling with the memory of pain, I found myself looking askance at the mug's handle. Studying it, assessing it for cracks and weaknesses. Then glancing back over my shoulder, hoping no one was watching.

I chuckled, tried to reason with my fear: *In all your long, happy years of coffee- and tea-drinking, you have never had one mug handle break. Not one broken handle out of hundreds. Maybe thousands. This was just a fluke, a onetime flaw in one dysfunctional mug.* But fear still prickled. At last, shaking my head, I picked up the mug, but not by the handle—I cradled the mug's warm, rounded body between two hands.

As I sipped, a little voice inside my head justified my fear: *I mean, you never can be too careful. You've been burned once; better not risk being burned again.*

I told myself it was just a temporary phase, my avoidance of mug handles. I'd get over it eventually. But every time I tried to lift a mug by its handle, my other hand swooped in to support the bottom of the mug, just in case. To keep me safe.

Weeks stretched into months, and I was still holding mugs—even familiar mugs I'd owned for years, mugs that had never, ever let me down—with two hands. The two-handed mug-hold was becoming a habit, a way of life.

I'd like to tell you that I had a Big Victorious Moment, a showdown where I stared down my fear of mug handles and won . . . but honestly, it just took time. More time than I thought it would. Time for the memory of pain to fade. Time for my self-protective instinct to settle down.

It's been years since the Mug Handle Incident, and I am happy to report that I no longer have trust issues with mugs. Today I almost always reach for mug handles one-handed, and I don't even go squinty-eyed. Most days I'd even say I grab mug handles with carefree abandon. It took a while, but I've put my fears behind me.

THE BOWL

The Sacred Worth Saving

The year before my grandmother died, I flew down to South Florida to visit her. Grandma and I knew these might be the last days we spent together, but we did our best to pretend otherwise. One sultry afternoon, with summer storm clouds pressing in, blanketing the house in the cozy darkness I always loved, Grandma crooked an arthritic finger at me, indicating I should follow her. Leaning on her walker, she shuffled into my grandfather's office and fumbled around in a drawer. With shaking hands, she pulled out a package and unwrapped a hand-painted, gold-tipped bowl. "Here," she said, her milky blue eyes bright as she flashed her trademark smile, "I want you to have this. It's very old, and I know you will treasure it the way it deserves."

"Grandma," I breathed, hugging it to my chest, then hugging her, "thank you. I will think of you every time I use it."

That bowl was Grandma's last gift to me on what was, indeed, our last visit this side of heaven.

Treasure it I did. I placed it on my desk in my kitchen so I could see it every day, use it every day, remember her every day.

Several years later, my seven-year-old was hunting for something on my desk. Suddenly I heard a crash and a wail. My stomach clenched; I could hardly bear to look, already knowing what I would see when I went to investigate. Sure enough, there lay Grandma's precious bowl, in pieces on my desk.

At first, I feared the bowl couldn't be salvaged. But I had to try. It was too special to give up on. Begging God to guide my fingers and go easy on my heart, I painstakingly began to glue that bowl back together, piece by piece. The process took prayer, skill, and several do-overs. After one failed attempt, I spent long, agonizing moments standing statue-still in my kitchen, barely breathing, pressing pieces together, praying the glue would still hold when it dried—and dry it did. Hold it did.

Today the bowl looks every bit as beautiful as it did the day Grandma gave it to me. If you didn't know it had once broken, you probably wouldn't be able to spot the cracks. But I know where the cracks are—where the weak points are—and so I treat that bowl even more carefully than I did before. I remember what happened when I didn't protect it the way it deserved.

The bowl is more precious to me than ever, because I've fought for it, prayed over it, and worked to preserve it. It feels like a gift I received twice: once from Grandma, and the second time from God.

THE HUMMINGBIRD

The Bittersweet Memory

March 12. The day I should have been in the hospital, giving birth to a baby. Instead, I sat in a garden, empty-armed and empty-wombed, and cried. My husband, not knowing what to say or how to help (there was nothing to say and no way to help), met me at the garden in the late afternoon and gave me a gift: a pink and green hummingbird figurine.

During my miscarriage all those months ago, I'd written a poem about my loss—*your tiny heart beating like hummingbird wings, though they never could find it, I never saw it*—and ever since, hummingbirds had come to represent our baby in our minds. The figurine was the perfect way to preserve the memory of the baby I still longed for and loved, to remember how his life had been cut short before he could fully take flight. To honor his would-have-been birthday.

I went home and placed the hummingbird on my nightstand where I would see it every day. We moved, and the hummingbird took up residence on a different shelf in our new house.

Several years later, around the same time as The Broken Bowl Incident That Shall Not Be Named, I heard another crash and wail—this time from my bedroom. I ran in to find my daughter in tears and my hummingbird in pieces.

The base was obliterated; the hummingbird lay helpless and tired, on its side. One wing was half gone; the bird's gorgeous beak was chipped at the end. I searched for pieces large enough to glue back on, but all the shards were miniscule. The damage was too great. This hummingbird would never—could never—regain its former shape.

After consoling my poor, clumsy, guilt-stricken child, I stood there beside the bathroom trash can, cradling the broken bird in my hand. *This figurine served its purpose,* a reasonable-sounding voice insisted in my head. *It helped you remember your baby for many years; now it's time to let it go.* For about five seconds, I thought I was going to do it—let it go and throw it away—but I couldn't. Instead, I placed what remained of the statuette on my dresser.

The hummingbird will never look the same, never regain its former shape and glory, but even so, my heart still gives a little bittersweet throb every time I see it. It's still beautiful to me, precious to me, broken wing and all.

SHELLS

The Beautiful Broken

My daughter and I were attempting to walk along the beach. We weren't making much progress because every few steps, she'd squeal and bend down to snatch up a shell or two or ten. "Oh, look at this one, Mommy!" Sawyer would gush, her little finger pointing out a streak of purple, a flash of iridescence, a jagged edge. Colorful though they were, every shell she loved was broken, some merely shards.

At first I tried to talk her out of her choices. "These are nice, but maybe you should slow down and only keep the undamaged ones. Wouldn't you rather collect shells like this one?" I showed her the single perfect shell I'd found—no chips, no cracks, a delicate pink ombre.

She shrugged. "Meh. I love *this* one!" She scooped up another broken shell and gazed at it rapturously.

Eventually I gave up trying to convert her to my perfect-shell-hunting ways. Sawyer carried on collecting—and of course she wanted me to admire every. Single. Shell. I did my best to see the beauty she saw, to come up with fresh adjectives and exclamations, though I confess my enthusiasm began to wane a bit after the forty-seventh shell. Meanwhile, I continued my own hunt, my hard-to-please eyes scanning the sand.

My hands stayed mostly empty while my daughter's quickly filled to overflowing; before long, she'd foisted fistfuls of shells on me, stuffing my pockets till they bulged.

At last I had to call it. "Okay, that's enough! I don't have any more room in my pockets. No more shells today."

"Okay," she agreed, then gasped. "But wait—one more!" She dropped to her knees, the collection of friendship necklaces around her neck swinging wildly; she scooped up another shell and handed it to me, delight sparking in her eyes. Before the handoff was even complete, her eyes drifted down; again she squeaked, bent, and scooped—two more, three more, four. "Okay, *these* are the last ones, Mommy." But already her besotted eyes were straying to the sand, filled with longing.

I placed a hand on her elbow and started steering her back to our towels. "C'mon, it's time to go."

Sawyer stumble-walked the whole way with her head tipped back, her gaze locked on the cloud-dotted sky. She moaned in frustration. "I can't look down, Mommy, or I know I'll see a thousand more pretty shells!"

"The struggle is real," I laughed, shaking my head.

Back home the next day, I rinsed and stored our finds; mine barely covered the bottom of a small jelly jar; Sawyer's filled an oversize mason jar, which promptly earned a prominent place on the bookshelf. Her collection was, indeed, beautiful: a kaleidoscope of wonder, every curious shape, all the sunset colors. And I couldn't help but think: *Maybe if I weren't so careful, so picky, I could see what my girl sees: perfect imperfection, beauty in broken, and endless possibilities—a world filled to bursting with treasures worth taking home.*

———

We sit in silence for a few minutes, you and I, a safe warmth between us even though our drinks have gone cold.

"I hope that helps in some way," I say. "I don't know which story fits yours, but maybe they can help as you think and pray through how to heal, and where to go from here."

You swirl the remains of your coffee around in your mug. I can see you pondering the four stories, the four broken things, trying to match up your own story to what I've shared.

"Will you pray through it with me?" you ask. "Will you ask God to make my path clear?"

"I will, and he will."

We smile.

Part 1

BEGINNING BROKEN

The Mug

1

WHEN A FRIENDSHIP FRACTURES

I told myself it was just a temporary phase,
my avoidance of mug handles.
I'd get over it eventually.
But every time I tried to lift a mug by its handle,
my other hand swooped in to support the bottom of the mug,
just in case.
To keep me safe.

My phone dings, and I pull it from my purse. The text from my friend is simple:

> I'm so glad God brought you into my life. I love how he planned for us to be friends.

I tuck my phone away and get back to work, but all day I hold her words close, a happy glow warming me inside, a joyful hum singing in my veins. Everywhere I look, life's colors seem richer, more exquisite. Everywhere I go, the world seems kinder, more welcoming. All because of friendship. All because I feel seen, known, and loved.

———

They say friends are the family we choose. And that choosing—the joy of loving and being loved by someone who isn't genetically obligated to share life with us—adds priceless worth to the relationship. Priceless worth—and great risk.

We meet, connection sparks, and suddenly we're thrown back to that fumbling middle school place: "I think you're cool; do you feel the same way about me? Want to be friends? Check yes or no." Over time, if we're brave enough, we pull back the curtain protecting our inmost hearts and invite this person inside—an act of terrifying vulnerability and trust.

We invite friends into our inner sanctum—and our home. They claim a favorite spot on our couch, rummage in our pantry for snacks, see us tearstained and sleep-deprived. We entrust one another with the secret heart places. Hold one another up in sacred moments of anguish, loss, joy. Along the way we may make lofty promises—*friends forever*.

But sometimes *forever* ends.

———

I haven't heard from her in forever. Forever and three days.

I check my phone again—nothing.

Dread crawls through my stomach, a twisting pain.

Insecurity haunts my thoughts, a cruel shadow: *How could this happen? Is our friendship really over?*

———

When a friendship falls apart, we experience a unique kind of loss. Other people may not take it seriously: "It's not like you were married or anything—you can always find another friend." Yeah, sure—lemme just put this book down and go pick a new friend off the friend tree. Like any time we want, we can just walk out the door and bump into another person who likes us, "gets" us, enjoys our quirks, and laughs at our jokes. Someone who is safe and understanding, someone we can trust with our unfiltered thoughts and deepest insecurities. Oh, and by the way, this someone has to be willing to make time for us in their life. And then (as if finding a person who fits all those qualifications weren't hard enough), *we* have to feel the same way about *them* . . . Yeah. Like I said. Easy-peasy.

HOW COULD THIS HAPPEN?

Even in the closest friendships, sometimes hurt happens. Misunderstanding. Distance. Disagreement. Even betrayal and deceit. Perhaps you have experienced this kind of anguish, this kind of brokenness, firsthand. Some friendships, like my grandmother's bowl, survive the fall, but others, like my friend's mug, stay fractured forever. The loss can be staggering, a blow not only to your happiness and way of life but also to your confidence and sense of identity. The pain may haunt you for years to come. Friendships fall apart in different ways, for many reasons:

Maybe you entered different seasons of life, and you no longer had much in common.

Maybe one Big, Awful Misunderstanding took a catastrophic turn—un-take-back-able words, dramatic door slams—and almost overnight the friendship was severed.

Maybe hurt feelings and unhealthy patterns snuck in over time, small fissures in your trust that eventually widened into a chasm that feels uncrossable.

Perhaps you grew—found God or made different lifestyle choices or overcame old weaknesses—while your friend stayed the same.

Perhaps she changed, going places you couldn't follow: into addiction or bitterness or ungodly choices.

Or maybe nothing happened at all—and that's the problem. You just . . . drifted. Stopped calling, stopped hanging out, stopped making time for each other. One day you looked up to find an ocean between you.

However brokenness entered your friendship, it's a wound. A loss. And the loss of a friendship is often accompanied by a host of unwanted companions: insecurity, anger, isolation, bitterness, guilt, regret. The closer the friendship, the greater the pain. And the greater the pain, the longer its memory may haunt you, change you, leave you reaching for mugs one-handed. It's a lonely loss, a private grief, like a divorce no one can see. No one's going to send cards or flowers. Hallmark doesn't make a Friendship Breakup sympathy card; churches don't offer Friendship Loss Support Groups. It's not something we can announce on social media, seeking emotional support or prayers; in fact, chances are, the broken friendship was intertwined with a larger group of friends, so it's tricky to talk about it anywhere, to anyone.

And when the relationship is between two faithful Christians, two people seeking to honor God in all they do, the pain is compounded, the fallout even more complicated. Godly friendships aren't "supposed" to fracture, but sometimes they do.

Friendships are precious to me—worth fighting for, praying about, and working through. But sometimes, in spite of my best (yet imperfect) efforts, I've had friendships falter and fail. Some have ended unexpectedly, the pain sudden and sharp, a gutting; others have faded with time, the pain low and throbbing, lingering for long years and then reigniting unexpectedly, ages after I thought I'd let the friendship go.

———

It's the day before my wedding. The past few days—make that weeks . . . actually, make that months—have been a blur. A blur of excitement and planning and details and cake-tasting and flower-scrutinizing and stress-compounding and decision-making and complex-family-feelings-navigating fatigue.

A friend from my small group at church, a girl I've been friends with for a couple of years now—we'll call her Sasha—is about to move away for a summer internship. Life has been happier with Sasha in it: she's kindhearted, quick with a laugh, reliable. I know people in her new city, and she's eager to connect with potential friends before she leaves; I've promised to help her for weeks now, and every week I have forgotten to follow up. But here at the eleventh hour—like, literally eleven hours before my wedding day—I remember, and I call her.

"Hey! It's me, your long-lost, scatterbrained, about-to-have-a-new-last-name friend!" I joke when she answers the phone. "I've got those phone numbers for you! Sorry it took me so long."

A weighty pause on the other end.

Then: "Just forget about it." Sasha's voice is flat.

"I've got my friends' numbers right here, it's no trouble," I say, confused.

"I don't want them anymore."

"You don't . . . ?"

Sasha sighs into the phone. She doesn't sound angry, just . . . resigned. "Elizabeth, I'm tired of this. You've been lost in your own little wedding world for weeks now, and I think you're really selfish, and I'm just done."

I stammer and flush, apologies spilling out in a guilty flood. "I'm so sorry. I know I've been distracted and overwhelmed with all the wedding plans, and I've hurt your feelings."

"You think?"

"I'm so sorry. So, so sorry. I wish I could come over and apologize in person and try to make things right, but, um, I have my wedding rehearsal starting in a few hours." I sort of laugh, hoping she'll soften to the *this-is-a-lot-all-at-once-and-please-cut-me-some-slack-I'm-so-overwhelmed* in my voice, but she lets the silence stretch way past awkwardness. At last I say, "I don't know how to make this right with you today, but I really want to. Can we please talk when I get back from my honeymoon?"

"I don't think so," she says. "I'll be gone by then anyway."

I fumble with more apologies, more pleas to set up a future conversation, but she hangs up. I sit staring at the phone, reeling, a hurricane of feelings swirling inside:

I totally blew it. This is all my fault. I tried so hard not to be a self-absorbed bride, but apparently I was.

But—this is so unfair! Can she really not show me a little grace for all I've been juggling the past few months—graduation and a new job and wedding planning?

And . . . maybe I was selfish, but how selfish is she, waiting to dump this on me on THE DAY BEFORE MY WEDDING? It's like she wants to ruin this weekend for me—that's so mean.

I fall to my knees in prayer, feeling all kinds of guilty, attacked, and blindsided. I'm no good at conflict—as in, if a person looks sideways at me, I can't eat or sleep until the perceived conflict is resolved—and this out-of-nowhere punch feels emotionally insurmountable on a day when my emotions are already running on hyperdrive. I feel myself spiraling down into a toxic swirl of regret and fear and anxiety, with a heaping side order of hurt and resentment.

God somehow takes all the upset and guilt and frustration I feel into his all-encompassing hands and helps me to set it aside and still enjoy my wedding weekend. I promise myself I'll call Sasha when I return from my honeymoon. I tell myself she will have had time to cool down by then, and I'll apologize and ask for grace and another chance in our friendship.

When Kevin and I float back into town on the wings of honeymoon bliss, I know it's time to reenter life in the real world. Time to try to go back to work—and most importantly, to make things right with Sasha. I beg God for help, and I call my friend.

No answer. No call back.

I call again.

Still no answer. Still no call back.

I call Sasha's boyfriend and beg him to help me get in touch with her. He says she doesn't want to talk to me.

I never hear from her—or see her—again.

———

Fast-forward a few years. I've moved away, started a new (extremely stressful) job, and life is a whirlwind of exhaustion, transition, and homesickness. Young marriage, new city, new big-city traffic, new coworkers, new church, new job . . . At every turn I feel the need to prove myself, win people over, overcome my youth and inexperience, but all I feel is failure. Watching eyes. Criticism and mistrust. I long for the comfort of a familiar place and people who know me—and like me.

Finally, after several months, Kevin and I drive back home for a visit. Thrilled at the prospect of familiar faces and comfortable relationships, I call a close friend—we'll call her Carrie. For several years she has been like a big sister to me, a constant and comforting presence, a rock. We've shared countless hours of laughter and tears and life.

"Hiiiiiii!" I squeal into her voice mail. "I'm coming into town for a couple of days. I know you're busy, but do you have an hour or so to meet up? I'd love to catch up and just see a friendly face! I want to hear all the things about your life!"

I don't hear back from her, but I know she tends to burn the candle at both ends, so I choose not to feel hurt, and I call again.

At last I reach Carrie, and she says she'll be busy for most of my visit, but she can hang out for an hour on my last afternoon in town. "I'll take what I can get," I say, though I feel a little squeeze of sadness around my heart.

At the appointed time, I pull into Carrie's driveway and find her sitting in her car with the engine already running. "Hop in!" she says. "Come run errands with me."

"Okay," I say, a bit confused.

We spend an hour running around town, doing her errands, attempting to squeeze in a catch-up conversation between stops, but she is distant, distracted. When our time together ends abruptly—she has somewhere else she needs to be—I drive home bewildered. Hurt.

I try to write that visit off as a fluke. *She's just overwhelmed and over-scheduled,* I tell myself. *We'll get together the next time I go home, and we'll catch up properly.*

But there is no next time. I call her every few months, trying to hang on to the friendship, but I rarely get calls back. I get the feeling she's withdrawing not just from me, but from some other friends too, cocooning herself in isolation. I wish she'd let me in, let me support her through whatever's going on, but I can't get through. After a couple of years, with a deep-in-my-bones sadness, I realize I have to let go. Our friendship was a blessing in its time, but it no longer has a heartbeat. You can't have a friendship if only one person wants to be friends. So I stop calling. It's been many years, but I still mourn the death of that friendship. I will never stop missing it.

———

These are two of my experiences with broken friendships, though I've had others. In speaking to many women about this topic, I've been repeatedly struck by a painful truth: we all face broken friendships. Sometimes a swift break, other times a slow drift. Sometimes our fault, sometimes not, sometimes a little of both. But always painful. Always confusing. Always dosing us with a complex concoction of pain, regret, anger, shame, frustration, insecurity, and confusion. As we struggle to digest the loss, we wonder: *How could this happen? And what do I do now?*

If you find yourself in the midst of a friendship that's falling apart or you're still struggling with past hurts and regrets, first, I am so sorry—my heart aches with yours. This book is for you, and I pray it's a comfort and help. In the pages to come, we'll explore questions like these:

How can Christians navigate a broken friendship in a way that honors God and allows our own hearts to heal?

When and how do we seek reconciliation, and when and how do we let a friendship go?

How do we guard against the poison of bitterness?

Perhaps scariest of all, how do we open up again and entrust our wounded hearts to new friendships?

WE'RE NOT THE FIRST, LAST, OR ONLY ONES

If I were to give the Bible a not-exactly-serious subtitle, it might be

The Holy Bible:
*A book about God's love for you, the astounding
life of his Son . . . and also how to get along with
(and sometimes just survive) other humans.*

I'm being facetious here, because of course Scripture is a profound and powerful book; we can forever plumb its wondrous depths and never reach bottom. But have you ever noticed how many Bible stories depict people in conflict with one another? And how much time God spends trying to help us get along? Helping us not do things like take advantage of each other, lie to each other, corrupt each other, speak rudely to each other, steal from each other, murder each other . . .

The number of people in Scripture who faced relationship crises is shocking-slash-oddly-comforting: Hannah, Sarah, Rachel, David, Mary, Martha, Paul, Barnabas, and many others. You and I are not the first, last, or only ones to struggle in friendship.

In Acts 15 we read about Paul and Barnabas, two leaders in the early church who disagreed so sharply that they ended a years-long ministry partnership. News of the split must have sent shock waves through the church. What heartache their story holds.

King David frequently lamented the loss of friendships in the psalms with words like these:

> My heart is in anguish within me. . . .
> If an enemy were insulting me,
>   I could endure it;
> if a foe were rising against me,
>   I could hide.
> But it is you, a man like myself,
>   my companion, my close friend,
> with whom I once enjoyed sweet fellowship
>   at the house of God,
> as we walked about
>   among the worshipers.
> PSALM 55:4, 12-14

Even Jesus, who loved perfectly, experienced broken friendships. On the night of his arrest, in his greatest moment of need, his friends fell asleep while Jesus wept alone; hours later, he was betrayed by one of his most intimate companions. "Do what you came for, friend," Jesus said to Judas, his betrayer—can't you hear the mingled love and hurt in those words? Almost before he'd finished speaking, the rest of his friends deserted him and fled (see Matthew 26:47-56).

Our compassionate Father knew our relationships would sometimes flounder, and in his grace, God went out of his way to include multiple examples in Scripture of believers whose friendships faltered and failed. Throughout this book, you'll find vignettes depicting relationships in Scripture, giving you a sense of how similar our Bible heroes' struggles were to ours. Some of these stories may sadden you; others will bring comfort; all will remind you that you're not alone.

OUR REALITY VS. GOD'S "IDEALITY"

Time and again, Scripture counsels us to be unified with our brothers and sisters in Christ: one in mind and heart, close like the Father and Son, connected by the bond of the Spirit. Jesus pleaded with God on our behalf: "I pray also for those who will believe in me through their message, that all of them may be one, Father, just as you are in me and I am in you" (John 17:20-21). And he called us to exemplify his love to the world through our relationships: "As I have loved you, so you must love one another. By this everyone will know that you are my disciples, if you love one another" (John 13:34-35).

Our relationships are God's testimony to the world, bright lights in dark places. We are called to be examples of forgiveness and reconciliation. And we try hard to be all those things.

But our reality doesn't always line up with God's "ideality." Friendship fractures can be especially painful—and complex—in a faith setting. We offer our hearts in especially vulnerable ways in Christian relationships, sharing weaknesses and struggles, doubts and fears; our daily lives may be frequently interwoven through church fellowship connections. So when we can't work things out with a Christian friend, we may experience an additional cascade of emotions: guilt, shame, doubt, isolation. To add to the convolution, we may even suffer division, misrepresentation, or misunderstanding in our mutual relationships with other believers.

If you've picked up this book, your heart has been wounded. You may be mourning, confused, and lonely. You need a friend to guide you through this time—perhaps you would normally turn to the very friend with whom you've had a falling-out—so now you find yourself with a paper substitute: this book. How I wish we could sit together over coffee (I have a cistern of coffee sitting here beside me as I type). I wish we could work our way through a box of tissues together, because as you learned in the prologue, I am an incurable sympathy crier. But since we can't do that, please know that I pray for you every time I sit down with these words.

Maybe you're struggling to figure out what reconciliation could look like. You don't want to get your hopes up, but hope is stubborn, and a girl can dream . . . But you wonder how to make those steps, have those talks, glue jagged fragments back together. We're going to dig into Scripture for ideas and instruction.

Maybe you're wrestling with bitterness. Even thinking about the person sends acid worming through your veins. You know the damage bitterness is doing to your heart, and you want help overcoming it. But it's like fighting the ancient beast, a hydra: every time you cut off one bitter thought, two grow in its place. We're going to tackle that multi-headed monster together. God knew how challenging forgiveness is for us, so he gave us a lot of guidance in his Word. We're going to hang out in those Scriptures together.

Maybe you're plagued by insecurity and regret, and you can't find a way forward. You long to put yourself back out there, but fear and self-doubt have coiled themselves around your legs till you can't take a single step. Every time you reach for the mug of a new friendship, a jolt of fear makes you pull back your hand. We're going to do our best to untangle those bindings, to ease the memory of past pain, and set you free to open your heart back up again. (I know how scary that sounds. I promise, we'll take it one baby step at a time. You don't have to do anything you're not ready for.)

BUT GOD

Knowing that even the most righteous of people can let one another down, God has provided encouragement and tools to help us. How blessed we are to live under the care of a Father who knows us far better than we know ourselves. He anticipates our failings and loves us anyway. He is merciful and compassionate past the stretch of time and space, beyond the scope of words. He, too, has experienced the intimate pain of hurt, betrayal, and rejection. Yes, he has an ideal plan for our relationships—never betray, never hurt or be hurt, never suffer loss or loneliness or isolation—*but*. But God knows that life happens, sin happens, and splits happen—and he has already prepared comfort and counsel to see us through the less-than-ideal.

In these pages, we'll seek guidance from God for our struggling friendships—the faltering, the fractured, and the failed. In *his* pages we'll seek counsel for handling complex dynamics with integrity and wisdom. Where possible, we'll seek reconciliation and restoration; and where those things cannot be found, we'll seek resolution, the resolution that comes from a clean conscience and the healing and peace only God can give, the "peace . . . which passes all understanding" (Philippians 4:7, RSV).

As we dive into some difficult topics in this book, let us draw near to the one who is aware of our pain, concerned for our hearts, and always available to comfort and guide. Let's seek his wisdom, embrace his ways, and rest safe in his care. Let's take our hurting hearts to the Friend who is never too busy, never insensitive, and never selfish; the Friend who hears our hearts' cries, knows our deepest needs, and meets them perfectly—now that's a friendship we can rely on.

THOUGHT QUESTIONS

At the end of each chapter, you'll find a few questions to help you apply what you have read to your own life. I'm a fan of actually putting pen to paper.[1] Seriously, though, I've found that the physical act of writing down my thoughts allows my heart and head to connect more meaningfully and memorably with the words. However you choose to answer these questions—in your mind, in your prayers, or on paper—I pray they help you to take this book's message off the pages and into your heart and daily life.

1. Take a moment to ponder, or write down, how you are feeling right now about your friendship issue. What hurts the most? What confuses you the most? What do you most regret?

---

1. You may be shocked (and by "shocked" I mean "not surprised at all") that I, being a writer, am heavily biased in favor of pens; may I recommend a nice colored gel pen?

2. How do you hope this book will help you? For example, do you most need encouragement? Help overcoming feelings of guilt and shame? Help conquering bitterness? Practical, biblical guidance for attempting reconciliation?
3. When you picture yourself in a place of resolution with your issue, with your heart beginning to heal, what do you envision? How do you hope you will feel?

2

TRIAGE

On the outside, you'd never know I'd been burned,
but on the inside, something had changed.

This is all my fault. I'm a horrible friend. I'm always so selfish, all about me, me, me.

Pace around the room, squeezing the phone in a death grip.

She should have spoken up. I would have changed if she'd given me the chance! And . . . how could she shut me out and refuse to forgive me? That's so un-Christlike.

Stare out the window, unseeing.

I really care about Sasha—is our friendship really over, just like that?

A flood of beloved Sasha-memories, suddenly tainted, momentarily drowns my thoughts.

Memories. I'm supposed to be making good memories today! Doesn't she know she's ruining my wedding weekend? I'm supposed to be happy today! And there I go, being selfish again.

I feel a twist of guilt, laced with self-loathing.

I wonder if she's talked to all the other girls in our small group about this.

And now a shock of terror, bordering on nausea.

I wonder if they're all feeling the same way about me. Have I ruined any other friendships without realizing it?

A swarm of flutters fills my stomach as I remember I am about to see several of those friends at my wedding rehearsal in a few hours.

And there I go again. Thinking about myself and my wedding instead of my friend.

Consider tossing my phone out the window. (Not really, but sort of.)

Welcome to my thoughts following my breakup conversation with Sasha the day before my wedding. A merry-go-round of misery in which I cycled rapidly from grief to self-blame to shame to finger-pointing to guilt to resentment to fear to insecurity to paranoia and back again. The break felt especially hurtful and bewildering because I hadn't seen it coming—perhaps you know the feeling.

Losing a friendship is an invisible heart-wound, a quiet bleed. Left untreated, it can be a silent killer. After some time in prayer that afternoon, I managed to put my feelings about the conflict on hold during my wedding, but the emotional fallout—sorrow, shame, regret—sat waiting to greet me in my new apartment like an unwanted houseguest when I returned from my honeymoon. And the fallout touched every area of my life: church, work, marriage, self-esteem.

When a friendship falls apart, we grapple with a cascade of repercussions and side effects: You may find yourself falling behind at work when you can't still your whirling thoughts. You may find yourself feeling wary in other friendships, wondering if they, too, carry invisible fissures. You may feel insecure and isolated at school, at work, at church—everywhere your broken friendship has touched. You may feel inexplicably worn down as the loss takes a physical toll.

This chapter is all about helping you in that moment when your friendship break is still a fresh wound, the gash in your heart open and bleeding. Your pain is acute; your wound needs immediate care. When you check into the emergency room with an injury, the first steps are to identify the wound, stop the bleeding, and get your pain under control. Once the initial crisis has passed, you can map out a plan for long-term treatment and recovery. Let's take some similar steps in addressing our friendship wounds.

IDENTIFY THE INJURY

When my friendships with Sasha and Carrie fell apart, I wish I'd known then what I know now: that a powerful first step toward healing is defining what went wrong—diagnosing the nature of the injury. Because different wounds require different treatment. You don't put a cast on a burn or rub chicken noodle soup on a broken arm.

Even if we never share our insights with anyone but God, clarifying the causes of our friendship breakup in our own minds helps us to mentally and emotionally categorize what we're dealing with. It helps us to figure out what (if anything) we need to change, what (if anything) our friend might need to change, and what we need to surrender to God. It helps us to point our emotions in the right general direction. (For example, am I feeling guilty even though the break wasn't my fault? Or am I feeling defensive instead of owning up to my mistakes?)

Diagnosing the reasons your friendship faltered won't fix the problem, but it can set wild thoughts at rest. Without clarity, the questions and what-ifs and *why'd-she-say-thats* hound us, stealing our sleep, our peace, and our ability to be present with other people. Eventually, diagnosing what went wrong may help you begin to pray and think through possible paths to making peace with your loss—maybe even making peace with your friend.

Let's drop in on a moment when two women in Scripture had a conflict and Jesus helped to diagnose its cause. Our first vignette tells the story of two sisters, Martha and Mary.

MARTHA AND MARY
Based on Luke 10:38-42 and Matthew 13:1-23

"Put that platter there. No, not that platter—the other one. Not there—*there*." Martha fights to keep the irritation out of her voice, a losing battle. "Ah, careful, you're about to—here, just give it to me." Martha rescues the platter from the confused servant girl's hands and carefully sets it on the table. The girl scurries away, tripping over her own feet.

With a sigh, Martha's eyes scan the food, mentally calculating. *It's not enough.* She releases a laugh-sigh. *Jesus always brings a bigger crowd than you expect.*

From the next room she hears the soothing baritone of Jesus' voice and a few muffled *amens* from his listeners. Her ears strain to hear—"farmer . . . some seed fell along the path . . ."

Oh, he is telling a story! Martha's feet move toward the doorway of their own accord. She leans against the doorframe.

"Birds came and ate the seed before it could take root."

Martha's eyes drift over the crowded room: Jesus seated on the cushion she'd chosen for him, the softest and best one in the house; his disciples seated in a ring around him; curious stragglers squeezed onto every couch and chair; and . . . Mary. Martha's sister, Mary, is hovering, just like Martha, in a doorframe across the room. Mary's eyes are rapt; Martha can almost see Mary's eager ears drinking in the Lord's words.

"Miss." A whisper at her elbow makes Martha gasp.

Sarah, the cook, stands wringing her hands. "Anna scorched the lentils."

Martha steps away from the doorframe. "Make up another platter of figs and cheese; we'll keep everyone snacking until another pot is ready."

Sarah bustles off, and Martha steps back into the doorframe.

Jesus keeps telling his story. "Other seed fell among thorns, which grew up and choked the plants."

A tap on her shoulder makes Martha jump, heart pounding.

"Sorry, miss." The servant boy stumbles backward, as if fearing her anger. "Sarah says we're out of goat cheese."

"Send someone to the neighbors to borrow some."

The boy sprints off.

Martha squeezes her eyes shut and presses fingers into her temples, feeling the beginnings of a headache. When she blinks her eyes open, two more servants stand in front of her.

"Gah!" she gasps. "What now?"

"Sarah said she can't find linens for the extra table."

When did Sarah become so helpless?

Martha holds up a finger. She needs help. She needs Mary. She turns to beckon to her sister from across the room—wait, where is Mary? Martha's eyes search the room for her sister's blue shawl. At last she finds a blue head bobbing up and down from a perch on a couch near the back of the room.

As if feeling Martha's gaze, Mary glances up, meeting her sister's eyes.

Mary grins, a grin that says, *Best day ever.* Martha sends back a head jerk in the direction of the kitchen, a head jerk that says, *I need you in there now.*

Mary's grin fades.

"Lord, tell us the meaning of the parable." Andrew's voice.

Mary turns back to face Jesus. Jesus begins to answer Andrew, but Martha's ears are buzzing with annoyance.

Is Mary ignoring me? Pretending she doesn't understand?

But wait. Mary is smoothing her skirts, standing up. The angry knot in Martha's chest loosens. *Oh, good, here she comes.* Mary picks her way past a few listeners, mumbling apologies.

Martha edges back toward the kitchen, her mind already whirling: *I'll have Mary supervise Sarah, and . . .*

Behind her, Jesus is saying, "The thorns represent all the distractions of life—if we aren't careful, we miss . . ."

Martha's thoughts prattle on: *I'll dig through the extra stores and—*

She glances back to check Mary's progress; her mouth falls open.

Mary is not making her way toward Martha; she is settling in on the floor just behind Andrew, spreading her skirts over her ankles and feet.

Martha's eyes refuse to believe what she is seeing.

She—she's sitting with the disciples! Acting like she's one of them! When she knows I'm here working myself to death trying to feed all these people!

Jesus' eyes settle on Mary, then dart over to Martha. Martha tries to send him a message with her eyes: *I need her; help me.*

But Jesus glances down again at Mary. He smiles at her; Mary beams back at him; Jesus speaks the next line as if only to Mary. "But the seed on good soil stands for those with a noble and good heart . . ."

Heat flares in Martha's chest; tears of frustration—laced with jealousy—prick her eyes. Maybe the Lord hadn't understood Martha's expression, but Mary definitely had. And Mary had chosen to deliberately ignore her. To leave Martha stranded, alone with all the work they usually share. To appoint herself a disciple instead of a servant.

How could she be so selfish?

With a deep breath, Martha wrestles down her feelings. There will be time to talk to the Lord about this later—he will make Mary understand. He will make Mary listen. To Jesus, at least, Mary always listens.

Martha pivots on her heel and marches toward the kitchen. Duty calls.

Scripture tells us that sometime after the moment when Mary sat at Jesus' feet to listen, Martha approached Jesus, seeking intervention. She said, "Lord, don't you care that my sister has left me to do the work by myself? Tell her to help me!" (Luke 10:40).

Jesus responded by helping Martha to see the situation more accurately. Martha thought the problem was her sister's laziness and selfishness, but Jesus diagnosed the problem differently. He said, "Martha, Martha . . . you are worried and upset about many things, but few things are needed—or indeed only one. Mary has chosen what is better, and it will not be taken away from her" (Luke 10:41-42).

Although Martha's heart to serve was admirable, Jesus discerned that her good intentions had devolved into worry and stress. Martha was not being mistreated by her sister; Mary was simply choosing to be present in her discipleship. Jesus' fair-minded analysis of the problem was a helpful first step toward possible resolution.

I invite you to begin your healing journey by clarifying what went wrong in your friendship. As you try to identify the cracks that led to your break, ask God to show you if any of the following issues contributed to your struggles:

Competitiveness—A vague undercurrent of trying to one-up each other, trying to prove yourselves to each other. Sometimes only one person is competitive; sometimes it's both.

Envy—One of you has success or receives a blessing or gets The Thing the other friend really wants (a boyfriend, an engagement ring, a dream job, a pregnancy, a house, a victory with one of your children—the list could go on forever), and the other person struggles to rejoice. Envy shows up in petty comments, resentful asides, mistrust, misinterpretations of your friend's motives, even gossip and accusations.

Moving into different phases of life and not figuring out how to bridge the gap—One friend gets a boyfriend or gets married and begins to neglect the friendship; one has a baby and is suddenly chained to sleep schedules, while the other friend longs for the days when they could go out together spontaneously, anytime they wanted; one friend takes on a structured nine-to-five-type career, while the other is still in school or choosing to work flexible hours or to stay home.

Unresolved hurt feelings—She hurts you and you don't get it; you hurt her and she doesn't get it. Maybe you try talking about it and it backfires . . . or maybe you keep quiet, and the hurts become fault lines, waiting to shift. Pressure builds silently under the surface, till one day the fault line triggers, and everything you've built comes crashing down.

Different definitions of friendship—One of you wants to hang out every weekend; the other can go weeks without talking and still feel close. You feel happy with the way things are, but it's not enough for her; or she feels happy in the friendship, but you feel distant. Disappointment and resentment build over time.

Not understanding or supporting a heartache—Your friend has never experienced the particular challenge you're going through and doesn't support you the way you expected. Maybe she neglects you, misinterprets you, says insensitive things, or even resents or criticizes the way you feel.

Unspoken insecurity—You started feeling insecure or weird (you might not even be able to explain all the reasons why), but you couldn't bring yourself to bring it up, so you just . . . gradually pulled away and grew distant. Or maybe your friend was the one who grew insecure. She started acting strange and taking steps back, but she wouldn't say why. (Or vice-versa.)

Do any of those descriptions feel familiar?

If you need a little more help thinking through your situation, maybe it'll help hearing someone else work through theirs. Here's what that analysis looked like for me.

In thinking about the Big Break Before My Wedding Day, I had some conversations with myself (yep, I'm one of those people who kind of talks to herself, but I usually do it on paper or by praying through my questions and answers); my self-talk went something like this:

What actually went wrong between you and Sasha?

It's all my fault. I got caught up in my own life and wedding plans and I neglected our friendship. I was self-absorbed, and I made her feel unimportant and ignored.

Okay, what else went wrong?

What do you mean, what else?

Well, why did the friendship end?

Sasha ended things. She didn't want to hear my apology or work things out.

Aha! So your selfishness got the problem started, but Sasha's decision not to forgive is what actually triggered the break. If she'd been willing to talk with you and give you a chance to change, perhaps things would have turned out differently. So it sounds like you both made choices that led to the split, which means the break is not *entirely* your fault.

I guess that's true. I really wanted to make things right and show her I could be different, but she wouldn't give me the chance.

And it sounds like she had been holding on to bitterness for a while before she ended things; is that right?

Yes. I guess I'd been hurting her feelings for a while, but I had no idea because she'd never spoken up.

So if we were to more accurately describe what went wrong in your friendship, we could say that what happened here was a combination of different definitions of friendship, entering different phases of life, and unresolved hurt feelings. You were selfish and distracted while planning your wedding, and this hurt your friend's feelings and made her feel neglected. For her part, she did not understand the stresses you were juggling, or speak up about her hurts, and she allowed bitterness to build in her heart. When she finally did speak up, she refused to engage in conversations that would have allowed forgiveness and grace. Sound more accurate?

That sounds about right.

Do you see how clarifying what went wrong can help you to begin processing a break? An accurate diagnosis sets us free from wild thoughts that place unfair, one-sided criticism and blame on ourselves—or on our friend. It helps us to "file" the loss in our heart; we are able to say, "This is what happened, and why." Even though that knowledge may not change the outcome, it may allow us to lay the loss to rest and think through any changes we want to make moving forward in our own behaviors—or in patterns we allow to develop in other friendships.

In my situation with Sasha, instead of sitting around flogging myself for being a selfish, thoughtless, neglectful friend, blaming myself completely for the break, an accurate diagnosis allowed me to take responsibility for my part and learn from it but also to recognize that my friend had made mistakes too. We'd both let each other down in different ways. We could have had a better outcome if I had been less self-focused *and* if she had handled her hurt differently. We might still be friends today.

When Jesus helped Martha to reconsider the resentment she felt toward Mary, I wonder if Martha was able to walk away and put her anger to rest. I hope she was able to receive the compassion and grace Jesus was offering her ("Martha, Martha," he said—can't you hear the gentleness and affection in his words?). I hope Martha managed to surrender her own need to perform and prove, to release her feelings of perceived injustice, and even begin to admire her sister's strengths: peace, trust, and an impressive amount of gumption.

STOP THE BLEEDING, MANAGE THE PAIN

Diagnosing the cause of your split is a stabilizing first step, but it's just the beginning of your journey to healing. We also need to stop the bleeding and manage the pain that comes in the aftermath of a breakup. For example, a broken relationship can make us more vulnerable to fear.

We may find ourselves unconsciously attributing negative qualities to our other friendships, making unfair assumptions based on The Bad Thing That Happened. We may become guarded, mistrusting, and self-protective. Maybe even a little paranoid. Just as my one bad experience with one faulty mug suddenly made me suspicious of all other mugs, so we may start viewing other people as potential threats and sources of pain. Fear flows, an internal bleed:

> *She wasn't honest with me; maybe my other friends are hiding their true feelings too.*
> *She didn't stick by me when I needed her; I can't trust my other friends' loyalty either. I should protect myself by assuming they're not going to be there for me.*
> *People talk a big game about forgiveness, but when you actually make a mistake, they hold grudges. I need to play it safe and not get too close to anyone else.*
> *I trusted her with my heart and my secrets—even my vulnerabilities and weaknesses—and she used them against me. I'm not going to make that mistake again. I'd better keep my real heart to myself from now on.*

We can't allow thoughts like these to float around freely in our minds, whispering accusations and stoking our fears. Even if we don't fully believe the thoughts at first (the reasonable part of us recognizes them as overreactions and exaggerations), they will begin to *feel* more true over time. And if we reinforce those feelings with our behavior—staying guarded, holding back, shutting down—we begin to lock into self-protective patterns that not only hinder our remaining friendships but also prevent us from cultivating new ones.

Cynical, insecure thoughts aren't going to get you anywhere closer to resolution in your broken friendship—or to victory in future friendships. Insecurity is a manipulative tool Satan uses to cripple us. It can even become a kind of self-fulfilling prophecy: we feel insecure, which makes us withdraw, which pushes others away, which makes us even more insecure . . . and so on.

We stop the bleeding by identifying unhelpful, fear-driven thoughts, and replacing them with God-focused, biblical truths. We're going to dig into these ideas even more deeply in chapter 4, "Flipping the Script," but here's the gist to get you moving in the right direction.

I've found it helps when I write down my fears as specifically as I can, and then find a Scripture to address each one. For example, a friendship crisis might make me worry, *I'm afraid that person is spreading gossip about me that could damage my reputation. I'm afraid other people might believe her instead of getting to know me for themselves.* To deal with that fear, I might seek comfort and guidance from Psalm 25:2-3:

> Do not let me be put to shame,
>   nor let my enemies triumph over me.
> No one who hopes in you
>   will ever be put to shame.

Our hope is in God—not people. God is aware of our relational struggles, and he protects us from slander.

When I'm feeling insecure, I might take a look at Ephesians 1, which reminds me of who I am in Christ:

> He chose us in him before the creation of the world to be
> holy and blameless in his sight. In love he predestined us
> for adoption to sonship through Jesus Christ, in accordance
> with his pleasure and will—to the praise of his glorious grace,
> which he has freely given us in the One he loves.
> EPHESIANS 1:4-6

We're not perfect, but we are chosen. Holy. Blameless. Free from accusation before God, embraced as beloved children. God knows us, and it gives him tremendous joy to call us his own.

I encourage you to find some Scriptures that address your specific fears, insecurities, or regrets. Pray through them, memorize them, and meditate on them. Choose to believe the Scriptures instead of your fears.

SET REALISTIC EXPECTATIONS

Before you can head home from the emergency room and start working on a treatment plan, the doctor usually comes in to give you some kind of a "here's what you can expect for your recovery" talk. She'll answer questions like, Will I ever get fully back to normal? When will I start feeling like myself again? When can I use that arm/leg/gallbladder again? In a friendship context, our questions might sound more like, When will I feel at peace about this? Can that broken friendship fully heal, or will it always walk with a limp? Will I ever be able to form another close friendship, or am I permanently wounded?

As I said from the beginning, I can't answer all those questions, but I do want to manage our expectations for future friendships. Can we please pause to acknowledge that, even when you're not wrestling with a difficult dynamic or breakup, friendships are a sore spot for a lot of people? The bookshelves and airwaves are flooded with books and podcasts celebrating friendship, calling us to make space in our hearts and schedules for friends, urging us to find our tribe, and . . . first let me say, Yay, and I agree. I love friends! More friends for all!

But sometimes all this talk about deepening your friendships and finding your tribe can make us feel . . . funky. Insecure. Left out. Less than. Like everyone else is in on something we're not. Like all these other people have I-would-give-my-right-arm-and-possibly-my-spleen-for-you friendships by the half dozen and we don't.

I suspect that books and posts and podcasts can unintentionally give us over-idealized expectations of friendship. We used to feel reasonably content in our friendships, but then we started hearing other people's epic descriptions and stories, and overanalysis kicked in, like, *Wait. Are my friends ride or die? Are we as close as those people are? If we don't go on epic biannual girl trips together, are we not truly close? If she can't read my thoughts across the room, are we even friends?*

As a former women's minister and now as a pastor's wife, I've had the privilege of working with hundreds of women over the years, and here's something I've noticed: the minute you start talking about friendships, women start crying. Almost everyone is insecure about their friendships. Almost everyone wishes they had more friendships, better friendships, deeper friendships. Almost everyone is convinced that everyone else has closer friends—and more friends—than they do.

I'm gonna take a wild guess and say, I bet you have better friendships than you think you do. Or at least, I'd bet your friendships are just as strong as those of the girl sitting next to you at church, school, or work. Yep, even the girl who's always posting pictures that make it seem like she spends every free moment laughing over coffee with a pack of supportive friends.

This book isn't about how to find your bestie tribe, but since a friendship fracture can leave you feeling a bit discouraged about your friendship future, it's important to check our expectations. I'd encourage you not to over-idealize others' friendships (especially as they appear on social media) and to let Scripture continue to guide your friendships and healing moving forward. The Bible offers powerful and practical guidance in forming, keeping, and forgiving our friends. The more you allow Scripture to guide you in loving others well, the more equipped and hopeful you'll feel about your friendship future.

A PRESCRIPTION FOR HEALING

Even if you still feel like the walking wounded, I hope this chapter has at least helped you to take a few steps toward healing. In time, I pray the pain will be less debilitating. In the chapters to come, we'll identify practices and perspectives that will continue to put the pieces of your heart back together and maybe get you brave enough to work your friendship muscles again, however weary and worn they may be.

Jeremiah's eloquent words express my prayer for you:

Blessed is the one who trusts in the LORD,
   whose confidence is in him.
They will be like a tree planted by the water
   that sends out its roots by the stream.
It does not fear when heat comes;
   its leaves are always green.
It has no worries in a year of drought

and never fails to bear fruit."

. . . Heal me, LORD, and I will be healed;
save me and I will be saved,
for you are the one I praise.

JEREMIAH 17:7-8, 14

THOUGHT QUESTIONS

1. Take another look at the list of issues that can cause friendship problems on pages 22–23. How would you diagnose the cause of your breakup?
2. How might this diagnosis change the way you think, feel, or speak about your loss in the future?
3. What is your biggest fear in friendship? What Scripture might help you to face that fear with a godly perspective?

3

TAKING INVENTORY

Hands tingling with the memory of pain,
I found myself looking askance at the mug's handle.
Studying it, assessing it for cracks and weaknesses.
Then glancing back over my shoulder,
hoping no one was watching.

Our church leadership group is circled up in our tiny living room, every seat and cushion and patch of carpet occupied. My husband leans forward on his elbows and says, "Okay, guys, we've all been working together for a few months, and I think we know each other well enough to do this now. I want us to go around the room and encourage each other one by one. Let's take a look at the fruits of the Spirit Paul wrote about in Galatians 5—love, joy, peace, patience, kindness, goodness, faithfulness, gentleness, and self-control—and let's tell each person which fruit of the Spirit they best exemplify."

My stomach twists into a knot. Ugh, I hate these activities. I love sharing about other people—this is a talented group of servant leaders, and I have a million great things to say about everyone here—but I wish Kevin would just skip me. I flash back to shards of bad social memories: times when I've felt unfairly criticized in a meeting, times when I've made a mistake and hurt a friend's feelings. Even though most of those memories are years old and should be long scabbed over, I still twitch with the memory of the pain; I still reach for mugs two-handed, just in case. All those memories have made me good at hiding, and this meeting is going to force me to fully participate.

I clench my fists and try to order the whirlwind thoughts away. *STOP! I'm just going to think about what I want to share about other people; hopefully they won't get to me before the meeting ends.*

I try to drown out the voice of insecurity by raising my hand and volunteering to share about someone else. Sure enough, within a few minutes I'm filled with warm fuzzies, thinking about how much I love and admire everyone in this group.

I almost forget I'm going to have a turn, when Kevin points at me. "Okay, what fruit of the Spirit do you see in Elizabeth?"

Inwardly I cringe, convinced people are going to offer a few insincere, throwaway comments. But Kim speaks up: "Kindness," she says, beaming at me. "Elizabeth is kind."

"That's what I was going to say!" says Elva. "That's one of my favorite things about her. And she's really encouraging."

As Elva and Kim go on to describe how they've seen me show kindness and encourage others, an odd, tingly feeling spreads through me. *I think they're serious. Maybe they actually see good things in me. Maybe they really think I am kind. Maybe I have something to give after all.*

When the meeting ends, I feel different. Different about myself, and different about this group. Safer. More seen and known. And more excited to offer my gifts to God and to friends.

When we've felt hurt or made mistakes in past friendships, the brokenness haunts our existing relationships, an unwelcome specter. The loss casts a sinister shadow, dimming and warping our perceptions of ourselves and others. Like my experience with the broken mug, the memory of the pain long outlives the pain itself. We engage in self-protective behaviors long after we have a rational reason for doing so.

Satan wants to use bad memories and past defeats to cripple us. He leans in close and fills our ears with lies, his "native language" (John 8:44): *This break proves you're a failure at friendship; you have nothing to offer. Don't bother trying to change—you'll always be this way.* But God specializes in truth. He helps us to see ourselves clearly, through eyes of faith; he helps us to see not just the people we are today but also the people (and friends) we can become. God specializes in redeeming the lost and restoring the broken: where we are gifted, he helps us shine; where we are broken, he pieces us back together.

In this chapter, we're going to take inventory of the strengths we have to offer our friends, the strengths we lack in friendship, and what it might look like to grow past our brokenness and into the kind of friend we hope to be.

INVENTORY YOUR STRENGTHS

The apostle Paul wrote often about the beauty and power of God's church, highlighting the way God's children are meant to use their gifts to encourage and strengthen one another. In 1 Corinthians 12, he explains:

> There are different kinds of service, but we serve the same Lord. God works in different ways, but it is the same God who does the work in all of us.
>
> A spiritual gift is given to each of us so we can help each other. To one person the Spirit gives the ability to give wise advice; to another the same Spirit gives a message of special knowledge. The same Spirit gives great faith to another, and to someone else the one Spirit gives the gift of healing. . . . The human body has many parts, but the many parts make up one whole body. So it is with the body of Christ. . . . Yes, the body has many different parts, not just one part. If the foot says, "I am not a part of the body because I am not a hand," that does not make it any less a part of the body. And if the ear says, "I am not part of the body because I am not an eye," would that make it any less a part of the body? If the whole body were an eye, how would you hear? Or if your whole body were an ear, how would you smell anything?
>
> But our bodies have many parts, and God has put each part just where he wants it. How strange a body would be if it had

only one part! Yes, there are many parts, but only one body.
The eye can never say to the hand, "I don't need you." The
head can't say to the feet, "I don't need you."
1 CORINTHIANS 12:5-9, 12, 14-21, NLT

When a friendship breakup makes us doubt ourselves and question
our worth, Scripture tells us the truth: we *all* have gifts to offer. When
the Spirit of God comes to live inside you, he gifts and equips you to
serve the body of Christ in your own way.

Satan hopes to use your friendship fracture to cripple you forever, to
manipulate you into keeping your gifts to yourself, hiding your light for
Jesus under a bowl (see Matthew 5:15). But as I was reminded that day in
my living room, each of us is gifted (even if we've made mistakes). The rest
of us need you and your gifts. Without you, God's people are incomplete.

First, I want to invite you ("invite" being polite-speak for "nudge-
slash-prod if necessary") to spend ten to fifteen minutes writing down
some of your friendship gifts. I see you squirming on the receiving end
of these words—*please don't skip this part or run away screaming.* Even
though you've suffered the loss of a friendship, you have relational gifts—
positive qualities you offer to anyone blessed enough to call you friend.
Please don't be shy or embarrassed. No one else is going to read what you
write except you. And the purpose of this exercise is not just to make you
feel good (though I do hope you feel encouraged); this exercise is going
to help you to give with confidence and intention when you're ready
to step back into the friendship arena. It's not prideful to identify your
God-given strengths so you can offer them more purposefully to others.

So please grab a piece of paper (I'll wait . . .) and humor me for a
few minutes. Got it? Now jot down some responses to these questions:

What do I do well in friendship? Here are a few ideas to get you
started. Maybe you . . .

- listen well
- remember important details
- make others feel special with your thoughtfulness

- give great gifts
- are generous with your time
- stay "present," giving yourself fully to whomever you are with
- draw out others' strengths
- bring God into your relationships
- help others see the best in themselves
- make people laugh
- give great advice
- bring people together

What have my friends told me they appreciate or enjoy about me?
Some of your answers may be profound:

- I'm an empathetic listener.
- I don't let people get away with small-talk-only conversations.
- I rarely forget important dates in friends' lives.

Some of your answers may be fun:

- I thoroughly educate my friends on all things 1980s epic rock ballad [insert your own quirky passion here].
- I send silly texts that make people laugh.
- I make killer gluten-free brownies.
- I buy thoughtful gifts.

What are my spiritual gifts, and how do I bring those gifts into friendship? Romans 12:6-8 lists a few spiritual gifts for us; perhaps you have some of these strengths:

In his grace, God has given us different gifts for doing certain things well. So if God has given you the ability to prophesy, speak out with as much faith as God has given you. If your gift is serving others, serve them well. If you are a teacher, teach well. If your gift is to encourage others, be encouraging. If it is giving, give generously. If God has given you leadership ability,

take the responsibility seriously. And if you have a gift for showing kindness to others, do it gladly.
ROMANS 12:6-8, NLT

- If you have the gift of serving, when a friend has a need, you're probably the one who drops everything to bring a meal, pick up a kid, or even clean a bathroom.
- If you have the gift of showing mercy, perhaps you help your friends find grace and a fresh start when they've made mistakes.
- If you have the gift of showing kindness, perhaps you excel at making friends feel loved and appreciated—your gift draws out others' gifts!

I hope you found that exercise helpful. It's not arrogant to say, "Hey, God made me good at this. Now how can I use it even more?" As Paul told Timothy, "I remind you to fan into flame the gift of God, which is in you through the laying on of my hands. For the Spirit God gave us does not make us timid, but gives us power, love and self-discipline" (2 Timothy 1:6-7). When you fight Satan's lies by identifying your friendship strengths, you are able to offer them more intentionally and effectively to others. The more you practice using your gifts in friendship, the more the Spirit breathes those sparks of giftedness into warmth- and light-giving flames. As you bring your gifts out from their hiding place under the bowl of insecurity, you "let your light shine before others, that they may see your good deeds and glorify your Father in heaven" (Matthew 5:16).

IDENTIFY AREAS THAT NEED GROWTH

One of my daughters once had some conflict with a friend at school, and in my totally unbiased maternal opinion, the fault lay mostly with the other child. After a day or so, I checked in with my girl, trying to evaluate whether or not I needed to get a teacher involved. She said, "Well, I talked to Shannon about it again today, and she said she isn't mad at me anymore about what I said, but she does think I'm bossy sometimes. And Mama," my daughter's face flushed a little, but then took on a resolved expression, "she's right. I *am* bossy sometimes. So I'm going to work on that. I'm already writing her a card saying sorry for being bossy before."

Teary-eyed and open-mouthed, I folded my child into a hug, amazed to see her demonstrating such self-awareness at a young age. She is a leader, a strong and confident girl—wonderful, God-given qualities. I didn't expect her to yet have the maturity to notice how bossiness can occasionally hijack her strengths. And I was astounded at the fair-minded perspective that allowed her to admit that, yes, she'd been hurt by her friend, but perhaps she, too, had things to grow in. Ways she could help a resolution come about. Yet another reason Jesus calls us to become like little children . . .

Self-awareness is a powerful tool for personal growth. Although none of us wants to experience conflict, it does provide an opportunity for self-reflection and growth. When you've been through a rough season in a friendship, it may expose some habits or traits that are hurting your relationships. You may discover some weaknesses or blind spots. But exploring and acknowledging our weaknesses isn't always the most fun process, is it? It's far more encouraging to think about our gifts and strengths, but we do ourselves (and our friends) a disservice if we refuse to pursue growth in our areas of strength *and* weakness.

We can't grow without some honest self-analysis. If you're a self-critical perfectionist like me, that process can feel intimidating and discouraging. If we see a weakness in ourselves—especially one that has harmed a past friendship—we are tempted to go belly-up in defeat. It may feel easier to wallow, overwhelmed by our insufficiencies, instead of having the courage to do some grace-laced self-reflection. It may feel easier to stay insecure—and alone—than to swallow hard and ask ourselves some gentle, how-can-I-grow questions.

When we become Christians, our spiritual journey has only just begun. One of my favorite things about being a Christian is that Jesus and the Spirit help us to grow. *We get to change.* When we discover a weakness or inadequacy in ourselves, we aren't bound to it forever. We get to overcome. God helps us develop new strengths; as Psalm 84:7

says, "They go from strength to strength, till each appears before God in Zion."

The apostle Peter noted in one of his letters that we get to add to our character over time. God doesn't just give us one set of gifts to work with; if we allow him to work on us and in us, he adds new strengths:

> For this very reason, make every effort to add to your faith goodness; and to goodness, knowledge; and to knowledge, self-control; and to self-control, perseverance; and to perseverance, godliness; and to godliness, mutual affection; and to mutual affection, love. For if you possess these qualities in increasing measure, they will keep you from being ineffective and unproductive in your knowledge of our Lord Jesus Christ.
> 2 PETER 1:5-8

As you take inventory of what happened in your broken friendship, it's helpful to ask yourself what you can learn from the break. I find it most helpful to write these things down—we think in a deeper and more focused way when we put our thoughts into sentences on a page. Just as you wrote down your list of strengths, try writing down your responses to some of these questions:

What can I learn from that broken relationship?
What do I want to do differently next time?
What character traits do I want to work on in myself?
What friendship qualities or habits can I tweak?
What new friendship qualities or habits do I want to cultivate?
What kinds of friends do I want to look for moving forward?

Perhaps, with hindsight, you'll realize that a lack of confidence led you to settle for unhealthy dynamics in a friendship. Low self-esteem meant you allowed someone to treat you badly, and over time bitterness grew, destabilizing the friendship's foundation.

Or maybe you'll realize you neglected something in the friendship or held back something your friend needed. Next time you make a new friend, you'll want to become more compassionate, more available, more selfless, or a better listener.

Maybe you realized you were a bit too . . . *something* . . . in your broken friendship. We all have ways we can be a little too much. Looking back, were you too . . . busy and distracted? Guarded? Demanding? Insecure? Self-focused? Naive? Controlling?

It may be helpful to ask yourself if you've had a similar struggle in other friendships—that may indicate a problematic pattern. If you spot an area where you've been "too much" (or too little) in the past, I hope you'll choose to view that revelation as empowering information. It's like the saying from the 1980s *G.I. Joe* cartoons: "Now you know, and knowing is half the battle." Now you know, so now you can grow.[1]

———

Lies keep us chained to shame and fear, but truth sets us free to love and trust. To help you find that freedom, I encourage you to keep your list of strengths handy—maybe tucked into your Bible or in the pages of a favorite journal where you'll see it often. When Satan hisses, *You're no good at friendship; you have nothing to give*, counter that lie with the truth of how God has gifted you. And when he insists, *You'll never overcome the weaknesses that made your last friendship fall apart*, remind him of all the ways you've already grown, and how God can help you to change.

The enemy has been using lies to drive wedges between people—and God—since the very beginning. His fork-tongued words draw strength from our brokenness. Where he finds a crack, he seeks to fill it with the poisons of shame, self-doubt, and bitterness. We've already begun the work of sealing the gaps and mending the breaks with the glue of God's Word. In our next chapter, let's continue to resist Satan's deceptions by dismantling more of the lies he tells after a friendship fracture, lies designed to multiply the effects of a break so it damages not just the one relationship, but all of them. The more we resist Satan's lies, the more the truth of God will set us free (John 8:32).

———

1. You, too, can experience the joy of a Saturday morning in 1985, eating a bowl of Fruity Pebbles with your Cabbage Patch doll in your lap, by watching this clip: https://www.youtube.com/watch?v=pele5vptVgc.

THOUGHT QUESTIONS

1. If you haven't already done so, write down your answers to the questions on page 34.
2. Which friendship strengths do you feel most excited about exercising?
3. What is one new friendship quality or habit you want to cultivate?

4

FLIPPING THE SCRIPT

I chuckled, tried to reason with my fear:
"In all your long, happy years of coffee- and tea-drinking,
you have never had one mug handle break.
Not one broken handle out of hundreds.
Maybe thousands.
This was just a fluke, a onetime flaw in one dysfunctional mug."
But fear still prickled.

This is entirely my fault . . .
  I'm a terrible friend, maybe even a terrible Christian and human being . . .
  Maybe I'm just not likable . . .
  Maybe I'm better off alone . . .
  But then . . . she wasn't exactly the Queen of Righteousness either. So maybe this whole thing is only 92 percent my fault.
  Which means she owes me an apology for her part—it was really hurtful! Why is she acting like I'm the only one who messed up here?

Do any of these thoughts sound familiar? I've shared with you some of the joy-filled (and of course by "joy-filled" I mean "soul-crushing") thoughts I've had in the wake of my friendship losses. Perhaps you can relate. The way we talk to ourselves *about* ourselves matters. The words we whisper to ourselves—and believe about ourselves—can either hamstring us or empower us.

I'm not sure which evil Satan finds more delightful: tearing friends apart, or using the aftermath either to cripple us with insecurity and shame or to shackle us with chains of bitterness and cynicism. Why would he settle for just a friendship breakup when he can *also* destroy our peace in the process? Two for the price of one!

Now that we've spent the last chapter reminding ourselves that we do have friendship strengths and we can grow stronger in our areas of weakness, let's continue to confound the enemy's efforts. Let's turn our attention to our internal dialogue and make sure it's godly and healthy. When we hear a negative, imbalanced, or unhealthy script running in our minds, let's flip it around and rewrite it so it aligns with the way God wants us to think. How will you choose to think about your friend—and yourself? Which attitudes and beliefs will you nurture, and which will you revise or disregard altogether?

This process will look different depending on the kind of brokenness you experienced and the way you respond to hurt and your own mistakes. The guilty souls among us will be tempted to take too much responsibility for a conflict, blaming ourselves and failing to see our friend's part in the problem. Those of us who struggle with defensiveness may want to deflect responsibility and point the finger at our friend without acknowledging our own part in the split. Or you may be tempted to sink into a slough of cynicism and isolate yourself from everyone. Let's address the internal struggles of all these perspectives and consider ways we can grow.

WHEN YOU'RE INCLINED TO SHOULDER ALL THE BLAME

Guilty souls see their own weaknesses, mistakes, and sins through a magnifying glass—always larger-than-life. If that's your tendency, let's take a look at some of the specific negative thoughts you may encounter, keeping this truth in mind: just as it takes two to tango (not that I have any idea how to tango in a nonmetaphorical sense), so it takes two to argue. Chances are, you have some regrets about things you said and did leading up to the break. Even if you tried your best to be righteous, to do and say the right things, you probably didn't pull it off the way you wanted to. You probably didn't choose all the perfect words or employ the ideal, not-the-tiniest-bit-defensive-or-sarcastic tone of voice in every conversation. You may look back through your hindsight goggles and encounter a list of *if-onlys*:

> *If only I hadn't done this or said that . . .*
> *If only I had gone directly to my friend first . . .*
> *If only I had spoken up sooner . . .*
> *If only I hadn't sent that email . . .*

Your lists of revelations and regrets may be pages long. Welcome to the Doing the Best We Can with the Information We Have but Still Bungling It Because We're Not Jesus Club. I've got a nice, shiny membership card in my wallet; maybe you've got one too. *We all have issues.* We are sinful humans with blind spots, insecurities, and quirks that can hurt others or even drive them away.

So let's reconsider the way we think about unpleasant revelations: instead of spiraling down into regret and shame, we can flip the script, using those truths as springboards to transformation. As a recovering perfectionist and guilty soul, I have to intentionally acknowledge weaknesses and mistakes in ways that leave me feeling empowered instead of paralyzed. As we saw in chapter 3, it's helpful to acknowledge our mistakes so we can grow and change. But there's a fine line between admitting weakness and harboring unhealthy, unproductive thoughts, especially thoughts that exaggerate our flaws and shoulder too much blame.

Let's get more specific, considering some of the thoughts we need to revise and possibly reject altogether with the help of God and his Word.

This is all my fault.

Mmm, probably not. It's unlikely that you deserve *all* the blame. Even if some of your words or actions contributed to the conflict, the other person probably said and did things that led to the break as well. Even if you grabbed that mug handle with a little too much strength, the handle still let you down. As we have said, trouble takes two. You may have made mistakes, but so did your friend. Proverbs 18:17 tells us, "In a lawsuit the first to speak seems right, until someone comes forward and cross-examines." In other words, every story has two sides.

So how might you flip the script on the *it's-all-my-fault* thought? Perhaps you might think, *I contributed to this situation, and my friend did too. We both need to take responsibility for our roles in the break.*

I always . . . I never . . .

You know that famous rule about how it's not fair fighting to say, "You always [fill in the blank]" and "You never [fill in the blank]"? Well, it's not fair to say those words to yourself either. Even if you have made the same mistake repeatedly in the past, God gives you the power to choose a different pattern moving forward. Scripture assures us that God doesn't just begin a good work in us; he sees it through. He can—and will— carry on his heart-work in us all the way to completion:

> In all my prayers for all of you, I always pray with joy because
> of your partnership in the gospel from the first day until now,
> being confident of this, that he who began a good work in you
> will carry it on to completion until the day of Christ Jesus. . . .
> And this is my prayer: that your love may abound more and
> more in knowledge and depth of insight, so that you may be
> able to discern what is best and may be pure and blameless
> for the day of Christ.
> PHILIPPIANS 1:4-6, 9-10

So what would be a more balanced way of thinking? Perhaps you can appease the Relentless Self-Honesty Policeperson inside you by revising your self-talk to say, "I sometimes . . ." or "I rarely . . ." That less extreme phrasing acknowledges the truth—yes, the truth—that even if you have a tendency to act (or not act) in a certain way, there are times when you rise above it.

Here are some specific examples of how you might flip the script on always-never thinking.:

Instead of, *I always gravitate toward unhealthy friendships with people who look down on me and take advantage of me. I never stand up for myself,* you might revise that thought to, *Sometimes I have settled for "friendships" where the dynamic is off-kilter and the other person doesn't appreciate me, listen to me, or value my perspective. In the future I am going to search for different kinds of friends and speak up when something bothers me.*

Instead of, *I always miss important cues and hurt people,* you might flip that script like this: *At times I have missed signs that my words or behavior were upsetting people. So moving forward I am going to pay closer attention, pray for discernment, and occasionally check in with my friends, giving them the opportunity to share things that may be bothering them.*

This breakup confirms all my worst suspicions about myself. Who's to say I won't do this again to someone else?

Even if you made ginormous mistakes in your friendship, your breakup doesn't have to be the end of your story. You aren't done growing. The things you are learning can make you an awesome friend moving forward. Now you know better. Now you can be different. And best of all, you have God and the Spirit on your side, eager to help you grow.

Paul wrote about leaving the past where it belongs—behind us—and setting our sights on the people (and friends) we're striving to become: "Forgetting what is behind and straining toward what is ahead, I press on toward the goal to win the prize for which God has called me heavenward in Christ Jesus" (Philippians 3:13-14).

Even if your breakup revealed some things you wish you'd done differently or a weakness in your character or some unhealthy patterns in the way you have conducted past friendships, now you know—which means, now you can start growing. You can't undo a mistake from the past, true—but you can avoid making it again in the future. As one of my literary heroines, Anne of Green Gables, said, "But have you ever noticed one encouraging thing about me, Marilla? I never make the same mistake twice."[1]

---

1. L. M. Montgomery, *Anne of Green Gables* (New York: Penguin Books, 2014), 245.

How might an Anne-Shirley-meets-Scripture perspective flip the script on your negative thoughts? You might think, *What a gift that God gives us forgiveness and fresh starts after mistakes. With his help, I am actively becoming a different person; I'm already a better friend than I used to be.* See how this revision process works? By capturing the unhelpful, self-critical thoughts that leave you feeling bad about yourself, trapped in a self-defeating pattern, and stuck in your situation, you can rewrite the dialogue in your mind.

Before we go on, let's pause for a story, the story of two women. One struggled with speaking bitter, crippling words over herself; the other extended grace to her friend as she grappled with her past.

RUTH AND NAOMI
Based on the book of Ruth

Dust glitters on the wind in golden swirls. Ruth strikes the braided rug again; more dust goes dancing. When Ruth is satisfied that she has pounded most of the dirt from the fibers, she pulls the rug down from its perch on a tree branch.

A dry cough rattles behind her. She jumps with a startled squeak, dropping her stick. Her mother-in-law, Naomi, stands a few feet away, wrinkled hands on her bony hips. "Hit that rug any harder and you'll beat a hole through it."

Ruth ducks her head, flushing. She can never tell if Naomi—*Mara*, Ruth corrects herself; *Naomi calls herself Mara now*—is teasing or truly angry. She used to tease often, back in Moab . . . Naomi and Mahlon, Ruth's husband, had filled the house with teasing and laughter. But now—here in their new life in Bethlehem, Ruth has learned to live on tiptoe. "Sorry, Mother. I hope the sound didn't wake you."

"Pssh." Naomi swats air with one hand. "Nothing gets through these ancient ears when I'm sleeping."

Ruth almost smiles but thinks better of it—she's still not sure if it's okay to laugh at Naomi, even if Naomi herself has cracked the joke—so Ruth smothers the smile, ducks her head, and moves to carry the rug back inside. Unconsciously, she gives Naomi a wide berth; Naomi needs her space, and

Ruth has grown used to giving it. That was part of Ruth's promise, all those months ago—to always give what Naomi might need.

"Hey, girl," Naomi says, her voice thick. Ruth turns slowly. *Girl* used to be a sweet endearment between them, but Naomi hasn't called Ruth *girl* since Mahlon died, along with his brother Kilion and their father, Elimelek. Naomi's whole world, gone. Their deaths had killed Ruth's girlhood, too—her wide-eyed hopes, her foolish dreams. Some days Ruth feels like she's died more than she's lived.

"I've been thinking," Naomi says, not looking Ruth in the eye. "You've done—so much—for me." Now her eyes find Ruth's and linger. "So very much." Her voice goes quiet and thin; her eyes go red and watery. Ruth blinks, her own eyes burning. It feels a lifetime since Naomi has expressed any emotion besides grief—the angry kind. Naomi chose the name Mara, Bitter, for a reason.

Ruth is afraid to breathe; if she does, this fragile moment will shatter, glass in her fingers.

"It's past time I find a home for you, a new husband to take you in."

Ruth's mouth falls open.

Naomi rustles forward, skirt brushing the grass. With one crooked finger, she pushes Ruth's jaw shut. "Don't gape, girl." Her fingertips brush Ruth's cheek and rest there for a heartbeat. Ruth leans into them, just barely. "Blessed girl," Naomi whispers. "My salvation. And I've never really thanked you . . ." Ruth's traitorous eyes fill completely; Naomi clears her throat and steps back, looking away. "I cannot keep you only for myself forever. You deserve a husband—and a home of your own."

Ruth fumbles for words. "Mother, I—"

Naomi cuts her short, holding up a finger. "Besides, you can't live off a grumpy old woman's charity forever, you know."

She barks a wheezy laugh, and Ruth sniffle-snorts a half laugh of her own. Her thoughts whirl in wonder: *All this time, God has been working. All these silent, angry months—Naomi so lost in her own grief I thought she couldn't consider mine—something was stirring in her heart. God has been moving where I couldn't see.*

Naomi rubs her hands together, her dry palms whisking like whispering leaves, sharing secrets. "Now, girl, draw some water and dig up your best clothes. Tonight, you're going out."

Scripture doesn't give us many glimpses into Ruth and Naomi's interactions as they adjusted to their new life as widows in Naomi's hometown, but when we first meet Naomi in Ruth 1, she can hardly stand beneath the crushing weight of her grief: "The Almighty has made my life very bitter. . . . The LORD has afflicted me; the Almighty has brought misfortune upon me" (verses 20-21). Sorrow, abandonment, loss: this is all she sees, all she feels, all she can say. With Naomi in such a depressed, hopeless, and possibly angry-at-God state of mind, Ruth (who was grappling with her own loss) probably had to show her mother-in-law extensive grace. And yet grace prevailed, Naomi eventually came to terms with her grief, and the love these women showed each other resulted in a powerful story of redemption and second chances.

By the end of the book of Ruth, the tenor of the women's conversations takes a dramatic turn; the script is completely rewritten; Naomi's lament, "The Almighty has brought misfortune upon me," is replaced by her friends rejoicing, "Praise be to the LORD, who this day has not left you without a guardian-redeemer" (Ruth 1:21; 4:14). Even Naomi's name has changed again: she is no longer bitter Mara, gritting her teeth through a bleak life without hope; once more she is sweet Naomi, cradling a grandson and dreaming of a joyful future. The conversation has changed because Naomi's life—and perhaps Naomi herself—has changed.

WHEN YOU'RE TEMPTED TO POINT THE FINGER

Maybe all our earlier talk about feeling guilty or blaming yourself doesn't really fit your situation. Maybe, like Naomi, you look at your story and see only the ways you've been damaged or wounded. Maybe you tend to react defensively, shielding yourself by casting blame. Maybe when you look back on your broken friendship, all you can see is one-sided mistreatment: *This was entirely my friend's fault, not mine.* It's certainly possible that the breakup was your friend's fault, but things are often more complex than that.

How can you tell if your view of a former friend has become too one-sided, pointing too much blame in her direction? It's always wise to ask God to help you see yourself and your friend clearly. And be on the lookout for thoughts like these; it's likely they need revision with a grace-colored pen.

I can't believe she did or said [fill in the blank]. I would never do that or say that to someone . . .

I once heard it said that we tend to judge other people by their actions, while justifying ourselves based on our good *intentions*. So even if we misspeak or make a mistake, we want credit for the good intentions behind our words and actions, but we may not extend the same grace to friends who hurt us. It might sound something like this: *I didn't intend to hurt her like that. My heart was in the right place; she just took things the wrong way.* Meanwhile, we obsess over every wrong thing our friend said or did, without pausing to consider *her* heart and intent.

Difficult as it may be, try taking a step back and considering the argument from your friend's point of view. Is it possible she had good intentions like you did, but they got muddled on the way out? Could she have a valid perspective you haven't yet considered?

Perhaps you can borrow Paul's fair-minded viewpoint here: "My conscience is clear, but that does not make me innocent. It is the Lord who judges me" (1 Corinthians 4:4). You acknowledge that *feeling* innocent doesn't *prove* us innocent, that God knows our hearts' true intentions, and that he is a wise and fair judge. In prayer, you can invite God to help you see yourself and your friend more clearly.

To rephrase a one-sided perspective, perhaps you could think, *I am still shocked and upset by what my friend did, but I also acknowledge that I have hurt people too, sometimes without being aware of the hurt I was causing. I am going to keep giving this painful moment to God, trusting that he can reveal and refine both our hearts.*

I just can't get over this one thing she said . . . that one thing she did . . .

I have a powerful imagination, but sometimes that imagination backfires on me. When I've been hurt, my imagination fixates on the most painful moments in the conflict, then replays them in an endless loop as my anger boils hotter with every replay. Ever been there? Stuck reliving the One Awful Thing? Trapped in the moment the hot tea sizzled against your skin, feeling like you're being scalded over and over and over again?

Consider this: Do you want your friend to judge you based on the worst thing you said or did, the low point in your interactions . . . or do you hope she will consider the broader scope of your actions and friendship? Do you hope she'll remember that the One Awful Thing doesn't represent your true character and usual behavior? Offer your friend the same grace. Chances are, she regrets her mistake and would welcome a do-over if you gave it to her.

Proverbs gives us this great nugget of advice: "A person's wisdom yields patience; it is to one's glory to overlook an offense" (Proverbs 19:11). Showing grace to people who offend us is a way we honor the grace God shows to us.

So how might you reframe this thought? Perhaps a better perspective would be, *I still feel hurt by that thing she said, but that one negative moment does not represent our entire friendship history. I also choose to remember some positive things from our past.*

She always . . . she never . . .

Again, it's time to flip the script. Just as it's unfair to criticize yourself, saying, "I always" and "I never," so it's unfair to make blanket statements about others. Maybe your friend does have some negative patterns, but be sure to give her credit for the things she has done right in your friendship. Here's where the Golden Rule can guide our perspective: "In everything, do to others what you would have them do to you" (Matthew 7:12). Perhaps in this case, we need to *think about* others as we would like them to think about us. To be evenhanded in our assessment of others, remembering both their weaknesses *and* their strengths.

Instead of "She always" or "She never," a fairer viewpoint would revise that statement to say, "She sometimes" or even, "She often."

She just doesn't understand . . .

Maybe your friend doesn't understand you or your perspective. (To be fair, can any human fully understand all we feel, all we have experienced? Full understanding only comes from God.) But perhaps you'll feel more empathy toward your friend if you switch this sentence around and ask yourself, "Maybe she doesn't understand me, but are there things I haven't taken the time to understand about her? Have I honestly considered her perspective with an open mind, or have I dug my heels in and refused to see things from her point of view?"

As Paul wrote to the church in Philippi, "And if on some point you think differently, that too God will make clear to you" (Philippians 3:15). When we don't understand—or feel understood—let's invite God into the conflict, asking him to help us bridge our differences. And let's reframe our thinking along these lines: *She doesn't understand the way I feel, but I'm sure I don't understand everything she feels either. As frustrating as our disagreement is, I'm going to pray that God's Spirit works in both of us to bring our perspectives closer together.*

WHEN YOU'RE TEMPTED BY CYNICISM

Maybe your struggle is less with placing blame and more with a cynical, jaded, throw-in-the-friendship-towel-and-also-the-mug-because-the-world-is-full-of-horrible-humans-and-untrustworthy-mugs perspective. Maybe, like Naomi, you find yourself stiff-arming others, muttering, "Call me Mara (Bitter)," because you can't imagine feeling happy, or like your old self, again. Maybe, like me, you're tempted to avoid mug handles for the rest of your life, because you never can be too careful. Here are a few cynical thoughts to guard against, with Scriptures to help you counter them.

People are fake, unreliable, and untrustworthy.

Can we go ahead and credit this line to our inner Drama Queens? Are some people fake, unreliable, and untrustworthy? Yep. But many, many people are not. They are honest. They are dependable. They are godly. We just have to pray to find them. David tells us about this kind of person in Psalm 15:

Who may worship in your sanctuary, Lord?
 Who may enter your presence on your holy hill?

Those who lead blameless lives and do what is right,
   speaking the truth from sincere hearts.
Those who refuse to gossip
   or harm their neighbors
   or speak evil of their friends. . . .
   Such people will stand firm forever.
PSALM 15:1-3, 5, NLT

I invite you to reword your cynical thought to something like this: *Some people are untrustworthy, but I know faithful people are out there. I'm going to pray God guides me to the right friends—and protects me from the wrong ones.*

I'm not friend material.

My friend, *everyone* is friend material. You have a heart that loves and needs love. You might collect three-legged cats, used toothpicks, and thimbles from all fifty states plus Scandinavia—but somewhere out there another person exists who, even if they don't share your hobbies, at least will appreciate and admire them. I'm being silly here, but please . . . you have lovable, likable qualities. How can I say that so confidently? Because you are a divine child of God, his special creation, "fearfully and wonderfully made" by his skillful hands (Psalm 139:14). You have gifts to offer to future friends, even if you've made mistakes in the past.

Here's one way to flip this script: *God loves the way he made me, and he doesn't like for his children to feel alone. I'm going to keep asking God to lead me to friends I can love, who will love me in return for the person God made me to be.*

I can't recover from this.

You may always carry a scar from this break. But God—and time—are powerful healers. The only way you can't recover is if you *choose* to stay stuck. Instead of stuck-ness (not a word, but let's pretend), you can choose forgiveness. And you can choose resilience, even if you're a big feeler like me who needs to spend a few months leaking snot and tears as part of your grieving process. Even if you've suffered stagger-ing losses like Naomi and Ruth did and it takes you a while to recover and rebuild.

You can start again. Give your heart again. Make new friends. You may be a bit wiser and a little more careful—you may spend a few months testing out mug handles before going all in with the one-handed hold—but you can still *have* friends and *be* a friend. As Naomi's friends rejoiced when her life took a turn for the good, so God can give you friends to share your joys. As David rejoiced in the way God helped him recover from a trial, so can you:

I waited patiently for the LORD to help me,
    and he turned to me and heard my cry.
He lifted me out of the pit of despair,
    out of the mud and the mire.
He set my feet on solid ground
    and steadied me as I walked along.
He has given me a new song to sing,
    a hymn of praise to our God.

PSALM 40:1-3, NLT

You can revise doomsday, I'll-never-recover thoughts with a new script like this: *This has been a difficult loss, but I trust that God can see me through it. He is helping my heart to heal, and one day these memories won't hurt as much. With God's help, I will be okay.*

WHAT DEFINES YOU?

Satan wants to take this one terrible thing and hold it over your head for as long as you'll let him. He wants your friendship crisis to plant seeds of insecurity that yield perennial blooms of self-doubt, fear, and isolation. He longs to leverage regret from past mistakes to accuse you forever, keeping you shackled to the person and friend you used to be. Don't let him manipulate you. Don't let him win. You are not chained to your past.

Naomi chose to define herself, for a while, by grief and loss. She couldn't bear her old name—maybe every time she heard it, she heard it coming from her husband's lips, "Naomi, my Sweet"—and so she shed the old name and wrapped herself in angry armor: *I am Mara, Bitter, and that's all I'll ever be.* And yet God used Naomi's daughter-friend, Ruth, to remind her of the openhearted woman she used to be, a woman who could plan and hope and dream.

If God could help Ruth and Naomi, two women who had lost everything, to find fresh hope on the other side of sorrow, he can help you too. If God could help Naomi to smile again, laugh again, love and trust again—to be sweet Naomi again—he can help you too. He can help you find your friendship footing, and your self-confidence, on the other side of a breakup.

As the apostle Paul so eloquently expressed it,

I press on to possess that perfection for which Christ Jesus first possessed me. No, dear brothers and sisters, I have not achieved it, but I focus on this one thing: Forgetting the past and looking forward to what lies ahead, I press on to reach the end of the race and receive the heavenly prize for which God, through Christ Jesus, is calling us.
PHILIPPIANS 3:12-14, NLT

We can learn from the past without living there. With God's help, we can press forward into greater strengths, new starts, and fresh hope. We can resist Satan's whispers, inviting God and his Word to reshape the way we think about ourselves, our friends, and our past. With his help we can overcome insecurity, resist bitterness, and conquer cynicism. We can take a scriptural red pen to our thoughts, crossing out the ungodly bits and rewriting them with more of God's heart in mind. Then, like Naomi, we can clean the cobwebs from our shuttered hearts and push open their rusty hinges to welcome love and friendship inside once more. And in spite of our imperfections and losses, we can still look forward to all God has in store.

THOUGHT QUESTIONS

1. Which do you most struggle with: the inclination to shoulder all the blame, the temptation to point the finger at others and overlook your own mistakes, or the tendency to become cynical?
2. List a few thoughts you know need some revision. How might you rewrite those thoughts so they reflect a more godly perspective?

5

LENSES FOR PROCESSING
FADED FRIENDSHIPS

A little voice inside my head justified my fear:
"I mean, you never can be too careful.
You've been burned once;
better not risk being burned again."

I miss you! How's life? I'd love to hear what's new with you!

I compose a let's-catch-up-soon text for the third or fourth time in a matter of months, knowing I probably won't get a response . . . again . . . but I feel like the friendship is still worth fighting for, so I press *send* with a sigh.

I don't hear back.

I'm not surprised, but it still stings.

I spend a few weeks—okay, it's months—pondering the relationship and how my friend seems willing to let it wither to the point of near-death. I try to resist the painful Carrie flashbacks, frequently reminding myself, *This isn't Carrie. Carrie had other issues. Don't give up on this friendship.* The confusing thing is, I know this friend still cares about me. We haven't had a falling out, and once in the bluest of blue moons, she does respond. After a while, epiphany strikes: *I get to decide how I'm going to file this situation in my heart. My interpretation of the drift is going to define how I feel and act moving forward. I can choose to view the decline in this friendship in several ways. I could describe it as . . .*

an intentional wound that rankles
a painful mystery that makes me insecure, leaving me wondering
 what she's thinking and whether I did something to cause
 the drift
a seasonal friendship that was great for a time
a friend whom I'll always love even if she has moved on
a friend who still loves me even if she's an "out of sight, out of
 mind" kind of person

I settle on some combination of the last three. For one thing, I just don't have the energy for a battle against bitterness. (Been there, done that; it's exhausting; see chapter 8.) And if I'm being fair, thinking through a rational lens instead of a personal one, I think the last three reflect different facets of what's actually going on in my friend's heart. Just as my broken mug handle didn't intentionally set out to harm me, so my friend hasn't intended to hurt me. She's not mad at me or intentionally sabotaging our friendship. She's just . . . not paying close attention. And perhaps, like my mug handle, she has an invisible weak point: she's not great at sustaining the friendships—the long-distance friendships, the both-of-us-super-busy-for-a-season friendships, or the different-places-in-life friendships—that take extra effort.

Processing faded friendships' demise has taught me a great deal about relational loss. Some friendships die with an explosion—huge fight! big lie! nasty betrayal!—but others suffer a slow demise by more passive forces: absence, distraction, distance, neglect. While some friendships crash and burn, others fade with the years, their once-vibrant colors bleaching into grayed-out, shadow-memories of something that used to be beautiful. Like my broken hummingbird, there's something about that friendship we can't quite let go of, something worth saving, even if it'll never fly the same.

In future chapters we're going to dig more deeply into the friendships that experience dramatic conflict—How do we resolve those conflicts? *Can* we resolve them? And if we can't find resolution, how do we find healing, peace, forgiveness, and the resilience we need to move forward?—but in this chapter let's take some time to consider the more "quiet" kinds of loss: the friendships that wither slowly, shriveling with neglect and languishing on the vine.

WHAT'S THE STORY?

When you haven't heard from someone for six months . . . a year . . . two years . . . it can be difficult to interpret the silence and even more difficult to pull off a conversation that gives you a sense of resolution. (What are you supposed to do when you can't reach someone for the hundredth time—call up and leave a message, saying, "Hey, so are we just not friends anymore?" Is there a GIF for that? Do you write a card?) For many reasons, we are left without the clarity we crave, and we are forced to settle for a lot of internal processing and prayer processing, in order to find peace.

For every loss, we have a story: a story we tell ourselves and a story we share with others. The definitions and descriptions we use in those stories hold great power. Is our tale one of betrayal and intentional cruelty? Misunderstanding and disappointment? Thoughtless neglect? Were we victims or victors? Blindsided or nearsighted? Sometimes the causes of conflict and distance are obvious, not really up for debate, but many times, they are more nuanced, even open to different interpretations.

WHICH LENS?

In working through my own losses, particularly the friendships that have faded with time, I have found that the perspective, or lens, I choose has a profound effect on the story I tell. And the story I tell has a profound effect on how I feel: how I feel when I look back on the friendship, how I feel about my friend, and how I feel about myself. Some lenses exacerbate our bitterness and insecurity, while others enhance our sense of grace and compassion.

A shift in perspective, tempered by the healing hand of time, can help us lay hurts to rest, offer forgiveness, understand our friend's standpoint (even if we still disagree), or release our own feelings of guilt and regret. An open-minded look back may help us to remember a fuller picture rather than just a few negative moments. Let's consider a few key lenses, or perspectives, that might help you make sense of, and make peace with, the faded friendships you've experienced.

Some people don't know how to maintain long-distance friendships.

My family has moved a million times, and I was forced early in life to learn how to maintain long-distance friendships. My friend Julie recently reminded me that when I was a preteen and my family moved from Atlanta to Boston, I used to record audio messages on cassette tapes and mail them home to my Georgia friends.[1] Miraculously, these cassette tapes did not melt in the mail. Julie and a few other girls would bring a tape player to church and huddle together in a corner after service to listen to my life updates together—and so we stayed connected from afar. I guess you could call it the analog version of Messenger Kids. Some of us are still friends, all these years (and technological developments) later. We've now upgraded to Marco Polo and FaceTime, but the principle of staying connected is the same.

Julie and I have maintained our friendship from across the miles; however, I have tried to remain connected with other friends after a move and gotten little response. I used to feel hurt by this and wonder if I'd done something to damage the friendship, but in most cases, I've realized: *They just don't know how to do this. In their mind, a move automatically severs friendships—it's in town or nothing. They're just planning to let our friendship go.* And sometimes, I *let* people let me go. It's not personal; it's just their way. Yes, it's their loss—if they were willing to put forth a bit more effort, we could probably still be close—but since it's not fun to chase people down, I have decided I'm okay with letting some out-of-town friendships fade.

Adopting this lens has protected my heart from hurt, bitterness, and

---

1. Yep, I used actual cassette tapes; I also loved *He-Man* and *The Last Unicorn*—so basically, think of my childhood as *Stranger Things*, but with fewer Demogorgons.

from making a friend's weakness about me. If you've lost some friend-ships after a move, this lens may prove redemptive. When you realize that the other person isn't intentionally rejecting you—they just don't know how to sustain long-distance friendships—the loss feels dramati-cally different. Less intentional. Less "This mug is inherently evil and destructive!" and more "What a shame that mug handle's bond wasn't stronger." Less "How could they treat me that way?" and more "Wow, it's too bad they haven't figured out long-distance friendship. They're really missing out."

Some people are "out of sight, out of mind" friends.

Ever had one of these friends? This lens might seem like it overlaps the long-distance issue, but it's a little different. Out of sight, out of mind friends may live in the same town as you, but they basically fall off the planet during busy school seasons, work seasons, or kid seasons. They don't mean to do it, but they kind of give you whiplash. When you're with them in person, you feel totally loved and close, and you feel dumb for ever questioning the friendship, but when you're *not* together for a little while, they sort of . . . vanish. They forget to call, text, respond, sometimes for weeks at a time. At first you think they're mad or ghosting you, but eventually you realize, they're just . . . dis-tracted. Spacey. Or maybe busy and overwhelmed, caught up in their own daily life.

More pointed truth? Maybe they are a bit selfish, and it would be great if they would grow and change . . . and maybe, thanks to your influence and constancy, they *will* grow. But honestly? Even if they make some changes, they may still sometimes lapse into forgetfulness and distance. It may always feel like they're less consistently engaged in the friendship than you are.

I understand people like this much better since marrying an out of sight, out of mind person. (I'm busting my husband here with his permission.) Kevin deeply loves all the people who have ever been in his life—and because he is a minister, that's a *lot* of people—but he is extremely present in his daily life. It's a great gift that means he gives his full attention and best love to the people right in front of him. But it can also be a challenge when life gets busy or his attention gets divided or people are no longer in his daily life and ministry. He doesn't mean to neglect those friendships; he's just mentally, emotionally, and spiritually engaged right where he is. He may not always remember to reach out, to wish someone a happy birthday, to remember their anniversary, or just to check in and say hi—but in his heart, his affection for that person has not changed. Seeing the way Kevin feels about people—and the guilt he feels when he realizes it's been a while since he's reached out to someone he doesn't see as often as he used to—has helped me show a lot more grace to the out of sight, out of mind friends in my own life. I get them better now. I know they still love me, and they may even feel bad when they realize how long it's been since we've connected.

To his credit, Kevin has worked on this part of himself. He's so much more consistent in friendships than he used to be, much more intentional and devoted. He makes an effort to remember birthdays, and he checks in with old friends more faithfully, just to say hi. I admire and respect his growth.

How might adopting this lens be helpful in your situation? This perspective may help you to feel less hurt by, and less angry toward, an out of sight, out of mind friend. You're not saying the way they treated you was loving or good, but at least you realize they weren't deliberately being cruel or selfish. This lens might also help prevent hurts with other friendships. With OOSOOM friends (that's a fancy new acronym I just made up), I've found that I just have to adjust my expectations. We probably won't be *best* friends, but we can still *be* friends.

Some friendships are seasonal.

The picture pops up in my Instagram feed, and my heart catches. *How have her kids gotten so tall?* My thoughts stutter forward in leaps and starts: *Last time we talked, they were way younger. I've missed so much!* Surprise gives way to a surge of guilt: *I've been a bad friend to her. I wonder if she's mad at me. But then—it's not like she's called either.* Guilt twists into insecurity: *Wait, why hasn't she called in so long? Are we okay? Is she mad at me?*

I ponder the friendship for a while until truth sets in: this friend and I relied on each other a great deal during a difficult season in our lives—*Wait, you too? I can't believe someone understands what I'm going through!*—and the friendship was a gift that encouraged us both through that long, lonely slog. Even back then, we didn't talk all that often, but when we did, it was meaningful. After a few years, God ushered us both into more joyful seasons of life, and we took turns rejoicing with each other, marveling at his goodness. We kept up for a while, but as time went on, we allowed more and more time between phone calls until . . . well, here we were. Several years past any meaningful communication.

It was then that I realized: that friendship was a gift that saw us both through a challenging season, and that's probably all it will ever be. We still love each other. Our shared prayers and journeys and victories weren't insincere. But life has gotten busy and we've both moved on to other friendships, *and that's okay.* The friendship isn't broken, just . . . somewhat faded. A little bit past tense. The affection is still there, but the "dailiness" of the relationship is gone.

I've found I can guard my heart against bitterness when I reword the way I describe a seasonal friendship. Instead of thinking, *That relationship is over,* a more accurate phrasing might be something like

That relationship was a blessing that saw me through a tough time.
That relationship still exists—it's just not a daily, active friendship right now.
That friendship is in airplane mode for now; maybe one day we'll take it back online.
God gave me that friendship at the exact time I needed it, and it served a wonderful purpose.
We both have other areas of focus right now, but that doesn't invalidate the sincerity of the memories and relationship we shared.

Although seasonal friendships don't last forever the way lifetime friendships do, they are still gifts we enjoy in their time. We can look back on our memories through the lenses of joy and gratitude, not regret and disappointment. Those friendships were blessings in their day, even if that day has ended.

Friendships (especially lifetime friendships) sometimes ebb and flow.
Solomon wrote beautifully—famously—about seasons of life and how different behaviors are appropriate at different times.

> There is a time for everything,
>   and a season for every activity under the heavens:
>   a time to be born and a time to die,
>   a time to plant and a time to uproot,
>   a time to kill and a time to heal,
>   a time to tear down and a time to build,
>   a time to weep and a time to laugh,
>   a time to mourn and a time to dance,
>   a time to scatter stones and a time to gather them,
>   a time to embrace and a time to refrain from embracing.
> ECCLESIASTES 3:1-5

Many of Solomon's observations apply to our discussion of friendships: a time to tear down and a time to build, a time to embrace and a time to refrain.

God has blessed me with several lifetime friendships, women who have shared decades of life with me. Each of these friendships has gone through different seasons. In some seasons, a friend and I will draw especially close: maybe we're going through a similar struggle or joy, and we need one another's support and companionship more than usual; maybe a job change or move has brought us geographically closer together for a time, so we are able to hang out more frequently; maybe we just feel extra connected for a season. Whatever the reason, we lean on one another more often, and what joy that enhanced closeness brings.

But each of those friendships has also weathered seasons where we aren't as closely connected. The affection is still there, our love and commitment to one another have not changed, but we don't talk or see each other as often. Maybe one or both of us is busier than usual, and phone calls and visits are difficult. Maybe one or both of us is going through a tough time, and for whatever reason we are leaning into other friendships that are better equipped to support us in that particular struggle. Or maybe one of us is struggling and has turned inward to deal with it, not yet inviting others in. I've experienced all these seasons and more with each of my lifetime friendships.

To be honest, when I first sense a distance—either in my own heart or in my friend's—my first instinct is usually insecurity laced with panic: *Oh no, is something wrong? Is she mad? Are we okay?* But panic and insecurity can lead to friendship missteps. When we feel worried and unsure, we are more susceptible to mistakes that unintentionally augment the distance between us.

Panic makes us push too hard when people need space.
Insecurity makes us act weird and self-focused, when the drift
    may be all about what's going on in our friend's life and not
    about us at all.
Fear makes us hold on tighter when people need breathing room.

When I sense one of my friendships drifting, sometimes I check in with them to rule out conflict or hurt as the source of the distance. But other times, by praying and paying attention, I figure out for myself what's going on, and it usually has nothing to do with me: she's stressed with work or school; her marriage is struggling; her kids are keeping her busy; her work is overwhelming; she's discouraged and not ready to talk about it yet.

I may or may not discuss the change with my friend, depending on our dynamic and what she needs. Sometimes a direct conversation is helpful; other times, I simply have a Note-to-Self Moment, offer up some prayers for my friend, then put on my patient pants and wait for time and the Spirit to work. That patience, that willingness to say, "This is a temporary drift that's not really about me"—could protect and preserve the friendship for a later time. It may mean the difference between pushing too hard too soon and losing the friendship altogether, versus waiting out a tough season, where the friendship is ready to be renewed on the other side.

Friendships sometimes ebb and flow. They come in close, then pull away for a while, but the best friendships, like the tide, come back to us.

———

They say hindsight is twenty-twenty, but I say hindsight is all about the lenses you use when you look back. Some lenses distort memory and reality; others clarify the truth. Some lenses promote bitterness and regret; others lead to grace and healing. Jesus said, "The eye is the lamp of the body. If your eyes are healthy, your whole body will be full of light. But if your eyes are unhealthy, your whole body will be full of darkness. If then the light within you is darkness, how great is that darkness!" (Matthew 6:22-23). The lenses we choose affect the way we tell our stories: magnifying hurt, sharpening regret . . . or helping us to see God's hand at work even through heartache, finding redemption even in broken things.

The way we choose to see our friends, our conflicts, and ourselves matters. The way we tell our story matters. As you decide how to tell the story of your faded friendship, I pray you view it through Christlike lenses, lenses that are clear, light-bringing, and life-giving.

THOUGHT QUESTIONS

1. If you've experienced a faded friendship, how might you look back on the loss with a different lens? How might choosing a different perspective affect the way you feel about the break—and about your friend?

2. Have you experienced ebb and flow in a long-term friendship? What helped to preserve your friendship in the time when the friendship wasn't as close as usual?

6

THE FRIEND WHO WILL NEVER LEAVE

Today I almost always reach for mug handles one-handed,
and I don't even go squinty-eyed.
Most days I'd even say I grab mug handles with carefree abandon.

I was in high school when I first began to realize that I wanted more from my relationship with God—and that there was, in fact, more to experience. So much more.

It was a revelation born partly out of necessity. By April of my sophomore year, I was already on my third high school in just two years. Cultivating meaningful friendships at turbo speed was challenging, and I often felt alone. (In my parents' defense, we did stay put after we got to our third city, so I enjoyed a little over two years at my last high school.)

Somewhere in the midst of all that mess of moving and change and trying to make new friendships but still feeling alone—plus feeling alone because I was a bit of an old soul, a bit more ponderous than the average sixteen-year-old—I realized that people couldn't fill the hole in my heart. People weren't really what I needed.

I needed a friend who would go along with me to the next state, the next new school. I needed a friend who would always go with me *everywhere* I went. I needed a friend who was willing to share the wild joys, agonizing humiliations, terrifying hopes, and crushing disappointments of life. I needed a friend who was never too busy to listen, whose voice mail never filled up so he didn't have room for my message. I needed a friend who would never be selfish or distracted or immature (but who would forgive me when I was).

In God I found all that and more.

Many of us don't realize this, but we have unconsciously spent our whole lives trying to fill the God-sized hole in our heart with people-sized relationships—and then we wonder why we're always left a little lonely, a little disappointed, a little let down. Why the hole never gets completely filled; why there are always hollow spaces, gaps where we feel unseen, unheard, unloved.

I'm not suggesting we become cynical about people or that we stop cultivating human friendships, but perhaps we need to reevaluate whether we are putting too much pressure and expectation on people. Whether we are trying to make people do for us things that only God can do.

Putting too much pressure on our human friendships leads to a lot of *shoulds*:

> *She should realize what I need without me saying it.*
> *She should drop everything and come over to help me.*
> *She should be more available . . .*
>   *more thoughtful.*
>   *more sensitive.*
>   *more selfless.*

Should.

I don't know about you, but most of my hurt feelings and friendship disappointments have been preceded by sentences in which the word *should* takes center stage.

And maybe people should, in fact, do those things.

But the problem is, people are imperfect. Sinful. Self-absorbed. Busy. Distracted. Overwhelmed by their own problems. And different people have different *shoulds* in mind when it comes to friendships—we all have our own expectations and definitions of what makes a good friend.

So friendships, even the best of friendships, can fall a little flat, leaving us wistful, wishing we could be closer, feeling we *should* support and understand each other better . . . and then if we lose a friendship, the hole gapes wider than ever. We crave affection, companionship, and understanding. We long to have someone hear our heart's song and know exactly which harmonies will make it complete.

Bottom line? People—even the people who love us most and best—can never do for us what only God can do. The minute we accept that, it somehow lets our friendships breathe a little. It takes the *should* pressure off. And once we start filling some of the lonely places in our hearts with God and his perfect love, some of our neediness goes away. We are able to accept and enjoy what our friends give us with gratitude, but without needing those friends to fill us up entirely. Without asking them to fill a role they can never fill because they were never meant to. Our friendship with God fills the biggest part of our love tank—our friends just top it off.

GOD AS A FRIEND

What are the things we most look for in friendships? Maybe you value compassion, insight, and honesty. Maybe joy, humor, fun, or a spirit of adventure are important to you. The list could run long, but let's consider some of the friendship qualities we find in God and how he exhibits them.

Understanding

One of our heart's deepest needs is to feel understood. To feel seen and known, loved and liked, in spite of our imperfections. Scripture tells us how God understands us more intimately than anyone else:

> O LORD, you have examined my heart
>   and know everything about me.
> You know when I sit down or stand up.
>   You know my thoughts even when I'm far away.

You see me when I travel
and when I rest at home.
You know everything I do.
You know what I am going to say
even before I say it, LORD.
PSALM 139:1-4, NLT

God takes the time to get to know you—the very depths of you.
The thoughts and needs and hurts and dreams and passions you hardly
know how to explain to yourself, much less confess to another human.
The New International Version says, "You have searched me . . . and
you know me." The Creator thinks you are worth knowing. You are
intriguing enough to search. And whether you realize it or not, you are
fully known and understood.

Companionship

A companion is someone who shares life with you, who goes along with
you—who literally walks beside you and keeps you company. Tells you
stories and jokes and listens to yours. God is the only friend who can go
with us all the time, everywhere, for all of our days. As Psalm 139 goes
on to explain,

You go before me and follow me.
You place your hand of blessing on my head.
Such knowledge is too wonderful for me,
too great for me to understand!
I can never escape from your Spirit!
I can never get away from your presence!
If I go up to heaven, you are there;
if I go down to the grave, you are there.
If I ride the wings of the morning,
if I dwell by the farthest oceans,
even there your hand will guide me,
and your strength will support me.

> I could ask the darkness to hide me
>> and the light around me to become night—
>> but even in darkness I cannot hide from you.

PSALM 139:5-12, NLT

As parents walk before and behind their toddlers, protecting and guiding, arms outstretched to catch them when they stumble, so our Father and friend surrounds us with his loving, protecting presence. Up in heaven, down in the grave, across the farthest oceans—no matter where we go, our God is with us—guiding and protecting us, sharing the journey so we're never alone.

Empathy

Sometimes I just need to have a ginormous, cathartic cry—the two-boxes-of-tissues kind, the kind where you flush all your feelings out through your eyeballs—but the catharsis doesn't feel quite complete without someone there to just . . . sit with me. Be in the room. Be my witness, care that I'm sad-overwhelmed-guilty-stressed-happy-grateful and a hundred other things at once. I have learned that even when a human isn't available—or willing—to fill that role, Someone always is:

> The LORD hears his people when they call to him for help.
>> He rescues them from all their troubles.
> The LORD is close to the brokenhearted;
>> he rescues those whose spirits are crushed.

PSALM 34:17-18, NLT

God is always near, but the more we hurt, the closer he leans. He hears our cries for help, and when sorrow comes, he invites us to weep into his broad shoulder. He hurts with us and for us.

Faithfulness

The loss of a relationship can make us wonder: Is anyone faithful? Is any relationship permanent? Know this: there is a friend who never leaves. Faithfulness is one of God's salient qualities, one he repeatedly emphasizes in Scripture because he knows how tempted we are to doubt it. Take a look at just two of many possible examples:

> He will cover you with his feathers,
>   and under his wings you will find refuge;
>   his faithfulness will be your shield and rampart.
> PSALM 91:4

> The LORD himself goes before you and will be with you;
> he will never leave you nor forsake you. Do not be afraid;
> do not be discouraged.
> DEUTERONOMY 31:8

A thousand different ways, God reassures us, "You can trust me. I'm never going to break on you or burn you. I'm never going to abandon you or change my mind. I'm never going to turn into someone different than the one you originally trusted. I'll always be here. I'll always be me. *I am.* And I always will be."

HOW GOD FULFILLS OUR FRIENDSHIP NEEDS

God is everything we long for in a friend: faithful, empathetic, understanding, a devoted companion. He is the one we can turn to, even when everyone else fails. Many years ago, a woman named Hannah showed us how.

HANNAH AND PENINNAH
Based on 1 Samuel 1

Hannah takes off her sandals and ducks into the tent Elkanah had the servants put up for her. Her eyes drift around the too-large space, noting how they've gone to great lengths to make it cozy, even pretty, though she'll only be sleeping here this one night on the family's way to worship at Shiloh. She slips off her outer garment and settles onto the sleeping mat, aware that Elkanah has given her the thickest of the blankets, the softest of the skins.

It should make her feel loved, make her feel happy and full—the favorite wife of her wealthy husband—but it only reminds her why he tries so hard. Because she will lie in this tent alone. No babe snuggled up at her breast. No toddler tucked in on a tiny pallet beside her. Not even Elkanah to hold her close and wipe her tears—"Help Peninnah with the little ones," Hannah had told him. "They'll be out of sorts from the travel. I don't mind."

"Really?" he asked.

"Really," she said, pretending even to herself.

"I'll come to you later," he'd promised.

"Don't," she'd insisted. "I just want to sleep. When I sleep, I don't feel." Which was not entirely true—even her dreams have darkened these past few years. With every child her rival wife Peninnah has borne, Hannah's hopes have shrunk smaller.

Elkanah drops a kiss on her forehead, and as she watches him leave, she wants to jump up, chase him, cry out, *I do mind! I mind it all, hate it all! Don't leave me in here alone. Come back to me. Peninnah has a tentful of children—I have only you.*

But what good would it do? What would it change?

A voice drifts on the air—a lullaby. Anyone else listening probably finds the song sweet, beautiful, all that is wonderful about motherhood— everyone says Peninnah has a gorgeous voice—but to Hannah, the voice is the dry rasp of a vulture's cry. *She's probably singing loudly on purpose, to spite me,* Hannah thinks. *To make sure I hear her and remember that I may have a bigger tent, but hers is full of children. Children she gets to sing to sleep. As if I could ever forget.* Resentment runs through her, a slow burn. She breathes deep, trying to fight it, not sure she has the strength.

Help me, Lord, she prays. *Just . . . help.* Snatches of psalms come to mind; she borrows them as her own prayers, whispering them to God, drawing strength from their words: "Record my misery; list my tears on your scroll. . . . When I was in distress, I sought the Lord; at night I stretched out untiring hands and I would not be comforted."

She tries to find more words, her own words, but all she can do is bleed emotion in a plea too anguished for human language. But somehow she knows God is taking it, understanding it, holding it—holding her—even when her husband is not. And for that she is grateful.

I'll go to the Tabernacle tomorrow, she resolves. *I need to be closer to the Lord. To stand in his presence. To speak with the only one who understands.*

Hannah did, indeed, go to pray in the Lord's Tabernacle at Shiloh. She took her lonely heart, her empty womb, into the place of worship and begged God yet again for a child. Her passionate prayer—tears streaming, lips moving with a plea too desperate, too painful, to speak aloud—got the attention of the prophet Eli. At first Eli thought she was drunk, but when Hannah assured him, "I was pouring out my soul to the Lord. . . . I have been praying here out of my great anguish and grief" (1 Samuel 1:15-16), Eli promised her that the Lord would grant her request. When Hannah poured out her soul to God that day, she showed us how deep friendship with God can truly go.

Let's step back momentarily from our talk of friendship with God to acknowledge an especially confusing aspect of Hannah's story: her husband had two wives. Honestly? To a modern reader the idea of polygamy is jarring, distasteful, and disturbing. It is difficult for us to comprehend, much less relate to. An in-depth study on polygamy is outside the scope of this book, but know this: it seems polygamy was a practice God tolerated for a time but did not condone.[1] Polygamous marriages often happened because of financial need or as a solution for infertility when a family needed an heir to protect property or to preserve a bloodline. Every time Scripture depicts a polygamous relationship, the practice is cast in a negative light, as an institution that harms women and divides families. But perhaps the fact that God does not shy away from including painful stories, like Hannah and Peninnah's, can comfort you if you've endured a particularly messy break. Some friendships break because of "mild" issues like gossip or hurt feelings; others shatter because of dramatic sin that carries awful repercussions: infidelity, theft, lies.

---

1. By New Testament times, church leaders were prohibited from polygamy, indicating that it was not upheld as a healthy or righteous practice. (See 1 Timothy 3:2 and Titus 1:6, which state that an overseer [elder] must be "the husband of one wife" [ESV, HCSB, and more].)

Is it any wonder that Hannah turned to prayer as a refuge in her suffering? Her example teaches us to draw near to God as our best and most reliable friend, entrusting him with our toughest emotions.

While the idea of friendship with God sounds nice on paper, even poetic, it may feel . . . theoretical. Like something only Holy People can experience. We long to see it, *feel* it, in our own messy, not-always-holy lives, with our own heartaches, hurts, and joys, but we don't know how. The encouraging news is, developing a friendship with God isn't all that different from cultivating a human one. If anything, it's simpler, because with God, reciprocation is guaranteed: "Come near to God and he will come near to you," James promises us (James 4:8). For every step we take toward God, however fumbling or unsure, he closes the gap and takes steps toward us too. Let's take a look at some specific ways we can begin to experience a feeling of friendship with God.

We can share all the details and emotions of daily life with him.

Sorrow and fear, joy and gratitude—there is no emotion or season God does not want to share with us. Hannah's example shows us that God is not put off by the deepest of sorrows; his hands are big enough, kind enough, to hold it with us and for us. But it's not just grief God wants to share; he's here for our joy too. "The blameless spend their days under the LORD's care," Psalm 37:18 tells us. The joyful days, the frustrating days, the silly, the mundane, the overwhelming days—he's here for them all.

It took my husband, Kevin, a long time to realize that I was the girl of his dreams. A *long* time. As in, I had to wait and pray and secretly swoon my way through two-plus years of an excruciatingly maddening yet delightfully thrilling friendship, rife with inconsistent and confusing romantic vibes. But when he finally (finally!) realized how he felt, he was head over heels, buying-me-Twizzlers-and-writing-sweet-cards-and-introducing-me-to-his-family in love. You have never seen a girl smile so big for so long.

At first, my friends and family, who had so faithfully put up with my years of angst and frustration, were eager to hear all the swoony details, but after a few weeks, I noticed their eyes glazing over when I tried to regale them with more "Listen to how Kevin dotes on me, and have I mentioned the way his chiseled jaw makes my heart go pitter-pat" stories. But I still needed an outlet—still needed someone to listen and celebrate and—well, maybe not squeal, but laugh and rejoice and savor it all with me. Waiting on Kevin had taught me to lean on God in heartache and struggle; now I thought, "Maybe he cares about the good stuff too." So I started sharing those moments with God in prayer. Praising God for his generosity and kindness, telling him how happy I was, thanking him for listening and caring. Odd as it may sound, it was a uniquely intimate time in my walk with God.

And I did the same thing several years later, when our miserable struggle with infertility finally came to an end and I became a mother at last. Every day with my babies held a thousand memories I longed to treasure and share—but who could make the time to listen to every one? God could, and God did. The same God who had held me through all the tearstained years I'd spent longing for a baby now rejoiced with me on the other side. Together we chuckled and *awww*-ed and rolled our eyes at the antics of these adorable babies he had entrusted to me. What a friend God was to me throughout the sleep-deprived nights, the exhausting-but-heart-soaring days. It was during those years that I began meditating often on this odd little proverb:

> Each heart knows its own bitterness,
> and no one else can share its joy.
> PROVERBS 14:10

This proverb acknowledges that people can never fully grasp all we feel—the weight of grief, sitting heavy on our chests, crushing air from our lungs; the buoyancy of joy, catapulting us heavenward to dizzying heights—*but God can*.

What if you tried communicating with God more often as you go about your day? Many of us feel only a vague sense of half-comfort at the idea of God watching over our lives, because we picture him squinting down on our ant-sized selves from some distant heavenly throne, possibly needing divine binoculars to even find us in a crowd . . . but what if we invited him in closer? I encourage you to welcome God into your thoughts, your feelings, your fears. Share with him your commentary on the business meeting. Laugh with him about the awkward exchange with your classmate. Lament your kid's struggles in school. Intentionally connect with him moment by moment, inviting him to participate in your life, sharing each day's journey with you.

We can trust he's fully present when we're hurting.

One of the reasons Jesus came to earth in human form was to teach us—to show us—how to draw close to God. The night of his arrest, Jesus knew what was coming. Knew it all, foresaw it in excruciating, overwhelming detail. And what did Jesus do? He asked his three closest friends to keep watch with him while he prayed. To keep him company.

Isn't that what we all need from our friends? Someone to keep watch? Someone to sit, their shoulder warm against ours, and hold our hand when words fail?

Jesus' friends weren't there for him in his hour of need, so guess who stepped in to fill the void? *God.*

Take a look at the scene:

He walked away, about a stone's throw, and knelt down and prayed, "Father, if you are willing, please take this cup of suffering away from me. Yet I want your will to be done, not mine." Then an angel from heaven appeared and strengthened him. He prayed more fervently, and he was in such agony of spirit that his sweat fell to the ground like great drops of blood.
LUKE 22:41-44, NLT

God sent an angel to comfort his Son. Where people failed, God stepped in.

And God didn't just step in to comfort his Son—Scripture gives us countless examples of God showing kindness to other hurting hearts. When Hannah stumbled into the Tabernacle, praying so desperately that she could not fit her grief into words, God showed up. He showed up through the prophet Eli, who promised Hannah a baby at last, an answer to her years of prayers.

David assures us in many of his psalms that God shows up for all of his people, including me and you:

The salvation of the righteous comes from the LORD;
    he is their stronghold in time of trouble.
The LORD helps them and delivers them.
PSALM 37:39-40

God is ready and eager to comfort you, no matter what you're going through. He'll never get tired, never run out of time or energy, never accuse you of being too needy. He's here for it—all of it.

We can be confident that God likes and understands us.
We all long for that glorious feeling of being chosen. Being loved by someone who has absolutely no obligation to do so. They just . . . *like* us. They enjoy our company. And best of all, they "get" us. As C. S. Lewis put it, "Friendship . . . is born at the moment when one man says to another 'What! You too?'"[2]

How precious close friendships are, and how difficult to find. As kids, we're like, "Do you like hide-and-seek, wiggly teeth, and the color purple? Yay!"—*et voilà*, instant bestie—but in adulthood, it gets more complicated. More nuanced. Kindred spirits are harder to come by, rare treasures.

But take comfort from this: even if you don't have a best friend in your life right now, you do have a friend who likes and enjoys you, quirks and all. You have God. I have always believed that God loved me (the Bible is pretty clear on that), but unconsciously, I used to wonder if God really *liked* me. For years—years!—I felt like God was half-heartedly putting up with me with a vague sense of disapproval, constantly sighing to the Holy Spirit, "This one's a handful. Way too emotional and complicated. And what's with her mug-handle phobia?

2. C. S. Lewis, *The Four Loves* (San Francisco: HarperOne, 2017), 100.

Talk about weird! I guess we'll let her stick around and hope she gets it together, but don't get attached to her—we'll probably have to kick her out one of these days."

But a morning spent meditating on Psalm 139, a passage that has already given us great encouragement in this chapter, changed my perspective. I sat in my prayer chair, pondering the meaning of these words:

> You have searched me, LORD,
>   and you know me.
> You know when I sit and when I rise;
>   you perceive my thoughts from afar. . . .
> For you created my inmost being;
>   you knit me together in my mother's womb.
> I praise you because I am fearfully and wonderfully made;
>   your works are wonderful,
>   I know that full well.
> My frame was not hidden from you
>   when I was made in the secret place,
>   when I was woven together in the depths of the earth.
> Your eyes saw my unformed body;
>   all the days ordained for me were written in your book
>   before one of them came to be.
> How precious to me are your thoughts, God!
>   How vast is the sum of them!
> PSALM 139:1-2, 13-17

Somewhere between moonfall and sunrise, a heart-healing shift clicked into place:

> You perceive my thoughts from afar. *God knows my deepest, most complex and tangled and even sinful thoughts.*
> You knit me together in my mother's womb. *He knit me together with his powerful hands: quirky humor, compassion and sensitivity, a huge love for language and family and dark chocolate. An oversentimental romantic streak.*

My frame was not hidden from you when I was made in the secret
place. *He saw me before I drew breath. He knows me—all of me.*
I am fearfully and wonderfully made. *God knows, and intentionally
designed, everything about me. He adores the person he made me
to be. He calls me wonderful.*

We all want to be seen and known, understood and enjoyed. We
can't always find that experience perfectly with friends—does any friend
ever understand everything about us?— but we can always have it with
God.

With God we never have to explain the backstory. With God we
never have to hem and haw and feel embarrassed, wondering what he's
thinking. With God we never have to think, *Was that TMI? Did I just
overwhelm him?* With God we never have to say, "You had to be there
to get it"—because he *was* there.

You can't overwhelm God. Can't overshare. Can't overstay your
welcome.

He'll never grow tired of you. Never "move on" to someone else.
Never forget you.

He is the perfect friend, the one you've been looking for your
whole life.

A REAL FRIEND IN THE REAL WORLD

You may be thinking something like, *All this talk about God being a
friend sounds so . . . mushy and vague. That's great and all, but I need
someone I can see. Someone I can sit down to have coffee with. Someone
who can shop with me and give me opinions! Friendship with God sounds
nice, but it's utterly impractical and doesn't make me feel better in the real
world.*

Honestly, I've felt the same way, had the same thoughts. But here
are a couple of practices that have helped me feel closer to God in my
real-world life. Perhaps they will also help you to sense God's friendship
more actively at work in your daily life.

Start praying more often throughout your day.

When something happy happens, thank God for it, acknowledging it as a gift from him—or even just smile toward heaven and say, "Did you see that, God? How cool was that?!"

When something stressful happens, take it straight to God in prayer, confident that he wants to hear about it (however small or insignificant it may seem), confident that even if he doesn't take away the problem, he can help you to manage the stress.

When something sad happens, take it to him—throw it onto his broad-as-the-universe shoulders. He can help you carry the load.

Take your relationship with God out of the morning devotion,
"quiet time" box.

Morning devotions are fantastic—I get up before the sun many days because I love having mine—but there's so much more to friendship with God than a half hour in the mornings.

And let's be honest: not everyone loves sitting in a chair reading and praying. So give yourself permission to try some different things, to experiment with connecting with God in different ways. Just as human friendships grow stale if we always do the same thing and rehash the same conversation every time we meet, so our friendship with God can grow stale too.

Here are some fresh ideas to try:

Turn your walk with God into some actual *walks* with God.
   Go take a walk and talk to God as you go.
Write down your prayers like letters.
Try praying out loud.
Go somewhere inspiring to spend time with God: a park, the
   woods, a pond, the beach, the mountains, somewhere with
   a pretty view.
Go out for coffee with God . . . Take your Bible and a journal
   and hang out with God in a café.
Listen to music that helps you connect with God.

These things may feel uncomfortable at first, and you may not connect with them all, but if you want a deeper friendship with God, it's worth investing more time and creativity. You've got nothing to lose and the best friendship in the world to gain. Why not give some new things a try?

You may not be ready to put yourself out there to make a new human friend, but in the meantime, I pray you lean into the one friendship that will never let you down. You may not be able to repair the broken friendship you're mourning, but you do have a friendship that will never break and never fail. God is here to fill the gap—all the gaps—that the broken friendship left in your heart.

He's here to listen as you process the hurts of what happened.

He's here for the part where you learn to forgive.

He's here for the part where you begin to heal.

He's here for the part where you reach out an anxious hand and take that mug by the handle.

He's here for all the other stuff you need a friend for along the way: laughing at silly moments, celebrating victories without a hint of envy, offering a hand to ease sorrow's load.

You could spend a lifetime looking for a friendship that will never disappoint . . . but the wondrous truth is, you already have one. I pray you begin experiencing that friendship more fully today—what a treasure awaits!

THOUGHT QUESTIONS

1. What quality of God's friendship do you need the most right now? How might you seek to experience and enjoy that quality a bit more?
2. When have you felt the most emotionally close to God? What helped you feel that way?
3. Which of the suggestions for connecting with God would you like to try?

Part 2

ATTEMPTING REPAIR

The Bowl

7

THE PATH TO HEALING

I heard a crash and a wail.
My stomach clenched;
I could hardly bear to look,
already knowing what I would see.

I'm sitting cross-legged and blanket-draped on my bed, praying. Praying about the broken relationship for the I've-lost-count time. Anger blazes, hot as ever, and I try to work myself through it . . . again:

Jesus calls you to forgive.

Forgive as God forgave you: generously, completely, without expecting an apology or restitution.

Let it go.

Let. It. Go.

After struggling to shake free from the strident voice of Idina Menzel, my mind hitches on two words:

Apology.
Restitution.

I start exploring those words in prayer: *Lord, if they would only apologize, I think I could feel differently. Is it too much to ask that I hear the words? If they would only set things right, I could move on.*

And the truth strikes, lightning-bolting my heart: *I'm not going to have the conversations I need in this situation. I may long for those healing talks, and they would really help, but if I'm being realistic, they're not coming. And that means I have to go ahead and let go without them. I have to decide to forgive. And I need to do it today.*

So here's what I'm getting at—this is the call you probably knew was coming (insert ominous music here; I'm thinking Darth Vader's Theme, aka "The Imperial March").

We have to choose to forgive.

Want to hear a horrible secret of mine? I love talking about forgiveness—until *I'm* the person who needs to do the forgiving. How righteous it feels to talk about theoretical forgiveness, to extol its lofty virtues from the pulpit or on paper . . . but when it's time to practice forgiveness in real life, when we ourselves are cut by the jagged dagger of real-life hurt wielded by the hand of a friend, we discover just how difficult forgiveness can be.

Maybe you already feel slightly annoyed-slash-defensive, the way I started out feeling that day on the bed: *I already know what you're going to say. I need to forgive, or God won't forgive me, yada yada. I didn't pick up this book to be preached at; I just need my hurts ministered to.*

Maybe you feel too hurt and overwhelmed to even consider forgiveness: *I'm still processing. I can't even name all the ways that friend hurt me—how can I forgive hurts I can't yet express?*

Maybe you feel guilty because you know you should forgive your (former) friend, but you're not there yet: *I know I should be more like Jesus. I should be able to let this go, but I can't. What's wrong with my heart?*

Maybe you feel exhausted from trying—and failing—to forgive: *I've prayed about this a thousand times, but the anger won't go away. Maybe I just can't do it.*

Maybe you feel hopeless and preemptively exhausted, the way I felt cradling the shards of my grandmother's bowl in my hands: *I don't think I can forgive, much less fit these pieces together again. I'm not sure I'm up for it.*

I have been in all of those places—sometimes all of them all at once. I cycled through every one of those thoughts that day on the bed.

Forgiveness is hard.

Forgiveness takes work.

Forgiveness fights against every instinct of our fleshly nature.

Is it any wonder Jesus spoke about forgiveness so frequently? Forgiveness was important to Jesus—you might even say it was central to his message, the very soul of it—so it has to be important to us too. Like it or not, we have to talk about forgiveness in broken friendships.

Ready or not, we have to dig in.

JESUS' TAKE ON FORGIVENESS

Early in his ministry, Jesus preached a message, or perhaps a series of messages, that we call the Sermon on the Mount. In that sermon, he explained to his followers, "Here's what it means to be my disciple; here's what you're signing up for if you want to be with me." And in that message, Jesus essentially prohibited bitterness for his followers. First, he told us to pray these words: "Forgive us our sins, as we have forgiven those who sin against us" (Matthew 6:12, NLT). He went on to say, "If you forgive those who sin against you, your heavenly Father will forgive you. But if you refuse to forgive others, your Father will not forgive your sins" (verses 14-15). (Here I picture Jesus walking off the stage after a mic drop, leaving the crowd to talk among themselves, trying to wrap their hearts around this idea.) We like to say that God offers us unconditional forgiveness, and certainly, there is nothing we can do to earn or deserve his grace. However, Jesus tells us there *is* a condition for our forgiveness: we must forgive others. Our ability to *receive* forgiveness is tied to our willingness to *offer* it. Holding a grudge is not a luxury Christians have—not if we want to be forgiven by God.

Later in Jesus' ministry, his disciple Peter, who was apparently still wrestling with this concept, came to Jesus and asked for clarification:

> "Lord, how many times shall I forgive my brother or sister who sins against me? Up to seven times?"
>
> Jesus answered, "I tell you, not seven times, but seventy-seven times."

MATTHEW 18:21-22

Of course, Jesus wasn't suggesting we carry around a little notebook, jotting down a tally mark for every time we offer forgiveness to each of our friends. In Jewish thought, the number seven symbolized perfection or completion, so saying "seventy-seven" or "seventy times seven," as some translations have it, would convey the idea of *"perfect* perfection" or *"complete* completeness." Jesus is essentially saying, "Forgive as many times as it takes. Forgive the complete number of times."

As followers of Jesus, holding grudges is not an option for you and me.

I know. This is hard to hear and even harder to obey. Here's where our big *but*s get in the way:

But she hurt me!
But what she did was wrong!
But she's not even sorry!

Our hearts cry all these words, and the words may be fully true. *Even so*, Jesus calls us to forgive.

JESUS' EXAMPLE OF FORGIVENESS

Before you fling this book across the room and reevaluate your Christianity, consider this: Jesus is not asking us to do anything he has not done himself—and to a much more dramatic degree. Jesus has modeled a higher level of forgiveness than most of us can fathom.

You and I may have been betrayed by friends, but we have not been betrayed to the death.

You and I may have suffered at others' hands, but we have not been flogged and crucified.

And here's the thing: Jesus forgave *even when* the people who hurt him did not admit wrongdoing. Jesus forgave *even while* he was being betrayed and killed. Jesus forgave *even though* he hadn't received the apologies he deserved. We, too, are called to forgive even when, even while, and even though.

Paul once wrote to the church at Colossae, "Bear with each other and forgive one another if any of you has a grievance against someone. Forgive as the Lord forgave you" (Colossians 3:13).

Forgive as the Lord forgave you.

That's a tall order. Paul described the Lord's forgiveness like this when he wrote to the church in Rome: "But God demonstrates his own love for us in this: *While we were still sinners*, Christ died for us" (Romans 5:8, emphasis added).

There's that idea again: *even while.* Christ paved the way for our forgiveness while we were still sitting unrepentant in the middle of the horrors of sin. Still wallowing in our own filth. Thank goodness Jesus did not wait to offer us a path to peace until after we had repented.

The Lord forgave us before we knew we needed forgiving.

The Lord forgave us without reservation. Completely. Forever.

And *this* is how we are to forgive.

Here's the part where we all fall to our knees before Jesus, saying with Peter, "Go away from me, Lord; I am a sinful person!" (See Luke 5:8.)

I write these words, I explain these high standards in all their that-sounds-impossible glory, not to shame or to frustrate us, but to call us to *God's* call. His call that speaks to the *best* parts of our hearts. Yes, forgiveness is difficult, but our struggle comes as no surprise to God. He knew this would be hard for us, yet he called us to it anyway . . . which tells us *we can do it.*

Because we have received such astounding, unmerited grace from the Lord, we can turn and offer it to others. We can do it because we realize that forgiveness isn't really about what your friend does or says or whether she's really sorry or whether she understands your pain. Instead, forgiveness is about our relationship with God. It's a holy offering, a sacred expression of gratitude, humility, and surrender. It's the most challenging way—but perhaps the most beautiful way—we imitate our Lord.

Now, hang on to these thoughts, because I know you might be hiccupping on them a little. I sure have. We're going to flesh them out in depth as this chapter goes on. But first: a story. A moment when a friend of mine struggled to forgive.

JAN'S STORY

Jan never thought of herself as someone who struggled with forgiveness. She loved easily, laughed often, and let things roll off her shoulders. But . . . she had started to change.

Jan had been best friends with Geri for a decade. Then hurtful realizations started knocking on the door of her heart quietly, one by one:

This friendship isn't what it used to be.
This friendship feels lopsided. She gives me advice and points out issues in my life, but I'm not allowed to do the same.
I don't feel as close to Geri as I used to.

For a while, Jan brushed her concerns aside, hoping they would go away.

They didn't.

Resentment built: an itch here, an irritation there, like an invisible rash. But time passed, and the rash kept spreading. Everything Geri did and said seemed to inflame the irritation. Before long, Jan had a heart-wound, ugly and infected.

Finally, she tried to speak up, but it didn't go well. In fact, it went badly. Geri couldn't hear her. Jan felt blown off—more proof that the friendship was lopsided. Days went by, stretching into weeks, weeks Jan spent stewing, reliving hurtful moments on repeat. And sometime in those weeks, Jan finally thought to herself, *This friendship is broken. I don't know if it can ever be put back together.*

Fast-forward in time, and Jan and Geri hadn't talked for months—going on a year. Geri had moved away a while ago, and her absence was a relief. An excuse not to deal with the issue. The problem was, the issue hadn't moved away with Geri. Jan was stuck on it. Jan was stuck, period.

Geri started reaching out, making some efforts to set things right. She sent flowers, wrote a card, sent an email, asked Jan if they could meet. She was finally ready to hear what Jan had to say. But now Jan wasn't ready to talk. Jan spent a lot of time talking *about* their not talking. And her hard feelings. And all the things Geri had done to hurt her. And all the things Geri needed to change. This went on long enough that Jan's friends, who had listened patiently for the past year, started gently suggesting that it was time to move on. Time to let go. Time to forgive.

But Jan couldn't. Or maybe she wouldn't. It was hard to tell.

"You should pray about this," her friends said.

Jan nodded like she was listening—what was she supposed to say, "No way, I'm still not ready to pray?"—but the truth was, she wasn't.

The truth was, she could hardly pray or even read her Bible anymore. Every time she opened the Bible, the pages seemed to fall open to verses about forgiveness. Verses she didn't want to read, much less obey.

And what could she say to God when she knew there was this big, angry elephant stomping around the room between them?

Jan was stuck. Stuck in bitterness. Waiting on an apology that might never come. Waiting on her former friend to change.

MISCONCEPTIONS ABOUT FORGIVENESS

Jan's story brings up a few misconceptions about forgiveness that we have touched on but need to debunk more specifically.

I can't forgive unless my friend changes.

I have nurtured this thought many times, and at first it feels reasonable and fair. But my perspective starts to change when I remember the call to "forgive as the Lord forgave [us]" (Colossians 3:13). When I remember that Jesus forgave us before we'd even tried to change. Paul describes Jesus' grace this way:

> You were dead because of your sins and because your sinful nature was not yet cut away. Then God made you alive with Christ, for he forgave all our sins. He canceled the record of the charges against us and took it away by nailing it to the cross.
> COLOSSIANS 2:13-14, NLT

God canceled our charges and offered us a path to forgiveness while we were still dead in our sins, still living the same old way we'd always lived. Now we get to offer that kind of pay-it-forward mercy to others.

Would it be ideal if your friend grew and changed? Of course, and you can continue praying for her, asking God to help her grow. But it is both Christlike and liberating to say, "My forgiveness is not dependent on anyone else's choices or actions. My decision to forgive is between me and God."

I can't forgive unless my friend understands how much she hurt me and apologizes.

Would it be ideal if your friend tried to grasp all the ways she hurt you, then apologized in a way that made you feel understood? Absolutely. But there's no guarantee she will do those things. You could be waiting a long time—maybe forever. Meanwhile the anger and hurt you feel will continue eating away at your heart. And here's a hard truth: even if they try, people who hurt you can never *fully* understand how you feel. They can't step inside your head and heart to access your memories and emotions. The moment you set yourself free from the expectation that a friend has to understand your hurt is the moment you set yourself free to begin letting go.

When I'm struggling with this, it helps me to remember that Jesus did not demand, "Until you understand the pain I suffered because of your sin, you can't be forgiven!" If Jesus had done that, we would never have received forgiveness. We can never fathom all Jesus suffered for us on the cross; we can never understand the anguish the Father felt as he heard Jesus' cries of pain. Even if we spend the rest of our lives trying to grasp it, trying to say thank you and honor Jesus' sacrifice, we'll never completely understand. Thank God he doesn't make us.

I can't forgive unless justice is done.

Some wrongs may not be set right for a while—or even in this life—but Scripture repeatedly assures us that God loves justice, and he will make things right in his time and in his way. As David put it,

Commit everything you do to the LORD.
Trust him, and he will help you.

He will make your innocence radiate like the dawn,
    and the justice of your cause will shine like the noonday sun.
Be still in the presence of the LORD,
    and wait patiently for him to act.
PSALM 37:5-7, NLT

If a former friend is lying about you or otherwise mistreating you, they will face a day of reckoning. In the meantime, Scripture calls us to keep our hearts clear of bitterness and our hands clean of revenge. To trust that God himself will set this right in the end.[1]

With God's help and Jesus' example, we can work through the myths that stand in the way of forgiveness. As Jesus fought for his final breaths on the cross, he managed to pray, "Father, forgive them, for they do not know what they are doing" (Luke 23:34). Jesus forgave the ones who killed him even though they didn't acknowledge their sin, apologize, or try to make things right—and it's unlikely any of them ever did *any* of those things. But that didn't matter to Jesus. Jesus' decision to forgive wasn't between him and those people—his decision to forgive was between him and God. And so it is with us.

WHAT FORGIVENESS *ISN'T*

As difficult as forgiveness is, sometimes we make it more difficult on ourselves than it needs to be. We get confused about what forgiveness actually is, and so we try to manufacture feelings or beliefs that are outside of our control. Let's examine a few misconceptions about what forgiveness looks like, misconceptions that can be barriers to our willingness to get started. Let's consider what forgiveness *isn't*.

Forgiveness isn't approving of someone's actions.
Sometimes we worry that if we forgive someone, we're implying that what they did was okay—or at least not that bad. If a friend has sinned against you, it wasn't okay. Not at all. Forgiveness doesn't mean you

---

1. See chapter 13, "When You're Being Maligned," for a more thorough discussion of this topic.

think your friend's sin was any less wrong. It was still wrong, perhaps horribly so. When Esau forgave his brother Jacob (see the vignette on page 97), he did not fold him in a hug and say, "What you did was fine, and I'm so glad you stole my birthright and inheritance." Scripture is clear that Jacob was a deceiver, and God seemed to refine Jacob's manipulative character by allowing him to suffer similar mistreatment at the hands of a deceitful relative, Laban. But in offering his brother forgiveness, Esau set his own heart free and saved his family from continued brokenness—even war.

Forgiveness simply means that you are letting go. You are refusing to allow bitterness and resentment to live inside you (because bitterness has painful consequences for our hearts). You are not allowing your former friend's actions or choices to dictate what you think or feel. You are leaving correction and rebuke, justice and vengeance, in God's hands, trusting that he will work on your friend's heart (whether or not you ever see that work happening).

Forgiveness isn't a feeling.

I can't forgive until I feel ready to forgive. To pretend otherwise would be insincere and fake. Ever bumped up against that thought? Sometimes Jesus asks us to do things we don't *feel like* doing—and things we may never feel like doing. He set the example for us by going willingly to the cross even though he didn't want to suffer. He didn't want to die. But he chose obedience to God in spite of his human desires (see Matthew 26:36-46).

If you think about it, we do many things for God that are based on decisions, not emotions. We sacrifice when we would prefer to be comfortable. We love others when we would rather be selfish. We tell the truth when a lie would make life easier.

The decision to forgive is not a feeling—it is a decision. A choice. An act of trust and obedience. I find that truth liberating. It sets me free from being enslaved by my unruly emotions and allows me to obey God's will regardless of how I feel.

Forgiveness isn't something you do once.

The initial decision to forgive is a powerful moment, but that's just the beginning. At first, you may have to renew your decision every day, even many times a day. You'll have to *remind* yourself that you've already decided to forgive.

Even when your head knows you've decided to forgive, your feelings may be stuck in the old pattern. Angry, hurt feelings don't go away overnight; they linger. Like caffeine, they buzz around in your veins long after you've finished your coffee. When you decide to forgive someone, you have to lay new neural tracks in your brain, to rewire the emotions you automatically feel whenever your friend's name comes up. Bitterness casts a long shadow, and it may take you a while to walk far enough away to escape the shadow's gloomy grasp. Again, you may not *feel* differently toward your friend right away, but that doesn't mean your initial decision to forgive was invalid. Stick to it. Reinforce it with thoughts and actions that promote grace and peace. Eventually, your emotions will catch up.

Let's imitate the Father's generous heart and offer fresh mercies to friends who have hurt us. Lamentations 3 speaks eloquently about the way God offers us new mercies day by day:

> Because of the LORD's great love we are not consumed,
>   for his compassions never fail.
> They are new every morning;
>   great is your faithfulness.
> I say to myself, "The LORD is my portion;
>   therefore I will wait for him."
> LAMENTATIONS 3:22-24

Let's renew our decision to forgive as often as we need to.

Forgiveness doesn't mean you're done processing how you feel.

A minister friend wrote to me recently, saying, "Forgiveness has gotten so much harder lately. People are taking so much time to 'process' that they won't forgive. It feels like 'I'm still processing' really means, 'I refuse to forgive and move forward.'"

Whew.

That's a tricky one, but I hear what she's saying. Does it sometimes take us time to heal and work through it to the other side of hurt? Of course it does. But does our need to process give us the right to withhold forgiveness from someone? Biblically, no it doesn't. Here's something to consider: you can fully forgive a friend who has hurt you before you've finished "processing." Processing and forgiving can happen simultaneously. That means you may have difficult feelings you are still praying about and working through, but in the meantime, you can be kind. You can be gracious. You can speak to (and about) your friend without being angry and miserable.

Perhaps you've been on the receiving end of a "forgiveness delay," so you know what it feels like. If we're not careful, words like "I just need time to process before I offer forgiveness" can end up being code for "You hurt me; now it's my turn to hurt you" or "You once held power over me; now that you're sorry, *I* have the power, and I'm not using my power to set you free from your mistake . . . not yet." Our forgiveness can become a weapon. A tool we use to tilt the balance of power back in our own favor and put our ex-friend back in her place.

Even if you still need time to process, to sort and pray through your own hurts, you can offer forgiveness. The relationship may never be exactly the same, but at least you aren't holding something over your friend's head.[2]

Forgiveness doesn't mean you have to be friends again.

You can forgive someone without obligating yourself to become BFFs again.

Some people just don't pair well. Their personalities clash constantly. One friend is significantly stronger than the other, creating an imbalance in the relationship. One friend is too insecure to speak the truth. Or the two don't speak the same emotional language no matter how hard

---

2. If you're still in the processing phase, check out chapter 14, "Mourning a Lost Friendship."

they try, and someone is always getting hurt. They bring out the worst in each other.

Perhaps your conflict has revealed some unhappy truths about a former friend: you have irreconcilable differences, or she is not a trustworthy person. Perhaps she damaged your trust in such a way that you no longer feel safe in the relationship.

You can forgive someone, then allow some space in the relationship—not out of unkindness or a desire to stick it to them, just . . . a need for elbow room. Healthy distance.

———

I pray discrediting some false definitions of forgiveness knocks down some of the unnecessary barriers that may have been hiding in your heart, hampering your forgiveness.

Once we tear down the false barriers, we still have to deal with the *real* roadblocks—the anger and fears that root in our hearts, then root our feet in place, preventing forward progress. Let's take a look at the story of brothers who were driven apart by deceit and greed. Jacob and Esau's relationship wasn't just broken; it was crushed to powder, destined for the garbage heap. The twin brothers, who had once shared a womb, now lived completely estranged, and we know that Jacob, at least, suffered a great deal during their time apart. (You can read more of his story in Genesis 29–31.) All of the milestones they should have shared—marriage, children, loving and losing and learning—they did it all on their own, without a brother to help share the joys and carry the burdens. But one day, life—or more accurately, God—forced them to meet again.

JACOB AND ESAU
Based on Genesis 32–33

"Come, my love, it is time." Jacob reaches out a hand; Rachel's small hand slips into his, a perfect fit. They begin walking in the night-tipped light of almost-morning, following ghostly plumes of dust rising from the flocks, herds, and people walking ahead of them—Jacob's vast household.

Rachel's worried eyes search Jacob's for reassurance; he gives her a tight smile—not nearly as reassuring as she'd hoped. "Do you really think—will Esau kill us all? Is he still so angry after so many years?" She casts an anxious look over her shoulder, eyes seeking their son Joseph, who is riding a donkey.

"I—I *hope* Esau is no longer angry," Jacob hedges. "And if he is, I hope the gifts I have sent ahead of us will appease him." He swallows his next words: *But Esau is bearing down on us with four hundred men. Four hundred men is not a welcome-home party; it is an army.*

They walk on in silence, Jacob's sore hip twinging with every step. He thinks back to last night, how he'd wrestled God's mysterious messenger, begging for a blessing. *I hope the pain was worth the promise—only God can keep my family safe.* Jacob keeps his face still for Rachel's sake, even as his mind runs panicked circles, reliving all the awful memories with Esau: Esau's fury when he understood what he'd lost in selling Jacob his birthright, Esau's heartbroken wails when Jacob stole his blessing, the fear in their mother's face as she'd urged Jacob to run away before Esau found him—found him and killed him. *What was I thinking, coming back here? There can be no reconciliation. I have wounded my brother too deeply, stolen too much. I can only hope he will leave some of my family alive.* Jacob releases Rachel's hand so she will not feel him tremble.

The waking sun pokes its fiery crown up from the horizon, bathing them in unforgiving light. They crest a hill, and Jacob's heart catches. Spread out beneath him he sees his flocks, his herds, his household—everything and everyone he loves—slowly descending into a valley. On the valley's other side, Esau's men swarm toward them, locusts ready to devour.

Forcing words past the knot of fear in his throat, Jacob says, "I'm going on ahead of you, my love. You stay here to watch over Joseph. I'll see you when it's over."

Before Rachel has time to object and Jacob's legs have time to become paralyzed by dread, he limp-sprints ahead, descending the hill to take his place at the front of the caravan. The crowd parts down the middle to let him pass.

As the hill levels out, Jacob sees a large man striding toward him. A murmur builds behind Jacob, a slow rumble of voices. Even from a distance, Jacob can see the wild red hair glinting in the sunlight like a blazing torch.

"Esau," he breathes.

Jacob drops to the ground, prostrating himself. Seven times he rises and bows as his brother approaches. When Esau is close enough for Jacob to hear his brother's footsteps, he remains on his knees, trembling. He will meet his brother like this, in submission. The sand beneath his knees is hot, but Jacob has never been colder.

Esau's booming voice rings out. "Can it be? Has my long-lost brother come home at last?" The voice is . . . gruff. Loud, but not shouting.

Jacob risks a glance upward. His brother is four strides away, his long legs eating up the space between them—three . . . two . . . Jacob ducks his head back down, pressing his forehead into the dirt.

Strong hands grip Jacob's arms, hauling him to his feet, planting him roughly on the ground. "Rise, brother, and face me!"

"My lord, I do not deserve to—" Shaking, Jacob raises his eyes to meet his brother's.

Esau's are streaming tears, wetting his beard.

"At last, you've come home!" Esau's thick arms enfold Jacob in a spine-crushing embrace. He lifts Jacob off his feet and swings him side to side till his legs flop and flail, exactly the way he used to when they were boys. Jacob stiffens, but Esau is . . . laughing through his tears.

Shock gives way to confusion, confusion to amazement.

Esau sets Jacob down on the ground but does not release him; he buries his bushy head on Jacob's shoulder, shaking with sobs. Jacob's arms remember how to move at last, and they wrap around his twin in a desperate, trembling, after-all-these-years hug. "I'm sorry, brother, so sorry," Jacob says into Esau's shoulder, the words muffled by wool and tears.

How long they embrace Jacob does not know, but time seems to peel back, second by second, year by year, reversing what was stolen, mending what was broken. When at last the brothers release and step back to look at each other, Jacob sees nothing but forgiveness in his brother's streaming eyes. Forgiveness and healing and home.

Jacob and Esau's story is an astounding example of God's redemptive might, the way his all-powerful hands can reunite people whose relationship seems broken far beyond the hope of healing. (You can read about the brothers' complicated relationship, and the years they spent apart, in Genesis 25:19-34 and chapters 27–31.) For long years, it seemed the rent in their relationship would never, could never, be mended. *But God.* God had other plans. God was working on each brother, as each man lived his own story. And God brought them together in the end. He mapped out a road back to relationship; he paved a path for forgiveness. Jacob and Esau's story gives hope to all of us who live with brokenness—hope that our story isn't finished. Hope that God isn't done working. Hope that forgiveness and redemption could still be waiting around the bend.

FORGIVENESS FINALIZED

Maybe all this forgiveness and reconciliation talk sounds . . . well, amazing, but in the way a winning lottery ticket sounds amazing: *That would be life-changing, but it'll never happen to me.*

But what if it did?

Let's take a look at what forgiveness can look like in our own world, between women like us, processing hurts like ours. Let's drop back in on Jan and Geri's story.

After three years of distance, three years without speaking, three years spent marinating in bitterness, Jan and Geri both attended the same Christian conference, a weekend-long event. On the first night, Jan probably talked to a hundred different people, but to her immense relief, she never even spotted Geri in the crowd. But even so, Geri was the only person Jan could think about.

Jan went to a Bible class the next morning. Halfway through the lesson, the speaker's words hit Jan's ears hard, and her heart harder: "The other person doesn't have to understand how much they hurt you in order for you to forgive them."

And several truths clicked into place:

Geri may never understand how much she hurt me, but that's okay.
Forgiveness is on me.
It's time to let go, time to forgive.

By the end of class, Jan's body was nearly trembling with conviction. *It's time.*

Jan walked to the front of the room to thank the speaker, and found her talking with a woman named Barb, one of Jan's friends. Jan sucked in a trembling breath. "I just wanted to thank you. You said exactly what I needed to hear."

The speaker offered a compassionate smile. "Which part did you need to hear?"

"The part where you said the person who hurt me doesn't have to understand how much they hurt me in order for me to forgive them."

The speaker's smile melted into confusion. She shared a sideways glance with Barb, who was still standing in their little conversation triangle. "I . . . I didn't say that."

Jan blinked at her. "Yes, you did! I heard it clear as day!" Jan appealed to Barb. "You heard her say it too, right?"

Barb shook her head. "No. She didn't talk about forgiveness at all."

Jan's mouth flopped open. She blinked from one woman to the other. "But—but I heard you say . . . I could have sworn . . ."

The speaker gave Jan a gentle smile. "I didn't say those words, but that doesn't mean God didn't want you to hear them. It sounds like he had a message for you, and he found a way to get it through."

Goose bumps tickled Jan's spine. "I—I guess he did." Blinking tears, she straightened her shoulders. "I'm going back to my room. I have some soul-searching to do."

Jan avoided fellowship and beelined back to her hotel room, opening the door just as her husband, Mitch, was heading out to his next class. "It's time," she told him. "Time for me to forgive Geri. I'll be in here with God and my Bible, and I'm not coming out until I've forgiven her."

Jan stayed sequestered in her room all day and all night. She finally emerged the next morning, red-eyed but lighthearted. Triumphant. She had let it all go.

She planned to find Geri and try talking to her, but Jan had already decided it didn't matter what Geri said or how she responded. Forgiveness was done. Jan didn't need to hear anything from Geri to be okay. She had given it all over to God.

———

Jan's story isn't the only one we left unfinished. We began this chapter with me sitting in bed, a bolt of truth hitting my heart with a painful insight: *I'm never going to get the conversation I need from the friend who hurt me. I can't withhold forgiveness based upon a conversation that's never coming.*

That first epiphany sparked a second: *I can do that. By accepting the fact that I am probably never going to hear the words my heart needs, I can release that unrealistic expectation . . . I can let go. I can forgive.*

And I redirected my prayer. I had attempted to forgive this particular hurt in prayer before, but this time was different. This time, I released all conditions and expectations. I simply knelt at the foot of the cross, remembering the grace I'd been shown, knowing I could never apologize enough or "make it right" with Jesus. It was time—*past* time—that I offered my "enemy" the unconditional grace Jesus had shown me. I couldn't offer it in person, but I offered it in prayer, with the Spirit as my witness.

I'm not usually a mystical, "I felt the Lord" kind of pray-er, but as I prayed, I felt a *physical* release, the sense of something snapping inside. It was as if a cord that had tethered my heart to bitterness, chaining me to anger and hurt and self-righteousness—had been cut by God's holy hands.

And just like that, my forgiveness was complete. I was set free. Painful as that situation once was, it no longer causes me pain. Over time it became a healed wound with a scar, but even the scar has faded, and most days I forget it's there.

Wherever things stand today between you and your friend, and whatever may be going on in her heart, I pray *you* choose to stand in a place of grace. A place where you are forgiven by God and have fully forgiven the people in your life. What a place to stand—a place of peace and freedom. What a victory—a triumph over Satan and sin, resentment and regret. And no one can take that victory from you. The loss of your friendship may have stolen many things, but it cannot steal this. The power, and the choice, to forgive are yours.

THOUGHT QUESTIONS

1. Which of the forgiveness myths resonated with you? How might a new perspective on that misconception (or misconceptions) make forgiveness feel easier?

2. How does kneeling at the foot of the cross and considering Jesus' example affect the way you feel about your own hurts?

3. What might it look like for you to forgive your friend even if you still have some difficult feelings to work through? How might you forgive even while you are still "processing"?

8

BITTERNESS

Sure enough,
there lay Grandma's precious bowl,
in pieces on my desk.

So-and-so's name comes up in casual conversation, and the name itself triggers the familiar response: clenched gut. Shallow breaths. Acid tracing through my veins.

It's a feeling I loathe and crave at the same time. My thoughts feed the beast: *I am totally justified in feeling this way. What they did was wrong, so very wrong—and unfair. And from what I can see, they aren't even sorry. They have zero plans to apologize, much less change. They're probably going to do the same thing to someone else.* With that thought the acid flares, hot and burning. Again, I feel justified, almost righteous, in my anger.

Ever been there? This, my friend, is more than anger, more than "I haven't forgiven her yet, but I'm working on it." It is bitterness—the gangrenous festering of a wound left untreated. Scripture describes bitterness as a dangerous root: "See to it that no one falls short of the grace of God and that no bitter root grows up to cause trouble and defile many" (Hebrews 12:15). Bitterness hurts everyone it touches—and when we embrace it, it *defiles* us. Yikes.

We use bitterness as a toxic salve for our pain and a false shield for our hearts, but with disastrous consequences. Bitterness changes us, takes over us. It ages our childlike hearts a hundred years. Imprisons our once-trusting hearts in suits of self-protective armor. It distorts our perspective with cataracts of suspicion and mistrust. It even transforms the sound of our voice, hard-edging it with cynicism and sarcasm. On the other side of bitterness, we find we've become a person we don't even recognize. As someone has said, "Bitterness is the poison we drink, hoping the other person will die."

When a friendship falters, it harms you in squishy, vulnerable places. The friend has seen parts of you few others have. You have allowed her into your inner sanctum; and so the betrayal feels more personal. More powerful. The more we make ourselves vulnerable in the friendship, the more exposed we feel, which leaves us even more susceptible to the temptation of bitterness. Our minds race with a litany of painful thoughts:

> *I can't believe she'd say that, knowing my past.*
> *How could she abandon me, knowing I've been hurt that way before?*
> *I can't believe she used my honesty against me.*
> *I told her things no one else knows, and she abused my trust.*
> *I let her see the real me. I thought she'd be a safe place—how could I have been so stupid?*

Feeling angry and hurt is a normal response to brokenness in relationships. God and Jesus both express anger when people are unfaithful or unloving to God or to one another (see Numbers 11:10, Judges 2:20, 1 Kings 11:9, John 2:15, Mark 3:5). And angry, hurt feelings may linger even after we've made the decision to forgive. But sometimes when we don't forgive, anger can descend into something darker and more damaging. When anger starts rotting, it putrefies into bitterness.

SIGNS OF BITTERNESS

Bitterness can be tough to define precisely. Diagnosing may be an inexact science, but you know it by its symptoms.

So what are some symptoms of bitterness?

- You feel angry whenever you think about your ex-friend.
- You have a physical response of some kind whenever you think about her (a stomachache; your gut makes a fist; you feel lightheaded or short of breath; you feel restless and uneasy, like you can't sit still).
- You can't stop replaying in your mind what she did or said or didn't do or didn't say.
- Every time your thoughts drift, they drift toward the friend or the situation.
- You keep talking about what happened. You may turn to gossip in the name of openness and seeking support or advice.
- You imagine confronting her or taking revenge.
- You avoid your friend.
- You fantasize about her getting some kind of punishment or payback for what she did.
- You feel yourself becoming cynical and mistrusting in general.
- You overreact in unrelated situations.
- Anger spills over into your other relationships. You feel misplaced anger toward your family or other friends.
- It's hard to pray about or for your former friend.
- It's hard to pray, period.

I knoooooow. I feel uncomfortable-slash-twitchy reading that list too. Let's all take a deep breath and maybe chug some comfort coffee. We have all been guilty of some (ahem, maybe all) of these things, prisoners of our own pain, drinkers of our own poison. But can we please review that list and gently, gently ask ourselves, "Is this the person I want to be? Is this the kind, trusting, compassionate person God planned for me to be—the person he intended before sin started wedging its way in?"

If your friendship breakup has started changing you, I have good news: you don't have to stay in this place. You don't have to stay bitter. Even if the shards of your friendship are too jagged, too small, to glue back together, your heart doesn't have to stay broken; your wound doesn't have to turn septic.

Let's step into the biblical story of Hagar and Sarah, two women who were driven apart by bitterness, a bitterness so damaging it split their family apart. These two women were in a tremendously complicated situation, both wives of Abraham. In this case, Sarah pressured Abraham to take her slave Hagar as his concubine, or secondary wife, hoping Hagar would bear the child Sarah could not conceive herself. God had promised Sarah and Abraham a child, but after years of desperate longing, Sarah had lost faith.

Theirs is the tragic tale of two women, both aching with anguish from different wounds: Sarah, adored by her husband but empty armed, unable to bear a child; Hagar, forced into a loveless marriage, a pawn used for her fertility. A vicious power struggle ensued, and bitterness warped everything about their relationship. While it's doubtful these women were ever friends, they didn't have to be enemies. When I think about their story, I wonder if there were moments when these women almost came together, moments when the armor shielding their hearts came down and they almost let one another in—almost.

HAGAR AND SARAH
Based on Genesis 16

Hagar's stomach roils. The room tilts. She launches herself off her bedroll and heaves her breakfast into the toilet basin on the floor. She stays on hands and knees, head hanging over her own sick, hair falling in her face. She tips sideways with a groan, curling into a ball beside the basin. Nausea still pulses in waves, though the waves are growing less intense.

"Hagar?" A voice overhead. "Oh no, sick again?"

Hagar cracks one eye open; Sarah's concerned face floats above her. "Yes," Hagar moans.

"Stay there; I'll get a fresh basin."

"Couldn't move if I wanted to," Hagar mumbles.

The rustle of skirts, the *whoosh* of the tent flap, a play of light-dark against her eyelids as the flap opens and shuts . . . moments later, Hagar feels a damp cloth on her forehead. "There now." Sarah strokes her face with the cloth, just the way Hagar's mother used to do when she was ill.

"Thank you," Hagar says, her voice thick with the mother-memory. "I think—I think I can sit up now." She begins to push off the floor.

"Easy, take it easy." Sarah's voice is soft—Sarah's voice, not her mother's.

Hagar sits up, and Sarah tucks pillows behind her back.

"There. Is that better?" Sarah's dark eyes are concerned, attentive, and—something more.

"Yes, better." Hagar should say thank you again, but the words die in her throat. She tips her head back, breathing slowly, testing herself—yes, she can sit; the worst has passed for now—and allows herself a moment of fantasy: the pregnancy brings them together, Sarah and Hagar, mistress and former-slave-girl-become-equal. They become friends. Sister-wives. Sarah, many years older, steps into the maternal void, the aching chasm at Hagar's center; Sarah dotes on her, comforts and guides her through the pregnancy, and loves the child as Hagar's mother would have done—as her own.

As her own.

Hagar chokes on an angry snort of laughter, tries to disguise it as a gagging cough.

The child is Sarah's—he will never be fully mine.

And Sarah will never be my mother.

I am just a borrowed womb.

Hagar shifts and watches Sarah watching her. If not for Sarah, Hagar might still be serving at her mother's side in a wealthy household in Egypt. If not for Sarah, Hagar would not be vomiting on the floor, the pregnant concubine of an old man she does not love. Something twists in Hagar's stomach, and she cannot tell if it is bitterness or nausea. Perhaps both.

Sarah's eyes drift from Hagar's eyes, down to the small bulge beneath her skirts. A riot of emotion glitters there: love, joy, and . . . hunger. Envy.

Sarah drags her eyes back up to Hagar's, as if it takes effort to remember that Hagar is here. "What else can I get you?" Sarah asks.

Hagar starts to say, "Nothing," but something flares inside, hot and vengeful. "Ginger tea would be nice," she says in a voice oversweet.

Sarah nods and bustles out again.

Who's the servant now? A sense of power sings through her veins, intoxicating and darkly comforting.

Sarah soon presses a hot mug into Hagar's hand. Once more, Hagar swallows the thanks she should say.

Sarah's hand flutters toward Hagar's waist, a tentative bird. "M-may I?" she asks. "Just . . . rest my hand on the babe?"

Hagar shakes her head no, again with that zing of power. A new smile twists on her face, an awful smile, a smile that makes her feel like a stranger to herself. "Not today. I am too ill. Maybe tomorrow." She strokes her belly, staking her claim. Every stroke whispers, *Mine.*

Sarah's eyes widen, shuffling through a rapid series of emotions: surprise, hurt, then—understanding. Her gaze sharpens, studying Hagar as if seeing her for the first time. As if realizing that Hagar is no mousy servant girl turned concubine but a competitor. Hagar stares back unblinking, defiant, hoping her mistress can read her thoughts.

This baby is mine.

With this babe I become the primary wife—I supplant you.

I am no longer your slave.

Sarah stands, towering over Hagar. "I will be back tomorrow," she says, her voice cold as a slice of moonbeam. She stalks to the tent flap, then turns back so fast her long braid whips round. "Now that he's done with you, Abraham has asked me to move you out of this tent. It's a bit . . . large, don't you think? I'll have a pallet added to the servant girls' tent. Your services to my husband are no longer needed."

Hagar gapes, speechless, as the flap falls shut.

So this is how it begins.

THE THING YOU *CAN* CONTROL

Sadly, the story worsens from here: Hagar despises Sarah; Sarah retaliates with abuse so severe that Hagar flees into the desert, risking her own life and the life of her unborn child (see Genesis 16). Sarah may have intended to take Hagar's son, Ishmael, into her heart, to love him as her own child, but instead her hatred and jealousy nearly led to the boy's death (see also Genesis 21:15-20).

Although Hagar and Sarah suffered in different ways, I can imagine that both women felt trapped by their circumstances, powerless to change the situation that was causing them so much anguish. Sarah could not escape infertility; Hagar could not escape slavery and a forced marriage. Neither woman was in control of her own destiny—so in the end they tried to control one another. Conflict and bitterness ensued.

Like Sarah and Hagar, I am more tempted by bitterness when I feel out of control. Maybe I've tried to resolve a conflict but been stonewalled. Maybe I've tried to express my hurt and been rejected—or worse, insulted or blamed. Maybe my efforts to show someone kindness, give someone the benefit of the doubt, or offer an olive branch—"Hey, can we try to work this out?"—have been rejected or ignored.

At first, I'm simply baffled. My brain can't wrap itself around this kind of behavior. I'm standing in the kitchen, staring at the beloved fragments in my hands: *How could someone do this to something that used to be so beautiful?* But how swiftly innocent befuddlement can shift to a feeling of entrapment: *This friend has me pinned down. She's pulled me into a drama I didn't want, and now she won't let me out. I'm stuck. No longer in control of my own life.*

There, on the stark door of that barren prison, bitterness comes knocking.

Maybe it sneaks in when I'm not looking, the way mold blooms in dark basement corners, a silent but toxic intruder. Or maybe it comes explosively, like a toddler's tantrum: THIS IS NOT WHAT I WANT! THIS IS NOT FAIR! However bitterness makes its appearance, it comes . . . and when it comes, it cannot be ignored.

My dad always used to tell me and my siblings, "You can't control what happens *to* you; you can only control what happens *in* you."

You can't control whether or not your friend chooses to talk to you again.

You can't control whether or not she apologizes.

You can't control whether or not she listens to, or accepts,
  your apology.
You can't control whether or not she forgives you.
You can't control who she talks to or what she says about you.
You can't control the story of your breakup—she may tell a
  different story than the one you lived.
You can't control what she thinks about you.
You can't control what she feels toward you.
You can't control whether or not the friendship is restored.
You can't control your friend, period.

I know. That list is frustrating—but before your heart rate skyrockets any higher, hear this: there is good news. There are still things you can control:

You can control yourself.
You can control the way you choose to think about the friendship.
You can control the way you speak about the breakup.
You can control who you become in the aftermath.
You can control the way you carry yourself.
You can control whether or not you become bitter.
You can control—and hang with me here—how you feel about
  the breakup.

A first step away from bitterness is to prayerfully release the things outside our control and ask God to help us embrace the things we actually can do something about.

BUT I CAN'T HELP WHAT I FEEL!

Before we can make more progress in our discussion of bitterness, we need to address a popular half-myth I've seen floating around on social media: *You have to feel what you feel. You can't help what you feel. Besides, you have a right to your anger and hurt.*

Well, yes . . . and no. Let's consider what God has to say about this.

God knows that we all have difficult, painful, and unruly emotions. But he also calls us to cultivate self-control, particularly in our thought life, which has a profound effect on our emotions. What we think affects the way we feel. I wrote a whole book on this,[1] so I'm not going to do this topic complete justice here, but please consider a passage Paul wrote:

> The entire law is fulfilled in keeping this one command: "Love your neighbor as yourself." If you bite and devour each other, watch out or you will be destroyed by each other.
>
> So I say, walk by the Spirit, and you will not gratify the desires of the flesh. For the flesh desires what is contrary to the Spirit, and the Spirit what is contrary to the flesh. They are in conflict with each other, so that you are not to do whatever you want. But if you are led by the Spirit, you are not under the law. . . .
>
> But the fruit of the Spirit is love, joy, peace, forbearance, kindness, goodness, faithfulness, gentleness and self-control. Against such things there is no law. Those who belong to Christ Jesus have crucified the flesh with its passions and desires.
>
> GALATIANS 5:14-18, 22-24

With these words, Paul points us toward love and away from biting and devouring—in other words, away from anger- or envy-driven behaviors that tear others apart. Walking by the Spirit and inviting his influence into our lives helps us to overcome our fleshly nature—the nature that bends toward bitterness, selfishness, and other unrighteous emotions. The closer we are to the Spirit, the more we see his fruit in our lives, helping us to overcome anger and replace it with forbearance (aka patience), gentleness, and self-control.

"But a friend hurt me, and I need to process my anger!" someone may say.

And I agree. You do need to process. You need to talk it out with God and most likely with a trusted, godly person, someone who won't just

---

1. Elizabeth Laing Thompson, *All the Feels: Discover Why Emotions Are (Mostly) Awesome and How to Untangle Them When They're Not* (Carol Stream, IL: Tyndale Momentum, 2020).

listen and tell you what you want to hear, but someone who will point you to Scripture and godly thinking and forgiveness. You need to mourn and wrestle and pray through the hurt. All this takes time.

When my grandmother's bowl broke, it was an accident. Simple clumsiness by a young child. I was upset but not angry; the break wasn't intentional or malicious. But your break may feel different, like your friend was rough with your precious friendship, careless or even callous with your fragile heart. Those breaks are tougher to forgive; they're the kind that sow seeds of resentment. Like Hagar, you may look at the one who hurt you and feel completely justified in your anger.

But even so, as we talked about in chapter 7, God calls us to reject bitterness and choose to forgive as he has forgiven us. Jesus insists upon it (see Matthew 6:15).

When does "processing" turn into "stewing and refusing to forgive"? I'm not sure . . . but I am sure that we all have to guard against it. Fiercely. I once spent several years processing a hurt by some friends—a legitimate, ongoing hurt, a wound that kept being reopened, so it couldn't quite heal—but honestly? I took too long. I fought against Jesus' admonitions to forgive. I talked around forgiveness, talked myself out of forgiveness, justified and fed my bitter attitude . . . and I hurt my own heart in the process. It's possible I hurt some other people with my un-Christlike example too.

Here's something to try if you're not sure where your heart is: ask a godly person you trust about your attitude. Ask them if they think you have become bitter. Pray that God guides their answer. Then *listen*.

PROTECT YOUR HEART FROM BITTERNESS

So what do you do if bitterness has already taken root inside? First: don't despair. Please don't read all this as condemnation, but as an attempt to help. I have choked on the sour bile of bitterness. I remember all too well the sense of being enslaved to a feeling I hated and coddled all at once.

As tempting as bitterness may feel, we can escape its grasp. Paul encouraged us, "No temptation has overtaken you except what is common to mankind. And God is faithful; he will not let you be tempted beyond what you can bear. But when you are tempted, he will also provide a way out so that you can endure it" (1 Corinthians 10:13). God knows how alluring sin can be, so in his faithfulness he always provides alternatives to temptation.

Bitterness is not an inevitable condition. We can find the "way out" by being proactive, by intentionally engaging in thoughts, practices, and relationships that guard our hearts.

Protect your heart with scriptural thoughts.

When my kids were little, they sometimes threw tantrums to try to force me to give them their way. (They usually waited to do this until we were in the most crowded aisle in Target, surrounded by side-eye-casting onlookers.) I found I could help avoid tantrums on the front end by giving my kids a small measure of control over their little lives. "You can choose one more toy to look at before we leave; you can either have apple or banana slices for a snack; you can do one more activity before naptime—the swings or the slide. Which do you choose?"

In a similar way, we can guard our hearts against bitterness by reminding ourselves of the power we *do* have and what Scripture says about our hearts and our choices. We can't control how our friend acts or who she becomes through our conflict, but we do get to choose the ways *we* act and who *we* become during this time. Try some of these reassuring thoughts on for size:

> I refuse to let this breakup change me. I may be hurt, but I will not give in to destructive thoughts and feelings that damage my heart (see Proverbs 4:23 and Hebrews 12:15).
> I will not let this broken friendship define me. God defines me, and he knows my heart (see Psalm 18:17-25).
> I trust the Lord to vindicate me (see Psalm 31:1-8).
> I won't allow my friend's choices and sins to drag me into sin (see Genesis 4:7).
> Because of God's grace, I don't have to be a slave to bitterness (see Romans 6:6-7).

This too shall pass. Right now, this conflict feels like the biggest
thing in my life, but it won't always be, and God will bring me
through this (see Psalm 31:13-15).

I will honor God through this time (see Joshua 24:15).

I will live in the shadow of the cross, with Jesus' sacrifice in mind
(see 1 Peter 2:21-24).

Protect your heart with the power of prayer.

The voice on the other end of the phone—my friend's voice—was thick
with unshed tears. "So-and-so and her husband have been saying the
most awful things about us—and some people believe them. There's
only so much we can say to defend ourselves without it just blowing
up even more. I think . . . I think we're going to have to get out of
this situation altogether. It's becoming too damaging. I don't think our
reputations can recover."

At first, all I could feel was shock. I'd never witnessed behavior like
that before, particularly among believers. I was indignant and appalled
on my friend's behalf. *How can people act like this and call themselves
Christians?* And those feelings soon began to harden into a little ball
that settled in my gut.

A few weeks later, when my friend called to tell me that she and her
husband had decided to quit their jobs and move so they could get a
fresh start, I felt a different kind of tug on my heart, a pull toward bitterness. *Hate the people who hurt them,* a sultry voice cooed. *They deserve
it. Wish evil upon them. They deserve to suffer just as they made your friends
suffer. Allow yourself to hope someone does the same to them—that someone
destroys their reputation and exposes them for the bitter people they are.*

My mind paused on those words: *the bitter people they are.*

And I realized: *If I don't take these thoughts captive, I'm going to become
bitter too. Just like they are.*

I realized what was happening, but the feeling remained, the draw of
bitterness like the pull of an undertow, trying to drag me down. It would
be so much easier to give in than to fight. And the pull was titillating,
like watching some awful disaster on television that horrifies you even
as you can't look away.

Desperate, I turned to Scripture, and my heart landed on Jesus' words in the Sermon on the Mount:

> You have heard that it was said, "Love your neighbor and hate your enemy." But I tell you, love your enemies and pray for those who persecute you, that you may be children of your Father in heaven. He causes his sun to rise on the evil and the good, and sends rain on the righteous and the unrighteous. If you love those who love you, what reward will you get? Are not even the tax collectors doing that? And if you greet only your own people, what are you doing more than others? Do not even pagans do that? Be perfect, therefore, as your heavenly Father is perfect.
> MATTHEW 5:43-48

Love your enemies.
Pray for those who persecute you.
Pray.
I fixated on that: here was something I could do. I could pray for the people who'd hurt my friends. It didn't feel like it would help—and I honestly didn't want to waste my precious prayer time on such people—but I decided to trust Jesus and give his words a try. I decided to *obey* Jesus.

At first, I prayed through gritted teeth and a boiling heart.

But I dug in, remembering how Jesus himself prayed for his enemies even from the cross: "Father, forgive them, for they do not know what they are doing" (Luke 23:34). If Jesus did it, so should I. And maybe, if it had worked for Jesus, it could work for me.

Day after day, I prayed for the people I wanted to hate, and to my surprise, I soon felt the angry ball in my stomach begin to soften and dissolve. I felt the fist around my heart loosen its grip. The pull of bitterness gradually grew less powerful and—surprisingly—less attractive. I didn't want to become like the people who had hurt my friends. In time, I found my thoughts shifting away from revenge fantasies and toward thoughts like, *I hope God will allow those people to change, to escape their own bitter chains. I hope God will show them mercy and help them to have a fresh start.*

Jesus' ways *worked*. His advice to pray, so simple and straightforward, was the path that led me away from bitterness and toward forgiveness. I can honestly say that I did not become bitter toward those people—God uprooted the toxic seed before it had a chance to root and grow its poisonous blooms inside my heart.

Now when I think about those people, I just feel sad for them. Sad at the way they chose to think and feel and treat my friends all those years ago. I don't know where they are today, but I hope they are doing well. I hope they have learned a different way of handling hurt. I hope they have moved on from the way they used to treat people. I hope they have grown in grace and, through that growth, found new joy and trust in undamaged relationships. I'll probably never know where life has taken them, but that is my hope for them. All thanks to prayer.

Prayer works. Jesus is not only wise; he is smart. He knew exactly what he was doing—and what we needed—when he called us to pray for our enemies.

As we pray about our damaged friendships, God begins to work, not just on the situation and on our friend but on our own hearts. The prayer begins to form a shield of sorts to protect our hearts from bitterness. Here are a few things that happen when we pray for friends who have hurt us:

- Prayer reminds us of our own humble station before God.
- Prayer reminds us of our own sins and need for grace. A friend may have sinned against us, but we have sinned many times against God and others.
- Sometimes praying through a situation allows us to see things from our friend's perspective. Even if we don't agree with their viewpoint, prayer may help us to understand why they feel justified in acting a certain way.
- Prayer may help our defenses come down long enough to identify some things we could have done or said differently. Humility tempers our bitterness.

- Through prayer we feel *less* powerless because we are doing the most powerful thing we can: drawing God's attention and might to a situation we can't change ourselves.
- Through prayer we find a sense of peace and comfort knowing God cares and is working even when we can't see what he is doing.
- Prayer helps us release our desire to fix our friend or show her the error of her ways. It reminds us to trust that God is powerful enough and righteous enough to do those things without us.
- Prayer reminds us of the nature of God: he is kind, compassionate, patient, and just.
- Prayer reminds us that God is not dumb and God cannot be mocked. Even if our former friend is fooling other people, she cannot fool God. That truth is equal parts sobering and scary.
- Prayer may help us reinterpret our tunnel-visioned experience—the experience that only sees how a situation affects us—with God's bigger-picture perspective.
- Prayer forces us to reword some things in more righteous ways: "I hate her" may become, "I hate the choices she is making"; "I wish something awful would happen to her" may become, "I pray you'll show her how she is making other people feel."

You won't feel these shifts happening right away, but stick with prayer. Pray for your friend every day, or at least every time you feel that pull toward bitterness. Keep praying, and you'll give God room to work—on the situation, on her, and on you. Over time, you'll see, and feel, a difference.

———

When you first start praying for a friend who's hurt you, it can be tough to know what to say. You may sit in silence, searching for words that won't come—or that come out all kinds of sinful. It's oddly encouraging to note that the psalms contain imprecatory prayers—prayers in which psalmists actually ask God to deal harshly with their enemies, to exact revenge upon them. These prayers are unfiltered, and to be honest, they don't reflect the kind of forgiving, praying-for-your-enemies spirit Jesus encourages. But God included them in the Bible anyway—just as he included difficult stories like Hagar and Sarah's. Perhaps one message we can take from the imprecatory psalms is that God can handle it when we're not there yet. He's not going to run away screaming or cancel our prayer privileges if we're struggling with bitterness. Similarly, Scripture doesn't indicate that Hagar and Sarah found resolution, and yet we still see God working in both of their lives, protecting and guiding them in spite of their struggle.

Here are some prayers you might borrow and make your own as you begin wrestling with your heart and praying for broken friendships:

Lord, please help her to see this situation and me and herself more clearly, with eyes of humility and grace and forgiveness.

God, please protect her other relationships from this same kind of damage. I don't want others to hurt as I do.

Father, please help her to repent. The Bible says you grant repentance to people—please grant her the desire and ability to change.

Lord, please forgive me for my part in this breakup. There may be things I have done, ways I have hurt her, that I don't understand. And please forgive her for her part—she doesn't know what she's doing, how much hurt she is causing.

God, I believe you are able to help anyone transform and overcome. You brought Peter back to Jesus after heartbreaking, repeated denials. If you can change Peter and restore his relationship to Jesus, you can change me and my friend and restore our friendship too.

Protect your heart by choosing your confidants with care.

When we feel hurt, we want—and need—to talk about it. To air our grievances. We need the reassurance that other people still love us, that all our friendships are not broken. That *we* are not broken, incapable of friendship moving forward.

But we must choose our confidants carefully. Of course, we need to guard against a spirit of gossip and revenge, of talking about another person while hoping to damage their reputation or hurt them as they have hurt us. But let's also remember this: the people we choose to confide in can either help us or hurt us. It's not wrong to want someone to hear your side and offer you words of wisdom and comfort. But some people make our attitudes worse, not better. They fan the flame of our anger. They don't point us to God or to Scripture. They don't pray with us. They don't offer us fair-minded analysis. They don't point out anything we need to work on or change. They don't gently call us to forgive when they hear us bending toward bitterness.

If you are having conflict with a friend who is part of a larger group of mutual friends, you may need to go outside that group for encouragement and support. You may need to open your heart to someone who has no connection to the friend with whom you are having conflict. If you don't have a person who fits that description, you may need to find a counselor you can talk to.

A friend of mine once had a lot of difficulty in a friendship at work. To make things more complicated, his coworker also went to his church, leaving him no safe, neutral place where he could get advice and support. All of his relationships felt intertwined on some level. Everyone was biased—either for him or for the other person. Anything he said could hurt the other guy's reputation or force their mutual friends to feel like they had to take a side.

After a few months of grappling with the situation alone, he realized he desperately needed someone to talk to, but it had to be a person who had no stake in the situation. My friend sought out a Christian therapist. The therapist became a safe place where my friend could share, grieve, and seek counsel. That therapist was a lifesaver and reputation-saver for my friend. Over time he was able to work through his feelings about the conflict. He managed to preserve both his reputation at work and his church relationships. He even kept the peace in the friendship at work, although it was distant and strained for a while. His proactive decision proved to be infinitely wise and healthy. He forgave the friend in his own heart and worked his way through all his feelings. Several years later, he was able to circle back to that friend and rebuild the relationship.

Protect your heart with proactive grace.

Benita slides two birthday cards and an anniversary card across the kitchen table. "Your autograph, please," she says to her husband, wagging a pen between his phone and his face. He looks up, eyes glazed, from the Wordle. Benita's pen is pointing toward his heart like a dagger poised to strike. "And try to add a couple of nice lines—no passive-aggressive sarcasm, pretty please."

Derrick's eyes narrow. "Just who are these cards for?"

Benita ticks names off her fingers: "James, Ben, and the Flannerys."

Derrick groans. "James and Ben are one thing, but the *Flannerys*? Seriously?"

"Yes, seriously," Benita says, her voice hardening into her I-shall-brook-no-argument tone.

"You *do* remember how these people treated us, right?" Derrick says. "Practically forced us out of town?"

"I remember," Benita says, her voice a little clipped. "Way better than you think I do. But doing this is good for our hearts. It . . . protects us."

Derrick mutters something under his breath.

"I'm telling you, Derrick, this is good for us. Writing kind words prompts kind feelings; it helps us stay committed to that decision we made not to be bitter. You *do* remember that decision, right?" Her tone mimics Derrick's from moments earlier, but she grins so he knows she's teasing.

Again, Derrick mutters under his breath, but he reaches for the pen.

Several years and many, many birthday and anniversary cards later, Derrick and Benita move back to the town they'd left, where they are thrust back into friend circles with James, Ben, and the Flannerys. Forced to face their bitterness, only to realize . . . the bitterness is dead and gone. Sent packing by the US Post Office.

Their first night back in their old town, Derrick pulls Benita close and whispers, "Thank you for making me write all those cards. If you hadn't encouraged me to reinforce our forgiveness so many times, I never could have done this. I never would have given these friendships another try."

Benita and Derrick decided to forgive early on, but they *fortified* that decision time and again. They chose proactive grace that not only protected their own attitudes, it also left room for reconciliation. Sometimes we need to find ways to keep offering grace, ways to reinforce our own decisions. Every card we write, every prayer we pray, every olive branch we extend, reminds our hearts: *I have chosen forgiveness, not bitterness. This is my path, and I'm sticking to it.*

Bitterness destroys the best of who we are, robbing us of the people we long to be. Way back in Genesis, God warned against the dangerous pull of bitterness: "Why are you angry? Why is your face downcast? If you do what is right, will you not be accepted? But if you do not do what is right, sin is crouching at your door; it desires to have you, but you must rule over it" (Genesis 4:6-7).

You may feel as though bitterness is "crouching at your door," eager to erode your heart and change you into a person you don't want to become. Like Sarah and Hagar, you may feel resentment turning you into someone you hardly recognize. My friend, please don't let bitterness conquer you. *Conquer bitterness instead.* Ask God and the Spirit to empower you to overcome. Beg if you have to. And as you pray, remember this: God *wants* to help you overcome. He wants you to be victorious. And with his help, you can be.

THOUGHT QUESTIONS

1. Bitterness presents itself differently in every person's heart. What symptoms tell you bitterness is becoming a problem for you?

2. You can't control the way your friend acts through your

conflict—you can only control yourself. Who do *you* want to be during this conflict, regardless of how your friend conducts herself?

3. Which do you most need right now to help protect your heart from bitterness: Scripture, prayer, choosing the right confidants, or showing proactive grace? How might you begin applying that protection to your heart?

9

RECONCILIATION

Begging God to guide my fingers and go easy on my heart,
I painstakingly began to glue that bowl back together, piece by piece.
The process took prayer, skill, and several do-overs.

In a world of ghosting and canceling, God calls his children to something higher. Something nobler. Something infinitely more challenging. God calls us to forgiveness and peace, and wherever possible, he calls us to reconciliation. He calls us to pick up the broken shards in our trembling hands and try. To line up the breaks, trace them with glue, ever so gently press them together—*wait, wait, wait, don't move a millimeter*—then hold our breath as we let go, praying the bond holds and the pieces stay connected.

Depending on the severity and nature of your breakup, the idea of reconciliation may feel uncomfortable, terrifying, or even impossible. Honestly? Your feelings aren't wrong. Attempting reconciliation will definitely be uncomfortable, possibly feel terrifying, and may ultimately prove impossible. But as we will see in Scripture, God calls us to seek peace—to do our part to mend fences.

Before you panic and throw this book across the room, let's just . . . talk. Let's take a step back from our feelings and ask ourselves, what does God want for his children's relationships? Many Scriptures provide principles for how we are to live at peace with others, whether through reconciliation or at least a resolution of the conflict at hand. We'll look at some biblical examples as well. Thank goodness, the Bible offers us stories of believers who attempted reconciliation—believers with fears and insecurities and hang-ups and anxieties and self-esteem issues and complex pasts and pride struggles that often feel surprisingly familiar to our own—with varying degrees of success. Taken together, these principles and examples will lead us to practical applications for reconciling our own broken friendships.

THE CALL TO PEACE

Let's start with the call to peace. Consider these words from the apostle Paul, which he wrote to Christians in Rome. I'm abbreviating the passage just slightly so we can home in on the juicy parts that apply most directly to broken friendships:

> Bless those who persecute you; bless and do not curse. . . . Live in harmony with one another. . . .
>   Do not repay anyone evil for evil. Be careful to do what is right in the eyes of everyone. If it is possible, as far as it depends on you, live at peace with everyone. Do not take revenge, my dear friends, but leave room for God's wrath, for it is written: "It is mine to avenge; I will repay," says the Lord. On the contrary:
>
> "If your enemy is hungry, feed him;
>   if he is thirsty, give him something to drink.
> In doing this, you will heap burning coals on his head."
>
> Do not be overcome by evil, but overcome evil with good.
> ROMANS 12:14, 16-21

In this passage, Paul reminds us that God desires harmony. That Christ followers are called to imitate the Lord in taking the high road, blessing people who we feel deserve our curses. He reminds us that others' sins do not give us an excuse to sin ourselves.[1] We are called to do what we can to forge peace. To avoid conflict in the first place if we can, but then to set things right if disagreement occurs. To seek restoration instead of revenge. To combat evil with good.

Paul summarizes his message here by saying, "If it is possible, as far as it depends on you, live at peace with everyone" (Romans 12:18). This sentence offers us insights on multiple levels, so let's wring out as much of its meaning as possible, breaking it down phrase by phrase. First Paul says, "If it is possible . . ." I'm grateful for the realism in those words: Paul acknowledges that sometimes, peace is *not* possible. Sometimes we do and pray and say All the Things, but our efforts fail. The broken pieces are too small, crushed beyond the help of glue; a critical piece is missing, and the shape cannot hold.

Then Paul writes, "as far as it depends on you." We are responsible for our part in keeping the peace, and the other person is responsible for theirs. Reconciliation takes two people, and it takes work. Both parties must have the courage to face a difficult conversation. And if that conversation is going to go anywhere productive, both people must have a heart that is humble and honest, gracious and forgiving. As I learned when my friend Sasha rejected my efforts to reconcile after my wedding, we cannot force another person to accept our peace. We may be ready to reconcile—desperate, even—but our friend may not. We can't *make* a friend make peace with us. Sometimes we have to leave room for God to work.

Here's another angle to consider: when you take a big-picture view of that sentence—"If it is possible, as far as it depends on you, live at peace with everyone"—Paul seems to be suggesting that we *initiate* reconciliation when we can. Jesus said so directly in the Sermon on the Mount: "So if you are presenting a sacrifice at the altar in the Temple and you suddenly remember that someone has something against you, leave your sacrifice there at the altar. Go and be reconciled to that person. Then come and offer your sacrifice to God" (Matthew 5:23-24, NLT). If we

---

1. If you'd like more on this, take a look at 1 Peter 2:21-23, and head over to chapter 13, "When You're Being Maligned."

know a friend has something against us, Jesus calls us to drop everything and go try to make it right. We need to go get right with people so we can approach God with a clear conscience. We aren't responsible for how others respond to our offer of reconciliation, but God is pleased when we make the offer.

Let's consider the last clause of Paul's sentence: "live at peace with everyone." This sentence does not say, "live as best friends with everyone"; in fact, it doesn't even say, "live as friends with everyone." Sometimes best friendship, or even casual friendship, is not possible in a certain relationship. God simply calls us to do our best to live at peace—in a place free from conflict and resentment. When we seek to mend a fractured relationship, we don't have to force friendship as the end result. We may long for it, pray for it, and work toward it, but our ultimate goal is simply *peace*.

RESOLUTION VS. RECONCILIATION

We've established that peace is our goal. Now we're going to explore two possible outcomes in our pursuit of peace: *resolution* and *reconciliation*. Reconciliation occurs when forgiveness is offered by both parties and the relationship is mended. Real relationship of some kind exists on the other side of reconciliation. Reconciliation may simply restore your friendship to a place of peaceful cordiality and casual connection, though you're not as close as you used to be, or reconciliation could draw you closer than ever, your conflict having brought greater depth and appreciation to your friendship.

But if your efforts at reconciliation are not yet bearing fruit, I propose there is another path you can pursue: resolution. Resolution comes about when forgiveness is offered and accepted (ideally on both parts) and conflict no longer brews. You have nothing more to discuss, nothing more to work out, and no hard feelings. Your relationship may be limited (or barely existent) moving forward, but not because you are still angry. When you cross paths, you may still feel some lingering sadness, haunted by ghosts of the friendship you used to enjoy, but you can interact without bitterness, awkwardness, unkindness, or pain. You no longer have a friendship, but you do have peace. Peace with each other and peace within your own heart. And that may be as far as the relationship ever goes. You wish each other well, greet one another with kindness, but you release all expectations and obligations.

RESOLUTION: PEACE WITHOUT FRIENDSHIP

Let's take a look at two types of resolution we find in Scripture: a truce and an impasse.

A truce

A truce means we aren't in conflict, aren't actively resenting, opposing, or otherwise hurting one another. We aren't BFFs, but neither are we enemies. Sometimes a truce is the best we can achieve. In Scripture, David and Saul provide us an example of a truce . . . or at least an attempted one.

As a teenager and young adult, David had lived a whirlwind. With dizzying speed, he'd gone from being a simple shepherd boy, to a young man secretly anointed Israel's future king, to a celebrated war hero (the upstart teen who killed a giant with a rock), to a warrior who earned the hand of the king's daughter in marriage. And then he became a man on the run, resented, reviled, and hunted by his jealous father-in-law, King Saul.

David had given Saul only respect, loyalty, and service. Saul's son, Jonathan, was David's closest friend, and David married Saul's daughter Michal, and so you would expect Saul and David to share deep bonds of both friendship and family. But Saul repaid David's every good deed with mistrust and accusation, slander and retaliation.

Ever been there? Utterly misunderstood by a former friend, someone who should have been a safe place? Cast aside because of fear and suspicion, your protests falling on deaf ears? David knew the feeling. Perhaps we can glean some comfort, hope, and guidance from the "man after [God's] own heart" (1 Samuel 13:14). How did David respond to Saul's persecution?

David repeatedly refused to seek retaliation. He ran from Saul, dodged his attacks, hid in caves, and just generally tried to stay out of Saul's way . . . but he never became the aggressor. Never mounted an attack or attempted to prematurely take the throne he'd been promised in his youth by the prophet Samuel (see 1 Samuel 16:1-13). David poured out his frustrations in prayer (see Psalms 69 and 109), but he left retribution and justice in God's hands.

Twice David attempted to make peace with Saul and put an end to their one-sided conflict. In 1 Samuel 24, we read about the first attempt: Saul enters a cave alone. David's men, convinced the Lord has delivered Saul into David's hands, urge David to sneak into the cave and assassinate him. Instead, David creeps up and cuts off a corner of Saul's robe—proof that though he'd gotten close enough to kill the king, he'd stayed his hand.

When Saul emerges, David waves the cutting aloft for Saul and all his men to see, bows, and says, "Why do you listen when men say, 'David is bent on harming you'? This day you have seen with your own eyes how the Lord delivered you into my hands in the cave. Some urged me to kill you, but I spared you. . . . May the Lord avenge the wrongs you have done to me, but my hand will not touch you" (1 Samuel 24:9-10, 12).

Saul weeps at David's display of mercy, saying, "You have treated me well, but I have treated you badly. . . . Now swear to me by the Lord that you will not kill off my descendants or wipe out my name from my father's family" (1 Samuel 24:17, 21).

With Saul's fury deflated, both armies go home.

The truce doesn't last; two chapters and an undetermined amount of time later, again we find Saul pursuing David. Again, we find David pursuing peace instead of revenge. This time, David and a companion sneak into Saul's camp while Saul and his army slumber, and they steal the spear and water jug lying beside Saul's head. Again, they announce their deed to Saul and the whole army—*We could have killed you, but we didn't; you were at our mercy, and we gave it*—and again Saul publicly apologizes to David and returns home. (You can read the whole story in 1 Samuel 26.)

This is their last recorded interaction before Saul dies during the battle. It was far from a reconciliation, but it was a truce.

Is a truce what God desired for Saul and David—or anyone? Probably not, but David's response helps us envision how we might honor God in a totally unideal situation. David wasn't an aggressor, but neither was he a pushover. He defended himself with words instead of weapons. And when Saul didn't fully repent, David left revenge up to God.

A truce is an undesirable outcome, but if a friend isn't interested in a more meaningful solution, a truce allows us to achieve peace while maintaining our own integrity.

My friend Sheila, whose story you will read in chapter 11, had to settle for a truce with a contentious girl from her small group. Sheila would have liked to take their conversation deeper and restore some kind of functional fellowship and friendship, but the other girl refused. The best Sheila could do was apologize over the phone, hoping the conversation would bring an end to the gossip and slander, and then move forward with her own life and different friendships.

An impasse

In a truce, both parties call "peace." With the argument settled, you go separate ways—perhaps not as friends, but as respectful noncombatants. But what if you can't even agree on the terms of your peace? What if you disagree on how to settle your disagreement? You talk and talk, but still fundamentally differ; not only does the original conflict still stand, you can't agree on how to move forward. You're stuck in your positions, unwilling or unable to see things a different way. The best you can do is agree to disagree. That's an impasse.

It may surprise you to realize that two righteous people may reach an impasse and leave it there for a time. In chapter 1, we briefly mentioned the breakup of Paul and Barnabas's partnership. These two brothers had shared the richest of friendship histories. When Paul first came to faith in Jesus and tried to join the believers in Jerusalem, they did not believe Paul was truly a Christian—they feared his conversion was a ruse designed to infiltrate their fellowship and destroy it. But Barnabas believed Paul. Barnabas vouched for him and convinced the brotherhood to embrace him. Sometime later, when Paul was forced to retreat to his hometown of Tarsus to escape persecution, Barnabas sought out his friend. He traveled to Tarsus, found Paul, and convinced him to come preach with him in Antioch. The friends ministered side by side for years, saving souls, building churches, spreading the gospel. But then an argument over Barnabas's cousin, John Mark, ended it all.[2]

PAUL AND BARNABAS
Based on Acts 15:36-41

Paul pinches his nose and breathes deeply, struggling to keep his tone even. "This is a spiritual issue, Barnabas. A character issue. Not to mention a financial one—he's a potential risk! John Mark abandoned us on the last journey. Gave in to cowardice and, I'm sorry to speak so plain, showed himself to be a mama's boy."

Barnabas spreads his palms. "His mother has always been emotional, Paul! She was overworried, and the boy felt responsible. Surely you understand that."

Paul shakes his head. "That's a cost we counted with him *before* he left home! The Lord himself said, 'Let the dead bury their own dead' and 'Whoever loves his father or mother more than me is not worthy of me'—the call is more important than a mother's fears, *brother!*"

Behind his bristly beard, Barnabas's cheeks flush red. "I don't appreciate the edge you put on that word, *brother*. And maybe John Mark did make a decision that was founded more in fear than in faith, but don't you think a young man deserves grace? The kind of grace I showed you when I vouched for you when no one else would?" Barnabas rises to his feet, pointing a trembling finger at Paul. "I made sure the fellowship trusted and welcomed you when they were terrified of you." With every *you*, a finger-stab. "Shouldn't we do the same for John Mark—show him grace, help him find his footing? Seems to me, showing grace is a spiritual issue. *Like you said.*"

Paul opens his mouth as if to respond, then clamps it shut. He draws in a deep breath and digs his fingertips into his temples.

Barnabas paces the room, anger pulsing off him in almost visible waves, but he keeps his silence too.

---

2. Acts 12:25 and 15:37 tell us that his name was John, but he was also called Mark—so I'm calling him John Mark.

Long minutes pass, Paul sitting, Barnabas pacing, neither speaking.

At last Paul coughs, breaking the silence; Barnabas jumps at the sound. "It is clear your mind is made up, Barnabas, and so is mine. I shall take Silas with me and go as planned to Syria and on to Cilicia"—Barnabas's head snaps up, a question in his eyes—"and I suggest you take John Mark and go . . . elsewhere." Paul's voice cracks; he clears his throat and looks away. "Perhaps Cyprus. They could use some encouragement."

"But, Paul—"

Paul drags his eyes to meet Barnabas's gaze; the anger in Barnabas's expression has quieted, replaced by a symphony of sorrow. Years of memories seem to pass between them—that first baptism in Antioch, meeting Lydia by the river in Philippi, convincing Timothy's mother to let the boy join their company . . . and all the times they'd talked of working side by side for the Lord forever, partners for always—Paul's ears fill with the echoes of the old promises as his eyes fill with new tears.

Barnabas reaches out a hand as if to hug Paul, then draws it back, unsure.

Paul stands and crosses the four steps between them—four steps that feel like a chasm. He spreads his arms, and Barnabas sinks into them, shaking with tears.

Paul's voice against Barnabas's shoulder is muffled. "I suggest we both continue to pray about this—perhaps the Lord will show us both things we cannot now see. Until then, my brother, I do love you, and I will pray for your journey. Mine will not be the same without you by my side."

Paul and Barnabas had reached a heartbreaking impasse. Neither man could—or would—change his mind. We don't know if they lost their tempers and said sinful things they regretted (the phrase "sharp disagreement" suggests heated words); we don't know if they harbored resentment afterward. Because these were two righteous men of God, we hope they both surrendered their anger to God and chose to respect their brother's right to hold a differing opinion. We hope they parted with words like we read in the vignette, words like, "Let's agree to disagree. I still respect and love you, and I wish you well." Whatever their attitude, they found resolution by parting ways, each man following his own conscience.

It is encouraging to note that Paul's relationship with John Mark was apparently restored after a time. In a letter to Timothy near the end of his life, Paul wrote, "Get Mark and bring him with you, because he is helpful to me in my ministry" (2 Timothy 4:11). That brief sentence tells us so much: not only was Paul saying that John Mark was "useful" in his ministry; he also put those words into action, sending Timothy on a mission to bring John Mark back to Paul's side. Paul trusted John Mark enough that he wanted to work with him again. How I wish we knew what happened between Paul and Barnabas, but what a comfort it is to know that Paul and John Mark's relationship was eventually restored.

Paul later wrote to the church in Philippi, "All of us, then, who are mature should take such a view of things. And if on some point you think differently, that too God will make clear to you" (Philippians 3:15). Paul's experience with his friend Barnabas had taught him that even in God's church, we won't always think alike; sometimes we just have to give God time to work and clarify.

Resolution, whether through a truce or an impasse, may not be the ideal you long for, but it is worth seeking when you can't achieve full reconciliation. Resolution may not restore your friendship, but it does protect your heart from bitterness, allow you to offer and accept forgiveness, and help you to set a conflict to rest. It allows you to move forward.

MAKING PEACE WITH IMPERFECT PEACE

If you're struggling to make peace in your own heart with an imperfect peace; if you feel unsettled with resolution when you long for full reconciliation, keep this in mind: just because you move forward with your life and other friendships doesn't mean you have to stop praying about repair and restoration in the broken friendship. You can keep praying for your own heart, asking God to protect you from bitterness and to clarify any truths or solutions you may have overlooked. You can keep praying for your friend, asking God to work on her heart. You can keep praying for the miracle of reconciliation even if you can't fathom a world in which it happens. You can dare to have a little crazy faith in a God who specializes in surprises and transformations.

WHEN A FRIENDSHIP FALLS APART | 135

Your prayers might sound something like this:

Lord, you know my heart and hers. When the time is right—
if the time is ever right—please bring us back together. Prepare
both our hearts, and please give us an opportunity to talk again,
to try again, and to fully reconcile one day. Paul wrote that you
could help us when we see things differently; please do that for me
and my friend. If there are things I don't yet see about my part in
this conflict, please show them to me. If there are things I could
have done differently, ways I need to change, or mistakes I need
to apologize for, please make that clear to me. Please do the same
things in my friend's heart. I want the complete unity Jesus prayed
for in John 17—if it is possible, please help us to forge it.

RECONCILIATION: A RESTORATION OF THE RELATIONSHIP

So what does reconciliation look like? In my mind, reconciliation means a restoration of the relationship, a renewal of some measure of friendship—even if the friendship still bears some scars. If you've been sitting in brokenness for a while, the idea of reconciliation may feel like a fantasy. False hope that will do nothing but tease your heart and leave it disappointed all over again. But what if it isn't? What if, somehow, Almighty God could help you and your friend glue the pieces together again? Is this kind of healing even possible?

Jesus came, not only to save us but also to model how to live and love. He gives us a beautiful example of reconciliation in his own relationship with his disciple and friend Peter.

Peter had been in the inner circle within Jesus' inner circle. He wasn't just one of the Twelve, he was one of the three—Peter, James, and John—who had a special relationship with the Lord. They alone experienced some key moments with Jesus: the Transfiguration (see Matthew 17:1-9) and Jesus' vulnerable, anguished prayer in the garden of Gethsemane (see Matthew 26:36-46). Peter was poised to be Jesus' main guy, the future leader of the church (see Matthew 16:18-19).

But Peter failed his friend in epic, friendship-crushing fashion. At the Last Supper, Peter swore he would stand by Jesus to the death, but mere hours later, when Jesus was arrested, beaten, and put through a sham of a trial, Peter quailed—and crashed. He cursed, he swore, he disowned Jesus altogether: "I don't know the man!" (See Matthew 26:69-75.) And he didn't just falter once; he denied Jesus three times in a single night. The last time Peter denied his friend, he did not realize Jesus was being led out by guards; Jesus, apparently overhearing Peter's curses, "turned and looked straight at Peter" (Luke 22:61). I can hardly bear to picture the hurt, sorrow, and loneliness that must have radiated from Jesus' eyes. I can only imagine the shock and shame that must have lanced Peter's heart; Scripture tells us he "went outside and wept bitterly" (Matthew 26:75).

But after Jesus' death and resurrection, the Lord sought Peter out to set things right, to give his friend and disciple another chance. Peter responded enthusiastically—we're talking jumping-off-a-boat-fully-clothed-level enthusiasm (see John 21:1-19). Jesus was alive, resurrected; Peter was standing there on the beach, soaking wet. Grace seemed ready for the taking . . . but a conversation still needed to take place. Jesus didn't pretend the betrayal hadn't happened and move on; he addressed the issue. Three times Peter had denied Jesus; now three times Jesus asked Peter, "Do you love me?" It was as if Jesus wanted to give Peter a chance to wipe away the memory of those old, awful words, replacing them with healing words of love and devotion.

But it seems Peter didn't understand what his friend was doing. The Bible tells us, "Peter was hurt because Jesus asked him the third time" (John 21:17). Peter was hurt, *and yet Jesus asked*. The question needed asking and redemptive words needed speaking before reconciliation could take place. I love that the gospel writer, John, mentions Peter's hurt feelings, because reconciliation conversations can be tricky. Our pride, insecurity, and self-blindness can get in the way. Even when conversations are going well—and going to *end* well—there may be painful moments, awkward moments, moments when we misunderstand one another's intentions.

And consider this: Jesus was perfect, and he handled his conversation with Peter perfectly—sinlessly. He chose all the right words. And not only that, Jesus kept his *tone of voice* righteous, not descending into bitterness or sarcasm for even a single syllable. But even so, Peter felt hurt. I find this truth both comforting and discouraging at the same time. You can do everything right and say everything right as you try to reconcile with a friend, but she still may have negative feelings. Welcome to the intricacies of friendship! Truly Jesus understands everything we go through (see Hebrews 4:14-16). Jesus' experience with Peter encourages us to push through the awkwardness, work through the misunderstandings, and show grace through the stumbling—because even when the conversation doesn't go perfectly, reconciliation may still be possible.

Jesus ascends back into heaven soon after this conversation, and Peter soon assumes the role Jesus had long prepared for him: he becomes the leader of the Twelve. The keeper of the keys of the Kingdom, ushering new believers into a new church (see Matthew 16:13-20 and Acts 2). It's clear that Jesus has full confidence in Peter and that Peter is no longer hampered by insecurity, guilt, or shame. The two are reconciled, their friendship restored. And through their reunion we, too, are blessed, as one of Jesus' last acts on earth was to model reconciliation for us—what a parting gift.

REAL-WORLD RECONCILIATION

What might a reconciliation look like today? Here's what it looked like for . . . wait for it . . . Jan and Geri. Jan and Geri had been the best of friends, but misunderstanding and resentment had driven them apart. They had not spoken for three years. When we left their story, Jan had decided to forgive Geri no matter what. With or without a healing conversation. With or without reconciliation. But here's what happened . . .

———

Geri's husband, Sam, walks into his hotel room, fumbling an armful of books, and freezes in the open doorway. He can't believe what he's seeing. The books tumble from his arms as disjointed words tumble from his mouth.

"I—you—wait, what? I thought . . . but you . . . *Is this what I think it is?*"

Geri sits cross-legged on the bed, and there in a chair facing her sits . . . *Jan.* Jan, the subject of a thousand tearstained, regret-filled marital conversations over the past three years. Sam's keen eyes do a quick assessment: both women's faces bear tear tracks and—*smiles.*

"You can close your mouth now, Sam," Jan teases with her characteristic blunt humor. "But yes, this is what you think it is. We're talking things through. Making things right."

"What can I do? Can I help? Oh, this is—this is so great. Praise God."

"Sam, you're babbling." Geri laughs.

Sam breaks into a ginormous grin. "Already ganging up on me, just like the old days! This is such a good sign!"

Jan and Geri exchange one of their trademark conspiratorial giggle-glances. Another excellent sign.

"But how—how did this happen?"

Jan says, "We ran into each other in the lobby, and I asked Geri if she'd be willing to talk to me."

"This is wonderful," Sam says. "I can't even—I'll just—I'll just leave you to it."

Sam leaves his books scattered on the floor and begins backing through the door in a half-sprint. He starts to close the door, then pops his head back in. "Please talk about *everything* and get this over with once and for all. I can't live with this drama anymore!"

"That's what we're doing, honey," Geri says. She blows him a kiss.

As Sam closes the door, they hear him babbling—they're not sure if he's talking to them, to himself, or to God: "I'm so happy. So, so happy. It's about stinkin' time. Praise the good, sweet Lord in heaven."

Jan and Geri exchange another laugh, and their eye contact is easy, unguarded, just like it used to be. Geri feels the hint of a familiar warmth beginning to spread through her chest—the happy warmth of being with a friend she adores, a friend who knows her completely and adores her fully. She thinks, *How am I already feeling this way again?*

"Okay, what else do you need to say?" Geri asks, growing serious again. "I want to get it all out here, now, and leave it here in this room."

"There are a couple more things I'd like to express," Jan says, "but honestly, we've covered the big things, and that's all I needed. And then I have some major apologizing to do too. I put you through misery the past three years, and it was wrong. So very wrong. I held things over your head, and that was utterly un-Christlike of me. I gossiped, I resented . . . and the truth is, I was seeing the past through a distorted lens of bitterness. Some of the stuff I thought I was mad about"—she shakes her head, her expression sheepish and a bit bewildered—"I now realize it never even happened, or at least didn't happen as dramatically as I've been remembering it. It's like I put this angry filter over all our memories together, and now that it's gone, I can see our past more clearly. More fairly."

"Okay, but still, let's talk about all your stuff," Geri insists. "I want to hear it. I *can* hear it now. Three years ago, I wasn't ready, but I'm ready now."

They stay locked in that room for another few hours—hours in which a giddy Sam finds Jan's husband, Mitch, and they camp out in the hotel lobby over cups of coffee, praising God for the miracle he is working upstairs and asking him to continue guiding their wives' conversation.

Finally, Jan and Geri hold hands and pray. They release everything they've talked about in prayer. In the presence of God and the Spirit and the bland hotel wall art, each woman extends the other both forgiveness and apology. They hug. When they walk out of that room, they are exhausted. Their voices are raw, their makeup long gone, but their hearts are soaring, trembling with a did-this-really-just-happen joy.

But it did happen, and it stuck. It's been sixteen years since Jan and Geri made up in that hotel room, and they're still friends. Last month, Jan and Geri went on a girls' trip together with three other friends. They shopped, swapped stories, bragged about their genius grandchildren, sipped Chardonnay, and stayed up late giggling like teenagers.

Jan and Geri have never looked back on the old hurts. They don't need to. They forgave one another completely and left all their resentment in that hotel room. The only time they bring up their old conflict is when they share their story with others who need to hear it, with others who need hope that they, too, can reconcile.

I don't know if you will experience a reconciliation as delightful and redemptive as Jan and Geri's—but oh, how I hope you do. I share their story because reconciliation is possible. Even after utter brokenness. Even after botched conflict-resolution attempts. Even after years of feeling heartbroken, resentful, and hopeless. All the time Jan and Geri spent apart, God was working on both their hearts—"the God who gives life to the dead and calls into being things that were not" (Romans 4:17).

———

When I first started trying to glue my grandmother's bowl together, the bond didn't hold; the pieces fell apart and nearly broke into even smaller pieces. But the bowl was worth fighting for, so I swallowed my tears, rallied my patience, and tried again. With shaking hands, I lined up the two largest pieces, traced them with glue, and stood motionless for ages, pressing them together, barely breathing, praying for a miracle. At last, I let go, whispering, "*Please, please.*" When the bond held, I nearly wept with joy. But my work wasn't done—not nearly done. Half the bowl was still in pieces.

I waited all night, letting the new, fragile bond strengthen. The next day, I tried adding on another piece. Piece by piece, praying the whole time, I put that bowl back together until finally, the last triangle fit into place. Still a perfect fit, even after all the trauma. Still the beautiful bowl I remembered. Still a treasure.

When Jan and Geri started down the path of reconciliation, no one was more surprised than Jan and Geri (except maybe Geri's husband, Sam). The only one not surprised by the reunion was *God*. He saw it coming, he worked on both women's hearts separately, and after three years, when the time was right and their hearts were ready, he brought them back together at a conference.

I share Jan and Geri's story to give you hope. Hope that a friendship that has fallen apart can fall in step again. Hope that grace and love can defeat hurt and pride. Hope that God is working even when you can't see it—even when you can't *imagine* it. Hope that God's grace is more powerful than your weakness. Hope that even if today you call your friendship "broken," the God who "calls things that are not as though they were" is powerful enough to call it "reconciled."

THOUGHT QUESTIONS

1. Which type of outcome currently feels most realistic for your broken friendship: a truce, an impasse, or a reconciliation? Why?

2. If reconciliation feels impossible but you still hope to achieve it one day, how might you keep that door open? What conversations, decisions, or extensions of proactive grace might be helpful?

3. How are your prayers about your broken friendship going? What have you been hesitant or even afraid to pray about, and why? What prayers might help your heart begin to heal?

10

RECONCILIATION CONVERSATIONS

I spent long, agonizing moments standing statue-still in my kitchen,
barely breathing, pressing pieces together,
praying the glue would still hold when it dried.

Every time you walk past your phone, you almost pick it up. Almost.

Every time your mind's at rest, it's not at rest. At all. It's writing-revising-deleting-rewriting potential texts to your friend:

Hi. I miss you. Can we please talk and try to work this out?

Too honest. Too vulnerable.

Um, hello? Where have you been?

Too passive-aggressive.

Remember me? Don't you think it's way past time we talked? Do you even want to try to save our friendship?

Okay, now that's just aggressive.

Days pass. You long to reach out, but you're frozen in indecision: *What do I say? Where do I even start?*

As more time passes, it feels more and more intimidating to reach out. Every day, you sense the window of we-can-still-work-this-out opportunity closing a little more; every day, you feel the tiny flame of hope inside—hope that the friendship might be repaired—weakening, dimming, till it's barely an ember.

Ever been there? Aching to make things right with your friend but unsure where to begin? Wondering how to even initiate a conversation, much less a restoration of your relationship? In this chapter, we're going to talk about ways we might approach the path of reconciliation. We'll get practical, examining ideas for ways we can initiate healing conversations and then move them forward in productive directions. These strategies are gleaned from my own experiences as a sinful human working through difficulties in my own relationships, as a minister and preacher's wife who has counseled others through their struggles, and from wisdom lent to me from other Christians I respect.

My bowl was patched together with glue; friendships are glued back together with love, with grace, and with *words*. Reassembling my bowl was painstaking, difficult work; reconciliation conversations are even more delicate. You may have some false starts and failed attempts. You'll have to be more patient than you've ever wanted to be. You may stand over the pieces with tears in your eyes, questioning whether they can ever line up again. But if the friendship means enough to you, you'll do whatever it takes, as many times as it takes, until the breaks are mended, the beauty restored.

I don't know about you, but when I have emotionally loaded conversations, the neural pathway between my brain and mouth short-circuits. My brain struggles to deliver helpful information to my tongue, but the truth is, my brain has nothing to deliver anyway, because conflict usually sends my brain into hiding. I freeze up: no thoughts except "Get me outta here," no words except "thrugoo." Which is not Greek or Hebrew or even an angelic tongue—it's me babbling.

For all these reasons, I have found that I have to prepare my thoughts ahead of time. I have to think through what I want to say or ask and how, exactly, I want to say or ask it. (True story: sometimes, when I'm over-the-top nervous, I even practice out loud in my bathroom.) Since reconciliation conversations are some of the most complicated and emotionally loaded talks we'll ever engage in, let's walk through some questions, phrases, and talking points that may prove helpful.

REACHING OUT FOR RECONCILIATION

First things first: How do you even get the other person to sit down with you? How do you let your friend know you'd like to talk?

This may be the most difficult and intimidating step in the whole process. We can't even set one tentative toe on the path of reconciliation because we can't bring ourselves to send the text . . . make the call . . . put our wounded hearts out there where they might be hurt even more. I understand—oh, how I understand—the sleep-stealing, heart-pounding, ulcer-producing anxiety that accompanies the decision to reach out to a friend with whom you're having conflict.

What if she doesn't even respond?

What if she does respond, but she's angry or harsh?

What if she agrees to talk, but our conversation just makes things worse?

What if, what if, what if?

When I need to initiate a difficult conversation, I lean on Jesus' prayer in John 17 for comfort and strength. Jesus said, "I am praying . . . for all who will ever believe in me through their message. I pray that they will all be one, just as you and I are one—as you are in me, Father, and I am in you. And may they be in us so that the world will believe you sent me" (John 17:20-21, NLT).

Our unity matters to Jesus—it matters so much that mere hours before his arrest (an arrest he knew was coming, and dreaded), he took the time to pray for us. And so I appeal to *his* prayer in *my* prayers, asking God to fulfill his Son's plea in my friendship. I ask God to go before me and make my path straight (see Psalm 27:10-14 and Proverbs 3:5-6). I ask him to open up my friend to the idea of speaking with me, to soften her attitude toward me and prepare a way for my invitation. I ask him to send the Spirit to work on me and my friend—to give us both a humble, listening posture; to help us both desire to heal and forgive.

And then I leave the rest to God. (Full disclosure, the "leaving it to God and no longer obsessing" process takes approximately 537 prayers.) I remind myself that it's not up to me to respond on my friend's behalf; all I can do is initiate the idea of a conversation and see what she says. I can't control her response—I can only do my part.

Perhaps some of these prayers and mindsets can prove helpful as you summon the nerve to initiate a reconciliation conversation with your friend. Once you've prayed (and prayed and prayed), strapped on your courage and humility, and decided to request a conversation with your friend, how might you word that invitation?

Ways to initiate a conversation when you've been hurt
If you're the one who's been hurt, here are some phrases that might help you reach out:

Hey, can we talk about what happened between us? I'd really like to work things out. I know. This one is astoundingly profound and creative, isn't it? But this simple question can feel tremendously intimidating to say. We hem and haw all around it instead of being direct. If you want to talk, why not just . . . ask your friend if you can talk? No need to overexplain or overcomplicate the invitation.

It would really help me if we could talk through some things I've been feeling. Still simple and direct while also subtly appealing to your friend's compassion, indicating that this conversation would help your heart.

I hate that we're not right with each other. I miss you, and I'd love to talk and try to work things out. This one requires a little more vulnerability on your part, which can be hard to exercise when you're already hurting. But saying "I miss you" and expressing sadness at the state of your relationship can help to lower your friend's defenses.

Ways to initiate a conversation when you want to apologize

Breaking the can-we-talk ice can feel even trickier when you know your friend may feel so hurt and angry, she doesn't want to speak with you. If you know you owe your friend an apology (even if she owes you one too), it helps to go ahead and adopt a humble stance from the get-go. To let your friend know, "Hey, you deserve an apology from me, and I'm ready to offer it." Your humility may help to soften your friend's attitude and take down her heart-shields. Here is some language that might prove helpful:

> *I know we haven't been in a good place. I owe you an apology. Would you be willing to listen? No expectations on my end, no pressure to respond a certain way—but there are things you deserve to hear from me.* Not only does this message show humility, it also assures your friend that you aren't coming in with expectations or demands. It shows respect for her feelings. She may be more willing to hear you out if she knows you're going to give her space to process your apology in her own time.
>
> *I've realized some things about myself and the way I treated you. I'd love to share what I've seen and apologize if you're up for hearing it.* This is a simple way to show your friend that you've done some soul-searching, and you'd like the opportunity to apologize if she is willing to listen.

Once you send the message or make the call, you'll probably sit around stalking your phone, half-hyperventilating thanks to the miserable combination of relief, terror, and *what-was-I-thinking-why'd-I-do-this-to-myself* second-guessing. To this let me say, I am so sorry, I feel your pain, and as awful as those feelings are, they are normal responses to conflict and stress. But as you wait to hear back, I encourage you to "pray continually" (1 Thessalonians 5:17). Be relentless in bringing your situation to God's attention, asking him to soften your friend's heart and guide her response as she considers your invitation. These prayers will help to calm your thoughts and take the edge off your anxiety.

If your friend says she's not ready to talk yet, as frustrating and disheartening as that answer may be, I'd encourage you to resist the temptation to give in to pettiness and try to hurt her back. Do what you can to keep the door open for a future conversation. You might respond by saying something like, *I'm sorry you're not ready to talk yet, but I understand that you need more time. I care about you, and I'm here when you're ready to talk.*[1]

But what if your friend says yes, she's willing to talk? What happens next (besides a swarm of butterflies taking over your stomach)?

WHEN IT'S TIME TO LISTEN

If your friend has agreed to meet with you, a passage from James can help prepare you to conduct yourself wisely and righteously during the conversation:

> My dear brothers and sisters, take note of this: Everyone should be quick to listen, slow to speak and slow to become angry, because human anger does not produce the righteousness that God desires. Therefore, get rid of all moral filth and the evil that is so prevalent and humbly accept the word planted in you, which can save you. . . . Those who consider themselves religious and yet do not keep a tight rein on their tongues deceive themselves, and their religion is worthless.
> JAMES 1:19-21, 26

Short passage, so much wisdom! This passage helps us approach conflict resolution with a spirit that honors God and promotes peace. James tells us to *listen first*. As we enter difficult conversations, we have to ignore our fleshly instincts—talk first, talk fast, talk most—and begin by listening. Listen well, and listen with an open, humble heart. Keep your anger in check, ask the Holy Spirit for an extra measure of patience and self-control, and take time to think before speaking.

Difficult as it may be, we have to resist the temptation to speak when it's our friend's turn to express her feelings. We have to fight the urge

---

1. More on this in chapter 11, "When Your Friend Won't Reconcile."

to interrupt in order to correct her, defend ourselves, or clarify "what really happened." If we do those things, we risk shutting her down or blowing up an already tense situation. We have to let her get it all out. We may eventually need to correct misinformation, explain or defend ourselves, or clarify a misunderstanding—but it's usually best to wait our turn. Even if we disagree with our friend's perspective and want to correct a misunderstanding later in the conversation, we can begin by (clamping our teeth down on our tongue and) listening as patiently and thoroughly as we hope our friend will listen to us. Let her finish without being interrupted. (Remember the Golden Rule in Matthew 7:12: "So in everything, do to others what you would have them do to you.")

WHEN IT'S YOUR TURN TO SPEAK

Responding to your friend's feelings

Once you've heard your friend's side of things (and before you share your own side), here are some ways you might address the hurt your friend is feeling:

> *What I'm hearing you say is . . .* Summarize what you have heard.
> People's defenses come down when they know you have
> heard them out and made a sincere effort to understand their
> perspective and feelings.
>
> *I'm sorry you felt that way.* This sentence is helpful when your friend
> expresses feeling hurt, and you want to acknowledge her hurt
> even though you don't think you did anything wrong. This
> sentence does not admit wrongdoing or accept blame, but it
> does validate the way your friend feels.
>
> *Looking back, I now realize that . . .* This is a way you can express
> sorrow or take ownership of anything you now realize was a
> mistake or sin on your part.

Sharing your own hurts

Once you've acknowledged your friend's hurts, you may need to share your own. When it's time to express your side of things, I'd encourage you to do so with wisdom, kindness, and self-control, choosing language that promotes reconciliation. Some words are more likely to make people feel angry, defensive, or shut down; other words can keep people open and listening. Here are some ways to share your hurts without raising the temperature in the room:

I felt _____ when you _____. There's a big difference between saying, "I felt sad when you didn't text me back," as opposed to, "You didn't text me back, and that was rude." The first sentence shares your feelings in a way that appeals to your friend's empathy; the second slings a criticism that could put your friend on the defensive. When sharing your hurts, it's wise to keep the primary focus on what *you felt* rather than on what your friend did. (Remember: more "I felt"; less "You did.") When you structure your words like this, you are simply sharing your feelings instead of accusing your friend of wrongdoing.

When you said (or did) _____, it reminded me of _____, so I responded with a lot of emotion. Sometimes it helps to explain the background behind our reactions. We all have triggers, and sharing your history and emotional baggage may help your friend better understand why you reacted so strongly to something she said or did.

BRIDGE BUILDING

Sometimes we need language that clears a path for peace, language we can both agree on. These words build a bridge from our perspective to our friend's. Even if we don't see everything the same way, we can find points of agreement that move the conversation (and friendship) toward forgiveness and unity.

I think we were both doing the best we could with the information we had at the time. This is a helpful thing to say when you realize you can't go back to change how things unfolded, but now you have a better understanding of where your friend was coming from. Maybe you both didn't know everything you needed to know, and you would have responded differently if you'd had more accurate information. Neither of you handled things perfectly, but you acknowledge that you were both trying your best. And using the word *we* is a helpful way of putting you both on the same team. You both made mistakes; you both have new realizations to process.

I think we were both doing the best we could with where our faith was at the time. Again, note the use of the word *we* to put you on equal footing and on the same team—the team of friends who want to make things right. This is a helpful perspective to embrace when you realize that you have both matured and would now handle things differently, but you are willing to accept where your friend used to be just as you hope she will accept where you used to be.

THINGS TO SAY BEFORE YOU CONCLUDE YOUR CONVERSATION

When you've both finished sharing what you came to say, it can be tricky to know how to end the conversation—how to leave your talk in a way that feels, if not completely resolved, at least somewhat settled. At a good stopping point. Here are some questions and statements that may help you conclude your conversation:

Is there anything else you need to say to me? This is a hard sentence to say—it requires humility and bravery—but it ensures you have fully cleared the air so you don't have to revisit issues later. As a person who struggles to advocate for myself when I've been hurt, I sometimes need people to ask me this question. I need permission to share everything on my heart. The conflict-avoider in me would rather swallow that One Thing that's still bothering me and leave feeling unresolved—but if a friend invites me to speak up, I'll find my courage.

Is there anything else you need to hear from me? If you know you've
hurt or upset someone, this is a powerful sentence exhibiting
true humility and love. It helps to clarify what your friend
needs to hear from you in order to feel resolved. Sometimes we
think we have apologized, but the other person hasn't heard our
words that way; or we think we have made our friend feel seen
and heard and appreciated, but we haven't gone far enough.
This question allows your friend to express anything she still
needs that you might have missed.

I forgive you, and I'd like to move on. You may not be ready to say
this yet, but at some point, I pray you and your friend get to a
place where you can sincerely express these life-giving words to
one another.

I'd love the chance to try again and do better in the future. Again,
don't say this if you're not ready—but I pray you get there.

Before we go, can we pray together? You and your friend may still be
feeling a lot, processing a lot, as you finish your conversation.
Prayer softens and humbles our hearts. It provides a moment
of unity when you come together to agree on your requests
to God. Prayer invites God into your conflict and friendship,
reassures you that he is working, and reminds you to embrace
his ways of grace, forgiveness, and righteousness.

HOW MUCH DO YOU NEED TO HASH OUT?

You may wonder how intense and thorough your conversation needs to
be. Do you need to talk through every little detail of what went wrong?
Do you need to go back through your entire friendship history in order
to get resolution? No one can decide that but the two of you, but here
are a few thoughts to consider. I've always loved this fascinating nugget
of realistic wisdom from Ecclesiastes:

> Do not be overrighteous,
>   neither be overwise—
>   why destroy yourself?
> ECCLESIASTES 7:16

Practical Solomon tells us that there is such a thing as overdoing it—as being too righteous, too by the book. Sometimes I think we over-complicate our reconciliation conversations, and that's one reason we run away from them. We make them harder than they need to be. We set our standards so high we are bound to be frustrated and disappointed. Some people will insist that you have to talk through *every single moment* of hurt and misunderstanding; you have to hammer it *all* out. You have to apologize or extend forgiveness for every infraction, every broken promise or ill-advised word . . . and then, and only then, can you be reconciled. To be honest, that would not be my approach, but if you and your friend want and need to do it that way, you certainly can. If both parties are willing, you can take turns saying, "Next I need to talk about this conversation . . . and this moment . . . and this hurt." And you can ask each other, "What else?" a hundred times till you get it alllllllllll out. If you need to do it that way and both of you are up for it and your supply of tissues and coffee lasts long enough, then you can choose to walk that path together. If reconciliation lies at the end of that marathon conversation, amen.

If you take that approach, I would encourage you to insert a lot of grace into your relationship on the other side of that conversation. Please don't keep your relationship in that I-can't-move-on-till-I-tell-you-every-little-thing-that-bothers-me place. It's no fun being in a friendship where you are constantly worried about hurting the other person. I'd encourage you both to embrace these grace-filled words from 1 Peter 4:8: "Above all, love each other deeply, because love covers over a multitude of sins." As you rebuild your friendship, I pray you'll offer one another the kind of love that covers over (and sometimes overlooks) missteps and mistakes.

An alternate approach, the approach I'd encourage, would be to focus on the main issues, talking through the big picture of what went wrong and how you hurt each other. If you talk through the main points of misunderstanding, then perhaps you will feel comfortable letting go of some of the minor offenses, the not-such-a-big-deal hurts. Grace can cover some of the little things in the spirit of, "[Love] is not easily angered, it keeps no record of wrongs" (1 Corinthians 13:5).

I don't see this approach as dodging the hard conversations, but rather as exercising grace as God offers it. When I became a Christian and begged God for forgiveness, God didn't insist that I remember and apologize for every single time I'd sinned against him; if he had, I'd still be sitting here listing sins. I repented the best I was able—even knowing I still had blind spots, things I didn't know I'd done wrong or didn't understand were wrong—and God forgave me. He knew my heart was in the right place.

Bottom line, you're done talking when you're *both* done talking. When you both feel resolved and ready to move forward. If your friend is a believer, you can close the conversation by praying together, forgiving one another in the presence of God and asking for his guidance and blessing over a fresh start. When you say "amen," I pray you leave the past there in that room, on that park bench, in that café, choosing not to remember or bring up old sins. I pray you are able to walk away from that difficult conversation with your heart unfettered, your burdens lifted, and your friendship on the road to recovery.

THOUGHT QUESTIONS

1. What concerns or frightens you the most about initiating a reconciliation conversation?
2. What would help you feel ready to sit down and talk to your friend? Who can you turn to for guidance if you need help preparing for or following up on a difficult conversation?
3. James 1:19 says, "Be quick to listen, slow to speak and slow to become angry." Which piece of James's advice do you most need to focus on when you speak to your friend?

Part 3

WORKING WITH BROKEN

The Hummingbird

11

WHEN YOUR FRIEND WON'T RECONCILE

The hummingbird lay helpless and tired, on its side.
One wing was half gone; the bird's gorgeous beak was chipped at the end.
I searched for pieces large enough to glue back on,
but all the shards were miniscule.

"I know we've had some great times together in this small group, but since we're no longer small, it's time to split into two groups," Sheila announced, looking around at a roomful of women. It was difficult to read their faces—most were blank, processing the information. Sheila's phone dinged, and she glanced down. "Ladies, this is awful timing, but I've got to go. Something came up at home. I'm sorry! We'll work out all the details of our new small groups, and I promise we'll still have great fellowship! I love you all!"

Sheila rushed out, leaving the group to finish their coffee and ponder her announcement. Later that night, a text came in from a friend in the group:

I'm sorry to be the one to tell you this, but things went sideways after you left. Jennifer stirred up all kinds of trouble and got half the group upset about the split. They were saying all kinds of things about you, criticizing your leadership and your decision to split the group. I'm sorry—I just thought you should know.

Sheila read and reread the text, hands shaking, heart pounding. *Jennifer. I should have seen this coming. She's always gathering a little group of followers, always derailing our discussions from spiritual topics to worldly ones. It doesn't even feel like they're coming to the group to talk about Jesus—they'd rather just sit around yakking about the latest Netflix drama.* Righteous indignation heated inside till it reached a slow boil. *I have to take charge before this goes any farther. I need to speak up for what's right.*

Sheila sat down at her computer, pulled out her Bible, opened it to Matthew 18, and banged out an email to the entire group, fingers afire with righteous fury:

I heard about what happened after I left. Ladies, this is not the way Matthew 18 says to handle our conflicts. Those of you who had an issue with my decision should have come directly to me instead of talking behind my back. We need to do better than this.

With a *whoosh*, the email was sent.
The conflict went from small blaze to forest fire.
Jennifer forwarded the email to who-knows-how-many people.
Groups took sides.
Chaos and division ensued.
Sheila quickly realized her mistake and sent another email to the group, apologizing:

I shouldn't have emailed you all about something so sensitive—there I was, preaching about Matthew 18 but not following it myself. I should have gone directly to Jennifer instead of sending a group email.

Sheila reached out to Jennifer, trying to apologize. She called every few weeks for several months—no answer. She tried to chase her down after church—Jennifer kept leaving early. Even though Sheila knew the situation was not entirely her fault, she wrestled with feelings of guilt and shame for her part in exacerbating the conflict. She longed and prayed for resolution.

After several months, Jennifer finally answered Sheila's phone call.

"Jennifer! I'm so glad you picked up." Sheila was so surprised her words rear-ended each other on the way out. "I just wanted to say I'm sorry for the way I handled things that day. I never should have sent that email. I know I hurt you, and I'm sorry."

Jennifer sniffed into the phone. "Yeah. You blew it royally. Listen, I gotta go. I'm meeting Allison at the movies."

"Allison?"

"I don't think you know her. Anyway, I'm late, but I guess she'll understand when I tell her I was talking to you—she knows all about this situation."

Sheila sat silent on the other end. *Why does someone I've never met know about our disagreement? How many people has Jennifer gossiped with?* At last, Sheila gulped out, "Maybe I'll see you at church."

"Maybe."

Jennifer never apologized to Sheila. Never admitted any wrongdoing in the whole messy situation.

Perhaps you have experienced the same frustration as Sheila: you've tried repeatedly to repair your broken relationship, only to have your efforts rejected. If you made mistakes, you've swallowed your pride, faced your own demons, taken responsibility for your part, walked the difficult road of soul-searching and repentance. You've fought to embrace humility and forgiveness, only to have them thrown back in your face. Your humility, trampled. Your fragile courage, crushed. Your barely-scabbed-over heart, wounded afresh. Your precious hummingbird, bent and broken, flightless on the ground. And the agony of twice-baked rejection somehow brings ten times more pain.

You're stuck, gnawing the gristle of some miserable truths that are tough to swallow:

You can't make someone talk to you.

You can't make someone forgive you.

You can't make someone apologize.

You can't make someone reconcile with you.

You can't make someone be your friend.

So what do you do when you'd like to fix the friendship but the other person isn't interested?

GIVE GOD TIME TO WORK

In many cases, all we can do is let it go. If we've reached out, expressed a desire to talk and set things right, but the other person has refused or not responded, we can't force them to change their mind. That's not to say they *won't* change their mind, but unless and until that happens, we may have to accept their choice. We see this kind of patience modeled for us in Scripture:

> When the rich young man rejected Jesus' call to sell everything and follow him, Jesus let the young man go. He didn't chase after him (see Mark 10:17-23).
>
> When the Prodigal Son demanded his inheritance and ran away, his father, who represents God, didn't chase the boy down. He waited at home, always searching the horizon, always hoping today was the day his lost boy would return (see Luke 15:11-20).

In the meantime, as you wait for your friend to respond to your overtures, there is one thing you can do: Keep praying. Keep praying that God will soften her heart, ease her hurt, lessen her anger, humble her pride, open her eyes. Pray that God will change her heart so she desires reconciliation. Praying like this will not only help your friend, it will also protect your heart. Again, we see Jesus' wisdom in calling us to pray for our enemies (see Matthew 5:44-45). He knew some relationship struggles might linger, or never be set right, and prayer would be the only medicine potent enough to neutralize the virus of bitterness.

Praying like this will also keep the Father's special attention on the issue. It reminds him, "Hey, we have an unresolved problem here, and we need you to work on both of us." Sometimes that work happens quickly; sometimes it takes a long time.

God is working even when you can't see it.

In the book of Genesis, we find several stories of broken relationships that are restored after suffering years of separation—and by "years" we don't mean two or three; we mean *decades*. In Genesis 25, we meet the twin sons of Isaac and Rebekah, who were named Esau and Jacob. We've already touched on their story in chapter 7, "The Path to Healing." Esau was so angry with Jacob that he plotted to kill him, and so Jacob fled.

God worked on these brothers for *twenty years* before they were ready to reconcile. We don't know what God did to soften Esau's heart, but we do know that God put Jacob through two decades of misery at the hands of a relative named Laban. In Laban, Jacob met his match: someone as devious, greedy, and manipulative as he. What probably felt like out-of-nowhere unfairness and injustice to Jacob was actually God's hand at work on Jacob's character, allowing him to experience life on the receiving end of deceit and trickery. Through Laban, Jacob experienced some of the pain he'd put his brother Esau through all those years ago.

God was working on Jacob's heart.

And when the time came for Jacob to return home, he was in a humbler place. He was eager to make things right with his brother, though he didn't know if Esau was still nursing a murderous grudge. Instead of rage, Jacob found grace; instead of resentment, welcome. Scripture doesn't tell us much about Esau's life during the years when Jacob was away, but in their reunion we find a different Esau from the rash, angry brother Jacob had fled from all those years ago. Esau has transformed. He has become a gracious, generous man, a man who loves his brother and has apparently forgiven everything.

God's work didn't stop with this generation of brothers. Sadly, Jacob's sons experienced similar brokenness. Ten of Jacob's sons ganged up on the favored son, Joseph, and sold him into slavery in Egypt. For his part, Joseph was a bit . . . overconfident. Arrogant. Ignorant of others' feelings. God spent years working on Joseph and his brothers before reuniting them decades later in Egypt. Here's how the story played out.

JOSEPH AND HIS BROTHERS
Based on Genesis 45

"Out! Everyone, out! Leave me alone with these men."

Reuben and his brothers throw one another fearful, confused looks.

The Egyptian guards hurry out; the carved doors swing shut with an ominous slam.

The sons of Jacob unconsciously bunch closer together in the middle of the cavernous room.

"What's happening?" Benjamin whispers to Reuben; Reuben silences him with a look.

For long moments Zaphenath-Paneah, who might as well be Pharaoh himself for all the power he wields, sits staring down at them from his gilded throne. Behind the kohl-rimmed eyes, his face is impossible to read. The brothers wait in anguished silence, keeping their eyes averted, as if eye contact might draw his wrath.

Is this it? The moment the unpredictable Egyptian official levies another unfounded charge, finds a reason to toss them all in a prison, as their father feared he would?

Reuben has nearly mustered the courage to speak, to ask a question—"My lord" is perched on his lips—when Zaphenath-Paneah begins to tremble. His shoulders shake; he buries his face in his bejeweled hands. A snort escapes him, then a loud, keening howl.

Reuben's heart begins to pound. This man is truly unhinged. If Reuben did not know better, he would say this man was sobbing.

The man removes his hands to reveal eyes raining tears—black tears, trailing streaks of kohl down his face.

The man *is* sobbing.

Panicked, Reuben drops to his knees. His brothers, fully terrified, follow his lead.

The man's sobs reach ear-piercing levels. Surely the entire palace can hear his cries.

Reuben staggers to standing, head bowed, knees rattling, and stammers, "My lord, can we serve—that is, what is wrong?"

With a shuddering gasp, the official stands. Raises his arms wide, as if preparing to make a pronouncement.

"It is I!" Zaphenath-Paneah shouts, through a warbly voice. "I am your brother! Joseph! The one you sold into slavery!"

A chill sets every hair on Reuben's neck quivering; his stomach turns to water. *Joseph*. How does this man know about Joseph?

Beside him, Judah stiffens with fear. Issachar moans. Someone—probably Asher—retches. Reuben can smell the terror leaking from his brothers' pores.

Reuben's thoughts are a sandstorm: *We are caught at last after all these years. And now this is some twisted Egyptian way of making us face our deeds. They will torment us, then kill us.* His thoughts flit to his wife, his children—how they will miss him. A strange calm settles on him, stilling his trembling body, slowing his racing thoughts. *This is what we deserve.*

The official's voice is less warbly now, and . . . speaking Hebrew, their own tongue. "Look up, my brothers! It is I—Joseph! Is my father still living?" Zaphenath-Paneah dips a towel into a bowl, wipes the kohl from his face. Removes the official headdress. Without the Egyptian trappings, he is clean-shaven, square jawed, and . . . smaller. Familiar. Something in the eyes . . .

He steps off the dais, taking one step down. "It is I, your brother, Joseph," he says again in Hebrew. "Come near to me. I will not harm you. Please—come here to me."

And in those words, Reuben hears it: the voice, long stifled in his memory, of his brother, pleading from the cistern, "Come back! Please come back!"

Now Reuben sees it plain: his brother's eyes, almond-shaped, just like those of Joseph's mother. His brother's jaw—thicker than it was at seventeen, now manly and full.

A rush of joy—*Joseph, alive!*—is quickly strangled by a sick twist of terror—*surely seeking revenge*. Reuben's ears rush with sound; the room swirls; he staggers sideways into Judah, grabs onto him. He doesn't know if Judah holds him up or if he holds up Judah, but he knows if he lets go of his brother, they both will fall.

"Come close to me!" Joseph's voice now rings loud, strong, commanding. "Come close to me, all of you! Do not be distressed and do not be angry with yourselves for selling me here, because it was to save lives that God sent me ahead of you. For two years now there has been famine, and for the next five years there will be no plowing and reaping. But God meant me to save your lives by a great deliverance."

At those words, Reuben looks up. Dares to find Joseph's face. It is tear streaked once more, but smiling. Warm. Radiant with hope and—is that affection?

He is not angry. He is . . . glad. Glad to see us.

Joseph descends the rest of the steps, all the way down to their level. "It was not you who sent me here, but God."

Could it really—but no. Could all this—all we did, all I failed to do, all the ten thousand lies to Father, pretending Joseph was dead—could it all somehow be part of God's plan? Could it be redeemed?

Something shakes loose inside, a knot Reuben has lived with so long—breathed around so long—he's forgotten life without it. So many nights he's woken gasping from a nightmare of Joseph—bloody, pale, too-late-to-save Joseph. Reuben lets go of Judah and drops to his knees.

Joseph steps closer, so close Reuben can smell the spices on his robes. Reuben doesn't know when he began weeping, but he can hardly breathe past the tears. He buries his face in his hands.

He feels a warm hand on his head. Looks up into Joseph's streaming eyes.

"Oh, brother," Reuben chokes, "can you forgive me?"

Firm hands grip his elbows, tugging him to his feet. "I already did, long years ago," Joseph whispers.

And Reuben is in Joseph's arms, sobbing into his shoulder. *My brother—alive! My sin—redeemed!*

God worked on Jacob's sons over a lifetime, just as he had worked on their father: Joseph spent decades being refined in Egypt, and the rest of the sons spent those same years living with their father's grief, their own guilt eating them alive. When the brothers are finally reunited, we see a different spirit in all of them.

Biblical stories like these help us find peace even when we're in the middle of an unresolved conflict. They give us truths to cling to while we wait for resolution. As difficult as it is to be patient when a conflict is unresolved and a relationship dysfunctional, we can trust that God is at work—on us and on the other person.

God may have plans for your brokenness you never saw coming.

Where we see only heartache, God may see an opportunity. Sometimes God reveals purposes for our suffering we could never have imagined. In Joseph's story (found in Genesis 37–50), which unfolds over a span of decades, God restored relationships and redeemed Joseph's suffering, using it for a powerful purpose—to rescue countless lives from a devastating famine. Joseph's foresight in storing Egypt's grain during abundant years, then distributing it judiciously during years of famine, prevented mass starvation. We don't know exactly how close Joseph and his brothers became after the family relocated to Goshen under Joseph's care, but at the very least, fellowship was restored. Forgiveness was offered and embraced.

I love what Joseph said to his brothers: "Do not be distressed and do not be angry with yourselves for selling me here, because it was to save lives that God sent me ahead of you. . . . So then, it was not you who sent me here, but God" (Genesis 45:5, 8).

So then, it was not you who sent me here, but God. Joseph saw the hand of God at work even in his broken family life. God had a bigger purpose in mind, and apparently the only way to accomplish that greater purpose was through the crucible of brokenness. Who knows? Perhaps God has a bigger-picture end in mind, a purpose for your suffering that you couldn't fathom now if he told you. As Joseph and his brothers did, I pray *you* will one day uncover some redemptive purposes in all you have suffered and lost. Perhaps you'll realize some personal growth you might not have achieved another way; perhaps you, like Joseph, will help others through your suffering; maybe you'll forge a new relationship from the old one's ashes, a phoenix rising.

God works over a lifetime.

Reconciliation may seem impossible from where you stand, but never count God out. If Jacob and Esau could make amends, so can you. If

Joseph and his brothers could reunite, so can you. You may not see progress right now, but that doesn't mean it won't come about one day. A reconciliation that may seem impossible now may still come to fruition later.

I am usually ("usually" meaning "pretty much always") in a bigger hurry than God is. I want things resolved now, today—actually, yesterday—but God often works more slowly than that. Your friend may not be ready to resolve things now, and you may see zero evidence of progress, but that doesn't mean God is not working on her heart. God is creative. He can use other people, other circumstances, and other heartbreaks to shift her perspective and reshape her character. (And of course he's working on you too.)

Long after we've given up on situations, declared them dead and buried, God—the ultimate optimist—is still working. Ever patient, ever persistent, ever determined, he doesn't give up. He still sees potential, still has hope, still sees what can be. He rests that hummingbird, crooked and one-winged, in a bowl, not in the trash; he still calls it lovely, still knows it can fly.

TRUST IN GOD'S JUSTICE AND MERCY

I can only imagine all the bitterness and despair Joseph must have wrestled with during his years of slavery and imprisonment. When he looked into his future, he didn't imagine himself walking down Pharaoh's hallways, he saw himself rotting in dungeons. He had no hope of ever seeing his family again, much less setting things right.

In times like that, when redemption feels impossible, we can find peace and comfort by remembering God's justice and mercy.

God is just, and he calls us all to account in the end.

If you feel mistreated or abused, and an apology and restitution haven't come your way, it may help to remember that your friend will answer to God for any harm she has done to you and your reputation. (For more on this, see chapter 13, "When You're Being Maligned.")

Consider these words from Paul. They are both comforting and sobering:

> You, then, why do you judge your brother or sister? Or why
> do you treat them with contempt? For we will all stand before
> God's judgment seat. It is written:
>
> "'As surely as I live,' says the Lord,
> 'every knee will bow before me;
>   every tongue will acknowledge God.'"
>
> So then, each of us will give an account of ourselves to God.
> ROMANS 14:10-12

God will hold us *all* accountable for our words and our actions. While this passage warns against a spirit of judgment, reminding us that we ourselves have made many mistakes and are in need of grace, it is comforting to know that God will also hold others accountable when they do harm. A person may get away with spreading rumors, lies, or unkindness on this side of eternity, but God will make them face those choices in the end. We should not *hope for* another person's judgment, or celebrate the idea of someone's condemnation, but the *fact* of God's future justice can give us peace when we witness or experience injustice.

God will always forgive you, even when people won't.
It's a heart-crushing feeling to know you've wronged someone, and it's even worse to have them withhold forgiveness when you have tried to make things right. As much as we may long to hear those healing words from human lips—*I forgive you*—we may never hear them.

And that's where God steps in to heal what sin (maybe even our own sin) has broken. He can wash it away. He can make us new:

> You who answer prayer,
>   to you all people will come.

When we were overwhelmed by sins,
  you forgave our transgressions.
PSALM 65:2-3

The LORD is compassionate and gracious,
  slow to anger, abounding in love.
He will not always accuse,
  nor will he harbor his anger forever;
he does not treat us as our sins deserve
  or repay us according to our iniquities.
For as high as the heavens are above the earth,
  so great is his love for those who fear him;
as far as the east is from the west,
  so far has he removed our transgressions from us.
PSALM 103:8-12

Even when we feel overwhelmed with guilt over mistakes we have made, God steps in to forgive. Even when we feel we can never escape memories and regrets from our past, God takes those sins far, far away. When people refuse to forgive, God's grace supersedes human frailty. When people withhold the words, "I forgive you," *I Am* forgives you. And he always gets the last word.

SIMPLE TRUTHS FOR TOUGH MOMENTS

I've mentioned that I'm a can't-eat, can't-sleep kind of person when conflict brews. You can imagine the delights I experience when a conflict remains unresolved long-term. I'm like a CD with a scratch in it (remember those, back in the days before digital downloads?): whenever I try to move on to the next chord, all I do is stutter on the same line, over and over and over. My thoughts become obsessive; my feelings spiral down into frustration, anxiety, and discouragement.

Of course, the ideal solution is resolution, but when that's not possible, I have to intentionally center my thoughts on godly truths. These truths calm me, comfort me, and give me peace. They take my eyes off myself (and my friend) and put them back where they belong: on God and his faithful promises.

Here are a few truths to cling to when you're stuck in an unresolved conflict:

> God is with me even when no one else is (Psalm 27:10).
> I don't have to reconcile this friendship to be okay. God is enough (2 Timothy 4:16-18).
> I can still be confident God forgives me and can continue to use me even if I've made mistakes (Psalm 51:12-15).
> I can still be confident even if I've been rejected (John 1:10-11).
> I can still have other friendships even if this one is never restored (Psalm 119:63).
> If there was anything to forgive, God has forgiven me, even if the other person has not (1 John 1:9).
> God will set things right in his way and in his time (Psalm 37:5-13).

———

Earlier in this chapter, I told the story about my friend Sheila and her conflict with Jennifer. Sheila couldn't control Jennifer's response to her—she could only control her own response to Jennifer. As much as Sheila longed to set things right, she had to accept Jennifer's rejection. It took a lot of prayer for Sheila to work through her regret and embarrassment, but eventually, she did come to a peaceful place in her own heart.

She now looks back on the whole debacle as a time when God allowed her to learn some tough lessons about leadership, forgiveness, and godly confidence. She wouldn't want to relive the conflict and its fallout, but she is thankful for the growth she experienced in the long run. She and Jennifer haven't spoken since that day on the phone, and maybe they never will—but because Sheila has brought the situation to God, she trusts that God is working, and so she has peace.

I cannot tell you what's going to happen in your broken relationship. I don't know if full restoration lies ahead or if you will have to live with this brokenness forever. I don't know if your friend will show up eons later, like Joseph's brothers did, in a Big Reveal Moment where God pulls back the curtain to give you a mind-pretzeling glimpse of all he accomplished through (and in spite of) your brokenness. I don't know if your hummingbird will ever fly again or if you will have to cherish its broken remains as relics of something that once was beautiful. But I do know that God is big, God is able, and God specializes in redemption. Even if God does not restore your relationship to a place of renewed friendship, he can renew your heart. He can prepare you for, and use you for, his good purposes even through this suffering.

> He can prepare you to be a compassionate confidant for someone else who is hurting.
> He can prepare you to be a faithful friend to someone else.
> He can equip you to walk a friend or child through a break, sharing your own experiences.
> He can refine your character, imparting lessons that are tough to learn but priceless nonetheless.
> He can transform the coal of today's suffering into tomorrow's diamonds of humility, empathy, and grace.
> He can use even broken pieces as powerful tools: to remind us what beautiful looks like, that precious things need protecting, and that we who loved once can love once more. Maybe the wings of some broken friendships can't fly, but new friendships await—and with God's help, we'll find them.

THOUGHT QUESTIONS

1. Describe a time when you have witnessed or experienced God working change slowly, over a long time period. What does that situation teach you about God's heart and his ways? How might those insights help your perspective on the situation with your friendship?

2. If you are currently living with an unresolved conflict, what is the most difficult part of that heartache? How might you give that pain to God in prayer?

3. If you are currently estranged from a friend, in what ways do you see or sense God working on you, on your situation, or on your friend? If you struggle to see anything happening, pray that God will help you to feel his presence and see his hand at work—even if his work is slow and quiet.

4. Even if your friendship is not restored, how might God eventually use the things you learn through this situation for some good? What growth or change would you like to see in your own heart as you work through this difficulty?

12

WHEN YOU NEED A BREAK

I stood there beside the bathroom trash can,
cradling the broken bird in my hand.

Alexa stands gaping at Tasha. Her sentences come in fragments, in jagged words: "Lindsay? Dating James? *My* James? I mean—he used to be my James till we broke up a few weeks ago . . . Are you *sure?*"

"Yes," Tasha says, placing a hand on Alexa's arm. "She told me herself. She told me because . . . she wanted me to tell you. She didn't think it would go well if she told you herself."

"Ha!" Alexa spits out the laugh. Her voice drips sour sarcasm, an unfamiliar taste. "*Not go well*—that's the understatement of the year. I can't imagine *why* she thought it wouldn't go well for her to tell me she's dating James, since James and I only broke up, I dunno, five minutes ago, and she knows—*she knows!*—how miserable I've been. How could she do this to me?!"

Tasha spreads her hands. "I'm so sorry. Please don't shoot the messenger."

Alexa's eyes widen as her stomach sinks. "Do you think they liked each other before . . . before James and I . . ." She can't even finish the sentence. It's too awful to think of her friend moving in on her boyfriend before they'd even broken up. But a voice inside hisses, *That's totally what happened. All those times you told her how much you were hurting and how badly things were going, she pretended to care, when all along she was inserting herself into his life, eager to take your place.*

Alexa's head begins to pound.

Tasha presses her lips together, then says, "So . . . you're going to talk to her, right? Try to work this out? I mean, you go to church together, you have lots of the same friends . . . it'd be really bad if you guys were—you know—fighting."

Alexa shakes her head. "I can't even imagine talking to her. Not yet."

Not yet turns into a month, then two, then four . . . For six months, Alexa and Lindsay manage to avoid one another, which takes some serious social gymnastics, considering they are members of the same college ministry and have many mutual friends. For several months, both girls dig into their positions:

Alexa feels deeply betrayed by her (former) friend, and she can't fathom finding words to say that don't involve shouting or some other thoroughly un-Christlike behavior.

Lindsay feels misunderstood, not given a chance—if the tables were turned, she thinks she would give Alexa the benefit of the doubt and at least try to talk things out.

Their friendship seems permanently broken.

Sometimes a broken friendship needs a break. Some breaks are temporary; others last forever. We've talked about times when a (former) friend refuses our efforts to reconcile, but what about the times when *you're* not sure about reconciling? Maybe you're standing over the trash can, friendship fragments in hand, debating what to do. Part of your heart still loves this friend, still clings to a tiny spark of hope; another part of you says, "It's over. It's done."

CAN CHRISTIANS TAKE BREAKS?

In those standing-over-the-trash-can moments, it can be difficult to know what's best: Do we need a clean break forever, or do we just need to take a break for a while to sort things out? Perhaps our first question should be, *Can* Christians take breaks? Is it ungodly to step back from a friendship that isn't working? We have seen how much God desires unity, how as a Father he longs for all of his children to get along, and yet when we search the Bible for examples of broken relationships, we don't have to search long. We hit the first conflict in Genesis 3 and the first murder in Genesis 4. Although disunity and separation are not God's ideal, biblical passages frequently encourage us to guard our hearts and even avoid certain types of people.

We find many such passages in the book of Proverbs. Proverbs offers practical, incisive, honest advice about daily life: business, integrity, family dynamics, purity, marriage, parenting, friendship, and so much more. Proverbs isn't afraid to call people out, using terms like "fools," "mockers," or even "wicked." Oof. Kinda rough, and yet the honesty is refreshing. Clear.

This tells us that we don't need to dance around the truth. When people, even former friends, show themselves to be deceptive or cruel, we don't need to turn a blind eye in the name of grace. Proverbs 12:26 tells us, "The righteous choose their friends carefully, but the way of the wicked leads them astray." Friends are powerful influences. A friend can lead us closer to God or push us away. A friend can influence us for good or drag us down. A friend can bring us joy and growth or make us all kinds of twisted up inside. Yes, we are called to love everyone, but we can love people without making them our besties. It's wise to choose friends wisely.

And Proverbs makes it clear that we may need to avoid or limit our relationships with people whose influence would harm us or our character, in passages like these:

> Do not set foot on the path of the wicked
>   or walk in the way of evildoers.
> PROVERBS 4:14

Drive out the mocker, and out goes strife;
    quarrels and insults are ended.
PROVERBS 22:10

A gossip betrays a confidence;
    so avoid anyone who talks too much.
PROVERBS 20:19

Wisdom will save you from evil people,
    from those whose words are twisted.
These men turn from the right way
    to walk down dark paths.
PROVERBS 2:12-13, NLT

Add all this together, and there is plenty of biblical support for limiting or even severing relationships that are causing harm or leading us away from the life God wants for us.

If you conclude that you need space from a relationship while you evaluate what's best, perhaps instead of presenting the split to your friend as an eternal, irreversible split, a break*up*, you can present it, and think of it, as a *break*. This allows room for God—and time—to work on both of you. It leaves space for change, forgiveness, and redemption—isn't our God the God of change, forgiveness, and redemption? Those blessings may not always come about, but at least you can leave room for them, making space in your heart for a miracle.

To be honest, writing this chapter was intimidating. Sobering. Breakups can break hearts. Breaking off a relationship, even temporarily, is no small decision, and such a choice should not be made flippantly. I want to offer God-honoring, Christlike perspectives to guide your decisions, and I encourage you to follow Scripture as your compass. A decision to take a break—or let go of a friendship altogether—shouldn't be made in the heat of the moment, with tempers flying. I encourage you to make your decision thoughtfully and prayerfully. Search the Scriptures and invite godly counsel from people who know you, know your friend, and understand your situation.

Because on the other side of the argument, we should acknowledge that we can find plenty of selfish or manipulative reasons for taking a break. Some of these not-so-good reasons might be to punish your friend, to feel a sense of power over your friend, to show her how it feels to be rejected or ignored, or to avoid having a difficult conversation. When we've been hurt, it's oh, so tempting to seek revenge. You may hear the manipulative voice of Satan luring you down that path, dressing up a desire for vengeance in falsely righteous clothing. For example, he might feed you the line, "Take a break from the friendship because she's not changing," even though your heart is secretly exulting, "If I tell her I need a break, she'll experience the misery of rejection she made me feel." If your primary reason for a break is to hurt your friend, then you may need to spend some time asking God to help you to uproot a seed of bitterness in your heart (see chapter 8, "Bitterness").

And to be fair, your motives for taking a break may be mixed or even too tangled to interpret at first. Sometimes we legitimately need a break, *and* we need to keep wrestling with our own hearts. We need some space *so that* we can work on ourselves with a clearer head. Here's where honest prayer, godly counsel, and some Bible-centered soul-searching can be powerful tools that protect our hearts—and our friends'.

So let's get even more specific. When might it be wise or necessary for a Christian to take a break from a friendship?

When sin and deceit are involved

So, to break or not to break? If sin or deceit is involved in your conflict with your friend, perhaps this passage can help guide you:

> A troublemaker and a villain,
> > who goes about with a corrupt mouth,
> > who winks maliciously with his eye,
> > signals with his feet
> > and motions with his fingers,
> > who plots evil with deceit in his heart—
> > he always stirs up conflict.

Therefore disaster will overtake him in an instant;
    he will suddenly be destroyed—without remedy.

There are six things the LORD hates,
    seven that are detestable to him:
    haughty eyes,
    a lying tongue,
    hands that shed innocent blood,
    a heart that devises wicked schemes,
    feet that are quick to rush into evil,
    a false witness who pours out lies
    and a person who stirs up conflict in the community.
PROVERBS 6:12-19

Whew, that's strong language: God *hates* these things. This list of ungodly traits may help to clarify your decision if you've been wrestling. If God abhors these qualities, it makes sense that we should stay away from them as well by either limiting a person's role in our life or stepping out of the relationship altogether. To be more specific, a break may be beneficial—or necessary—in the following situations:

Your friend refuses to listen or change (haughty eyes).
Your friend is dishonest and untrustworthy (a lying tongue, a false
    witness).
A friendship is causing harm to you or to someone else (hands that
    shed innocent blood).
Your friend is pulling you away from God and his ways (a heart
    that devises wicked schemes).
Your friend is engaging in behaviors that violate Scripture or your
    conscience (feet that are quick to rush into evil).
Your friend often causes trouble between others; she lives
    at the center of drama (a person who stirs up conflict in
    the community).

When time apart is dedicated to bringing you close again

Sometimes we may not need to take a break because of sin, we just need time on our own to think and pray and evaluate ourselves and the friendship. We need time to pray about whether or not to pursue reunion later. Friendship muddles our capacity for fair decision-making because feelings are involved. We dread hurting others and being hurt ourselves; we recognize our own imperfections and hesitate to pass judgment when we ourselves are so flawed. We may fear the potential social repercussions of a break or breakup—a broken friendship may affect a friend group, church small group, work environment, or family. All these feelings paralyze our ability to assess fairly and clearly. We may need a little time and space to do so.

Here are a few specific circumstances that might call for taking a break:

You've reached an impasse and can't take your conversation any further. Like Paul and Barnabas, you need to just go your own way for a while and let God work on both of your hearts.

The friendship is causing significant anxiety or stress that you can't manage. Overwhelming anxiety may be a sign of dysfunction and imbalance in the relationship. You may need breathing room while you clear your head, identify the issues, pray, seek godly counsel, and decide whether or not this friendship can (or should) be restored.

You simply need time and space to pray and think more clearly without actively navigating the complexities of the relationship.

As we said, breaks and breakups can break hearts, so if you choose to take one, please do so for good reasons, with godly intentions.

HANDLING A BREAK WITH WISDOM

If you take a break in a friendship, you may encounter some tricky situations. Mutual friends may ask uncomfortable questions; some may take sides; you'll struggle to define the line between gossip and advice; your friend may talk about you behind your back.

How can we take a break from a friendship in a way that honors God, avoids bitterness, clarifies your path, and leaves room for reunion (if that is the best choice) on the other side? Here are a few Bible-based principles that can protect your heart, and your reputation, while a friendship is on pause.

Take the high road.

George Bernard Shaw once reputedly said, "Never wrestle with pigs. You both get dirty and the pig likes it."[1] Ever heard that gem? It's one of my favorites. It's somewhat reminiscent of Jesus' aphorism: "Do not give dogs what is sacred; do not throw your pearls to pigs. If you do, they may trample them under their feet, and turn and tear you to pieces" (Matthew 7:6).

When we're on a break and a former friend mistreats us, it's tempting to stoop to that low level and start slinging dirt: "Two can play that game"; "I have to defend myself"; "I refuse to be a doormat"; "I'm not just going to stand here and take that; I have to fight back." I'm not suggesting you can't speak up or try to set the record straight, but as you weigh your options and choose your words, do your best to remain righteous. To avoid the pitfalls of gossip, slander, and revenge. If your former friend is resorting to unrighteous, unkind words and actions, don't get down in the mud with her. Don't sully your own character on her behalf.

Jesus was the ultimate example of taking the high road; his every word and action knit together courage and humility. Consider these examples:

> He still called Judas "friend" even as Judas was betraying him (Matthew 26:50).
> When false witnesses slung accusations during his trial, Jesus stayed calm. He refused to return insult for insult (Mark 14:57-61).
> When he was put to death, he prayed for his killers, saying,

---

1. "Quotable Quote," Goodreads, accessed May 11, 2022, https://www.goodreads.com/quotes/43033.

"Father, forgive them, for they do not know what they are
doing" (Luke 23:34).

How was Jesus able to remain righteous and humble? He trusted that
God would mete out justice at the right time; he knew he was in good
hands (see 1 Peter 2:23).

While your friendship is on pause, imitate the Lord and do your best
to keep the break peaceful. To avoid a feud. To sidestep conversations
and situations that might exacerbate the conflict.

Try to put yourself in your friend's shoes.

When we're hurt and mad, this is the last thing we want to do. The abso-
lute. Last. Thing. We want to dig into our position and erect a fortress
around it. We want to marshal all our mental energy pondering—and
proving—all the ways *we* are right and *she* is wrong, but . . . humor me
for a moment. Just imagine it is possible—perhaps in some alternate
universe—that your friend is just a *teensy* bit right. A break gives you
the opportunity to take down your defensive shields while no one is
watching and privately ask yourself, *If I experienced the situation from her
vantage point, is it possible I might see our issues a little differently?*

This exercise, as humbling as it sounds, can be powerful. Not only does
it protect your heart from bitterness, but it also tempers your response.
It helps you calm down and think more rationally, more righteously. It
helps you concede small points even if you need to stick to big ones.

Be "as shrewd as snakes and as innocent as doves" (Matthew 10:16).

I'm always surprised that this quote comes from Jesus—it sounds more
like cynical Solomon writing in Ecclesiastes. But Jesus, as we have noted,
is both an idealist and a realist. He urges us to strive for the ideal even
as we live in a broken reality among broken people—*as* broken people
who have been saved and healed by our loving God. Jesus reminds us to
preserve our innocent hearts—the hearts that still trust God, hope for
the best, and are capable of believing in and loving others—while also
keeping our eyes open. He's reminding us not to be naive.

The apostle Paul once warned his disciple Timothy to be careful

around a person who had harmful intent: "Alexander the copper-
smith did me much harm, but the Lord will judge him for what he
has done. Be careful of him, for he fought against everything we said"
(2 Timothy 4:14-15, NLT). If a former friend has resorted to underhanded behaviors—lying, slandering, intentionally harming your reputation, or manipulating you—be wise and be careful. As you evaluate
whether or not your break should turn into a breakup, remember this:
you should not stay in, or resume, an abusive friendship that is causing
you harm.

Pray for growth.

At first, it will be tempting to disengage altogether after all the stress of
the conflict. *Now I don't have to think about that issue, or that friend, at
all.* And maybe that's okay for a while—maybe you need to just . . . let it
rest. But as you catch your breath, I encourage you to pray consistently
about growth. Ask God to help you figure out what to do from here.
Ask him to reveal anything he wants you to do or say or change in order
to pave the way for peace.

In chapter 3, we talked about inventorying our strengths and weaknesses; perhaps a break will allow you space to revisit your needs and
goals in prayer. Paul wrote, "Each one should test their own actions.
Then they can take pride in themselves alone, without comparing
themselves to someone else, for each one should carry their own load"
(Galatians 6:4-5). Perhaps you can use this time to "test your own
actions"—to pay special attention to cultivating new positive qualities
and changing old habits and shortcomings.

Pray for patience.

I appreciate Solomon's real-world wisdom:

> Since a king's word is supreme, who can say to him, "What are
> you doing?"

> Whoever obeys his command will come to no harm,
>   and the wise heart will know the proper time and procedure.

> For there is a proper time and procedure for every matter,
>   though a person may be weighed down by misery.
> ECCLESIASTES 8:4-6

Solomon acknowledges that sometimes we have to wait things out even though we're miserable. We have to wait for the right moment. Maybe a break wasn't what you wanted, but here you are. Waiting. Your heart may be heavy; you may be frustrated, longing for clarification, vindication, and resolution immediately, today, five minutes ago—but the time isn't right. In the meantime, until the *right* time comes, you can pray God strengthens your patience.

Pray for God's intervention.

If you're growing antsy to get things resolved, but you realize that you or your friend still need more time, keep inviting God to intervene, to help you and your friend to grow as needed, and to see your conflict to a place of resolution. Jesus told the parable of the persistent widow, a woman who was being mistreated (see Luke 18:1-8). Time and again she presented her case to her local judge, begging, "Grant me justice against my adversary." As her suffering dragged on, she refused to drop the issue. She kept parading her concerns in front of the judge, downright nagging him until he was so desperate to get her off his back that he acted on her behalf. Eventually, she got the help she needed. Jesus invites us to do the same thing with our Father, comforting us with these words: "And will not God bring about justice for his chosen ones, who cry out to him day and night? Will he keep putting them off? I tell you, he will see that they get justice, and quickly" (verses 7-8).

God is not an uncaring judge; he is a compassionate Father. He listens to our pleas, and he cares about resolution. When he is ready, he steps in.

———

When we left Alexa and Lindsay, they hadn't spoken in months. For a long time, neither girl showed any sign of wanting to reconcile. But at the five-month mark, something starts shaking loose in Alexa's heart. Scriptures she's managed to avoid—"Bear with each other and forgive one another if any of you has a grievance against someone" (Colossians 3:13); "Do not let the sun go down while you are still angry" (Ephesians 4:26)—start needling her. Waking her up in the middle of the night. Making her feel uncomfortable when it's time to take Communion, to honor the Lord's sacrifice, to thank him for his forgiveness. She finds herself making small overtures: smiling at Lindsay when their eyes meet across the room at church, even eking out a small wave and "hello." *Maybe we'll sort of ease back into casual conversation, and that will be that,* she thinks, not wanting to resurrect the conflict.

But Lindsay wants more than casual conversation—she wants real resolution. She sends Alexa a text:

> Hey, can we finally talk? There are things to say, and I'd like to make things right.

Alexa has a heart-check moment with God: "I see what you're doing, Lord. Making me deal with this—not letting me brush it aside. I don't really want to dig up all these feelings again, but if this is what you want, okay. I'll talk with Lindsay."

They meet, and it's awkward, but they push through.

"I promise nothing happened between me and James while you were dating," Lindsay says, words spilling out in a jumble, as if she's afraid Alexa is about to jump up and storm off without letting her finish. "Things just moved really fast after you broke up." She pauses. "Too fast, if I'm being honest. I wish we'd done things differently. But I promise James didn't cheat, and I wasn't trying to—you know—steal him from you."

Lindsay begins to express how hurt she felt by Alexa's decision to take a break from the friendship, and as Alexa tries to find the words to explain that she hadn't been ready to talk yet, epiphany strikes.

Neither of us was trying to hurt the other, and neither of us handled the situation very well. We were both doing the best we could at the time.

I might not have chosen to do what Lindsay did in dating James so soon after our breakup, but to be fair, she wouldn't have handled things the way

I handled them either. She would have talked things out instead of taking a break.

We both messed up, but . . . we were both trying to do right in our own imperfect way. So maybe we don't have to hash out every detail and get to a place where we both fully understand each other's choices and perspectives. Maybe we can decide to trust each other's hearts, and just . . . move forward. Put all of this behind us.

And that's what they do. They give up trying to iron out every detail of who did what wrong. They apologize for hurting each other, and each girl acknowledges that the other girl's intentions hadn't been consciously evil or hurtful. And then they just . . . let the rest go. They put it behind them. They start hanging out a little here and there. Sharing laughs again. Going to movies in the same group. And a couple of years later, to their astonishment, they end up as roommates—and they're totally happy about it.

Looking back years later, Alexa told me, "I don't know if we could have done anything different at the time. Those six months when we weren't talking—I know it wasn't the ideal solution, but we both needed the space. We needed time to calm down, think more clearly, start healing—and honestly, we needed to grow up a little. We were both still a bit immature. I needed some distance from my feelings about James before I could even begin processing my friendship with Lindsay. But . . . I'm so glad we didn't let six months become six years. I'm thankful that we circled back to each other. And I'm so thankful that Lindsay pushed me to talk and get to a place of true resolution when I wanted to settle for a half-baked peace."

Was it ideal for Alexa and Lindsay to refuse to speak for six months? Not really. Should they, theoretically, have been able to talk and work things out earlier? Maybe. But was the six-month break what they were both able to handle, considering their maturity and faith levels at the time? Yes.

How grateful I am that God works with us when we're not at our best, that he is patient and working toward redemption even when we're stumbling along imperfectly. Even though it was messy at times, Alexa and Lindsay's break allowed them time to settle down, get some emotional distance from their conflict, and pray through their attitudes and perspectives. It also allowed them to seek advice from mentors in the faith who pointed them toward growth.

And they did a few crucial things right: *They both kept listening to God. They stayed open to his Word and his leading. They wrestled with their own attitudes and didn't indulge in long-term bitterness.* So after a time, with God working separately on each girl's heart, they came back together with more humble attitudes. Less consumed with their own hurt, more willing to hear the other girl's viewpoint. Better able to acknowledge that even if they didn't agree with the other person's choices, they either trusted the intention behind those choices, or trusted the sincerity of the apology afterward. And so healing eventually became possible.

If you're on a break and questioning yourself—*Ugh, I haven't done things the right way; I shouldn't have said that; I wish I could do that part over again*—don't despair. God is still working, and the more you invite him into your situation, praying for his intervention, the more he'll continue working. Alexa and Lindsay's story gives us hope for the reconciliations that stop and start, make messes, and don't follow a linear, perfect path. Even when we fumble through breaks and when we hurt each other a little more on the road to recovery, recovery and restoration may still be possible.

If you are on a break or if you choose to take one, I pray you continue to honor God in all you do. If the hummingbird of your friendship ends up in the trash can, I pray God refills the empty space left behind on your shelf. Even if that space stands empty for a while, gathering dust, I pray God brings a new friendship to fill the gap your old friend left behind. If your friendship ends up lying lopsided in a bowl, beak chipped and one wing gone, a bittersweet remnant you can't quite let go of, may God comfort your heart and allow you to appreciate what beauty remains, however broken. And if your friendship ends up fully restored, may God be praised for his goodness and grace.

THOUGHT QUESTIONS

1. If you are thinking about taking a break from a friendship, what are your reasons for doing so? What do you hope the break will accomplish—in your heart, in your friend's heart, or in your dynamic?

2. Who are some godly confidants and counselors you can turn to for guidance in your conflict?

3. If you take a break, how will you know it's time to reach out to your friend again? What would need to happen or change before you attempt to resume your friendship?

4. What will it look like for you to "take the high road" during a break? What situations or conversations do you want to avoid?

13

WHEN YOU'RE BEING MALIGNED

The damage was too great.
This hummingbird would never—could never—regain its former shape.

The news comes to me sideways, through an offhanded comment my husband makes.

"Wait, what?" I blurt, though he's already three sentences into a different topic. "Who's been saying bad things about you? Not—surely not Jerry?"

"Er, uh." Kevin's expression takes a decidedly dodgy turn. His eyes dart up, down, around—every direction but toward my face.

"Kevin, *please*. Has Jerry been saying negative things about you?"

Kevin sighs. "Yeah." He spreads his hands. "I mean, are you really that surprised?"

My mind flits back over years' worth of memories from before Jerry moved away: times Jerry played with our kids, ate at our table, wrote us cards. "Yes, actually," I say, my face hot with anger and shock. "I *am* surprised. We were friends. I knew he had a resentful streak, but this is . . ." My brain flits through multiple descriptions: *Next-level. Mean. Underhanded. Totally un-Christlike.*

"Unsurprising," Kevin finishes for me. "It's the nature of my job as a preacher—some people aren't going to like me no matter what I do. This is not something I choose to stress about. I hope you'll choose the same thing." He makes his cutest little-boy-wheedling face. "Now about that church email I need you to edit . . ."

I know this technique—the Distract Elizabeth from Obsessing Technique—but I am not fooled, and I am definitely not distracted. For days my mind keeps circling back to Jerry. Every time my thoughts are at rest, or my kids stop asking me five hundred questions an hour, my thoughts drift to Jerry.

What, exactly, has he been saying? And to how many people has he said it? We have dozens of overlapping relationships—has he been intentionally sabotaging Kevin's reputation? And do people believe Jerry? My thoughts freeze on one person in particular—a person who once believed a dishonest rumor about Kevin in the past, with deeply hurtful results. My stomach twists; a wave of panic washes over me. Are we going to relive that whole debacle again—because of Jerry?

At that point I realize my heart needs intervention. Protection. I'm dancing dangerously close to the edge of Resentment Territory—and I refuse to live there again. I breathe deeply, send a fragment of a prayer heavenward (the best I can manage at my current stress level), and grab my Bible. I know exactly where to turn. A smile dusts my lips. Another thing Dad taught me before he got dementia; another treasure to keep his memory alive in my heart.

I was in college, home for spring break, and complaining to my parents that I felt overlooked and unappreciated in a certain group (this was hardly a shining moment of humility and grace in my life). Later that evening, Dad pulled me aside and pulled out his Bible. "Remember how Mom and I were . . . sad . . . when we first moved here?"

I squinted, trying to remember my high school days. "I mean, sort of, but honestly, you guys did a pretty good job of protecting me from stuff like that."

Dad gave a relieved smile. "Well, that's good to hear. You know I usually wear all my emotions all over my face. And—pretty much my whole body."

"Apple, tree," I said, pointing first to myself, then to him, with a sheepish grin. "Guess I get my big-feeling ways from you."

"Anyway," Dad said, "what we didn't tell you was that we took a lot of criticism for some of our decisions. We were shunned by many people. At one point, someone even preached about us—not by name, of course, but everyone knew he was talking about us—telling people how selfish it was to put your personal needs and desires and your family's well-being over your ministry career . . ."

Dad paused, seeing my jaw dangling halfway to the floor. He shook his head. "Sorry. Anyway, you don't need to know all that, but what you do need to know is that Psalm 37 protected my attitude. And I know it will protect yours."

Dad's guidance that day gave me a biblical solution for a tough truth: sometimes when friendships fall apart, people—how can I say this delicately?—go off the rails. They trot out their inner Mean Girls. They start sharing your secrets, spreading half-truths and rumors, and even downright lying. They set out to protect themselves by harming you. To preserve their reputations by damaging yours.

I don't have all the answers for how to handle those scenarios. Should you confront the person? (Or will that make you look petty?) Should you speak up in your own defense? (Or will that backfire and make you look guilty?) Should you try to set the record straight? (Or wait for truth to prevail?) I can't tell you exactly what to do if you're being maligned, because every situation is complex and nuanced, but I can point you to Scriptures that will minister to your pain and help you guard your heart.[1]

In this chapter we're going to dig into three passages, one from the Old Testament and two from the New. These three passages have brought me great comfort when I've felt misunderstood, misrepresented, and maligned. They've helped me battle bitterness and discouragement. If you take them into your heart, they will serve as life preservers you can cling to when a former friend slanders you, when waves of gossip are battering you, and when public opinion is a whirlpool trying to suck you

---

1. I recommend, if it's possible, seeking advice from a wise, godly person who is familiar with your life and situation. They can advise you based on your specific circumstances and the needs of the people involved. A Christian counselor may be a great resource as well.

under. These passages will keep you afloat—faithful, sane, righteous, and maybe even peaceful—no matter how long the storm rages.

PSALM 37

Let's begin where Dad suggested: in Psalm 37. King David, who had extensive experience with betrayal and unjust treatment—not just from Saul, but from many others—wrote this psalm. It's lengthy, so I'll just quote the highlights here, but please do yourself a great big favor and read the whole thing.

We'll start with verses 1-2.

> Do not fret because of those who are evil
>   or be envious of those who do wrong;
> for like the grass they will soon wither,
>   like green plants they will soon die away.
> PSALM 37:1-2

I love that word, *fret*. It indicates more than worry—fretting stirs together a miserable mixture of worry, obsession, and anger. And isn't that exactly what we do when a friend begins spreading slander about us? We can't. Stop. Thinking. We ping-pong between stress—*What is she saying? Who is listening? What's going to happen to my reputation?*—and anger—*How dare she? This is appalling! I can't believe a so-called Christian would act this way.* We stare at the broken pieces of our friendship scattered on the ground, tempted to give full vent to our anger and crush the jagged remains underfoot: *Two can play that game. She doesn't know who she's messing with. Just wait till I tell everyone who she really is.*

David goes on from fretting to envy; isn't envy another temptation we face when we're mistreated? When it feels like an ex-friend is getting away with unkindness or slander, we don't feel envious in the sense that we want to be in their position, but we may feel resentful of the fact that they seem to have an eager audience clamoring for more of their vitriol while we stand alone backstage, helpless and isolated, not a soul listening to our side.

Eternal perspective is invaluable here: people who behave like this will not prosper—they will "wither" and "die away." Mean girls won't win. Their influence will be short-lived.

Let's move on to the next section of the psalm:

Trust in the LORD and do good;
    dwell in the land and enjoy safe pasture.
Take delight in the LORD,
    and he will give you the desires of your heart.
Commit your way to the LORD;
    trust in him and he will do this:
He will make your righteous reward shine like the dawn,
    your vindication like the noonday sun.
Be still before the LORD
    and wait patiently for him;
do not fret when people succeed in their ways,
    when they carry out their wicked schemes.
PSALM 37:3-7

Let these peaceful words wash over you: "Trust in the LORD and do good; dwell in the land and enjoy safe pasture." You can't control what your friend is doing or saying, but you can choose to trust God. You can find peace knowing you are safe in his holy hands. Commit your way to the Lord, and in time, he will make your righteousness shine. You will be vindicated. God will show you what to do with those broken pieces. As Jesus said, "The truth will set you free" (John 8:32).

It may not happen right away. You may have to wait in frustrated misery, choking down all the things you want to say but can't, watching as your ex-friend temporarily succeeds in spreading her rumors. I don't mean to suggest that you can't defend yourself, protect your reputation, or attempt to set the record straight. (See Acts 16:35-40 for an example of Paul legally defending himself against mistreatment.) But sometimes we are thrust into complex situations where we are unable to defend ourselves without making things worse or making ourselves look guilty. In those situations, we may have to wait for God to set things right.[2] Yet even when you are unable to silence the other person or defend yourself, you can trust that God's eye is on you and your situation, and he will make things right when he is ready.

Next the psalmist elaborates on the fate of the ungodly:

> The wicked plot against the righteous
>> and gnash their teeth at them;
> but the Lord laughs at the wicked,
>> for he knows their day is coming.
> The wicked draw the sword
>> and bend the bow
> to bring down the poor and needy,
>> to slay those whose ways are upright.
> But their swords will pierce their own hearts,
>> and their bows will be broken.
> PSALM 37:12-15

Whew. These words are intense. The Lord sees arrogance and cruelty for what they are, and he scoffs. Even when people are fooled by lies or swayed by slander, God never is. He knows every heart. And he cannot be mocked.

The part of you that aches for justice? God loves justice too. The part of you that longs to see lying lips exposed as the manipulative deceivers they are? God wants the same thing.

This Scripture assures us that people who plot against others are also wounding themselves. Every sharp word a former friend utters, intending to harm you, slices her own soul on the way out. We should not rejoice in this—Proverbs 24:17-18 warns us, "Do not gloat when your enemy falls; when they stumble, do not let your heart rejoice, or the LORD will see and disapprove and turn his wrath away from them." Still, the knowledge that there will be a reckoning may soften your frustration. Ultimately, injustice cannot prevail.

---

2. If you find yourself in a complicated situation where your reputation is being damaged in ways that threaten your work, your family, your mental health, or your other friendships, please seek out wise counsel as to how best to proceed.

It is unclear how, exactly, God will apply these sobering truths as he deals with Christians who make mistakes and seek to harm others—again, we should not wish ill upon our brothers and sisters, however sinful or deceived they may be—but we can take comfort in knowing that God knows what is right. He knows what to do. He will work on each of us in the right way and at the right time. The psalmist goes on to speak of God's tenderness toward us.

> Better the little that the righteous have
>   than the wealth of many wicked;
> for the power of the wicked will be broken,
>   but the LORD upholds the righteous.
>
> The blameless spend their days under the LORD's care,
>   and their inheritance will endure forever. . . .
>
> The LORD makes firm the steps
>   of the one who delights in him;
> though he may stumble, he will not fall,
>   for the LORD upholds him with his hand. . . .
> The LORD loves the just
>   and will not forsake his faithful ones.
>
> PSALM 37:16-18, 23-24, 28

A vengeful person may seem to have power over you now—harming your reputation, undermining other relationships—but that power will be broken. Meanwhile, you are spending your days in the shelter of God's compassionate care. He has gathered the broken pieces of your heart into his gentle hands for safekeeping. Pray that God opens your eyes to *see* the countless ways he is encouraging, helping, and protecting you in seasons of suffering.

God is making firm your steps even now. You may stumble—say the wrong thing, do the wrong thing, make a choice that backfires—but keep committing yourself to righteousness, and God will guide your steps. You will grow through this as you go through this. And God will not forsake you.

David concludes his psalm on a high note of hope, reaffirming that deliverance awaits and our future is good.

> The wicked lie in wait for the righteous,
>   intent on putting them to death;
> but the LORD will not leave them in the power of the wicked
>   or let them be condemned when brought to trial.
>
> Hope in the LORD
>   and keep his way. . . .
>
> Consider the blameless, observe the upright;
>   a future awaits those who seek peace.
> But all sinners will be destroyed;
>   there will be no future for the wicked.
>
> The salvation of the righteous comes from the LORD;
>   he is their stronghold in time of trouble.
> The LORD helps them and delivers them;
>   he delivers them from the wicked and saves them,
>   because they take refuge in him.
>
> PSALM 37:32-34, 37-40

What a comfort these words are when we fear that someone else's slander or lies will permanently wreck our reputation. When we fear we may lose trust, lose our job, or lose other friends. God's eye is on our pain, and he wants justice to prevail.

Yes, the wicked may flourish for a season. Your former friend may seem to get away with hurting you for a while, but make no mistake: God is watching, God cannot be mocked, and God delivers his people.

You have a heavenly helper, a stronghold, a savior. Cling to him.

In the midst of your struggle and heartache, I encourage you to meditate on Psalm 37 every day if you need to. You may want to pray your way through it, borrowing its words, asking God to fulfill its truths in your broken friendship; appealing to his heart for justice, pleading with him to intervene as soon as possible. The more we bring our anguish to God, the more he works—and the more he opens our eyes so we can *see* him working—on our behalf.

1 PETER 2 AND 3

Now let's dig into two more passages, both from the New Testament book of 1 Peter. These Scriptures remind us of Jesus' example and heart in the face of mistreatment.

> If you suffer for doing good and you endure it, this is commendable before God. To this you were called, because Christ suffered for you, leaving you an example, that you should follow in his steps.
>
> "He committed no sin,
>   and no deceit was found in his mouth."
>
> When they hurled their insults at him, he did not retaliate; when he suffered, he made no threats. Instead, he entrusted himself to him who judges justly.
> 1 PETER 2:20-23

These challenging words were actually written to first-century believers who were free in Christ yet living in slavery. Peter was calling these Christians to conduct themselves like Jesus even when they were being mistreated by their human masters. Let's pause for a moment to admire the courage and strength these brothers and sisters exhibited, sometimes in the face of harsh beatings or other physical and emotional cruelty.

You and I can draw guidance and perspective from their example and from these verses when former friends speak badly about us, when they seek to harm our reputations, and when we are insulted and falsely accused. In these moments, when we feel bewildered, baffled, and hurt, and we are tempted to retaliate in unrighteous ways, let us remember the Lord. He, too, was maligned. He, too, was lied about, betrayed, and abused. And yet he remained righteous. As quick-witted as Jesus was, he did not answer insult with insult; as powerful as Jesus was, he did not threaten those who lied about him. He did not sink to his opponents' level by seeking revenge. How did he do that? By entrusting himself to the one who judges justly. By remembering that God was aware and God would act in the end. When you and I are tempted to meet cruelty with cruelty or to pursue revenge, let us maintain our integrity by imitating the Lord's faithful attitude.

Let's take a look at a second passage from 1 Peter:

Finally, all of you, be like-minded, be sympathetic, love one another, be compassionate and humble. Do not repay evil with evil or insult with insult. On the contrary, repay evil with blessing, because to this you were called so that you may inherit a blessing. For,

"Whoever would love life
    and see good days
must keep their tongue from evil
    and their lips from deceitful speech.
They must turn from evil and do good;
    they must seek peace and pursue it.
For the eyes of the Lord are on the righteous
    and his ears are attentive to their prayer,
but the face of the Lord is against those who do evil."

Who is going to harm you if you are eager to do good? But even if you should suffer for what is right, you are blessed. "Do not fear their threats; do not be frightened." But in your hearts revere Christ as Lord. Always be prepared to give an answer to everyone who asks you to give the reason for the hope that you have. But do this with gentleness and respect, keeping a clear conscience, so that those who speak maliciously against your good behavior in Christ may be ashamed of their slander. For it is better, if it is God's will, to suffer for doing good than for doing evil. For Christ also suffered once for sins, the righteous for the unrighteous, to bring you to God.

1 PETER 3:8-18

This passage is jam-packed with wisdom to strengthen us through injustice. Let's highlight a few of the points that apply to the pain of being maligned by a former friend. First, verse 9 says, "Do not repay evil with evil or insult with insult. On the contrary, repay evil with blessing, because to this you were called so that you may inherit a blessing." Don't let a former friend's evil treatment change you or lead you into sin. Repay evil with blessing. Why? Because this attitude reflects God's merciful heart, and *you* will inherit a blessing.

Peter goes on to quote from Psalm 34. In verse 14, the psalmist urges us to "seek peace and pursue it." Whenever possible, let us choose words and actions that promote a peaceful resolution rather than exacerbating the conflict.

What a comfort to remember that "the eyes of the LORD are on the righteous and his ears are attentive to their cry" (Psalm 34:15). God sees everything that's happening to you, and he hears all your prayers for deliverance. He doesn't just hear them half-heartedly, like, "Yeah, here comes that girl complaining about her friend issues again"; he leans in close and gives you his best attention. He listens. He considers. He cares. It may be unclear why he is allowing your friend to continue mistreating you, but you can feel safe in his hands, knowing "the face of the LORD is against those who do evil" (verse 16).

In verses 15 and 16, Peter reminds us that when we defend ourselves or our faith, we should do so with gentleness and respect. We should keep a clear conscience, maintaining our integrity and self-control in the face of attack. Why? Not only does our righteousness honor God, but it may eventually win over our enemies' hearts, making them ashamed of their own behavior. It's not wrong to speak up and try to clear your name or clarify your side of the story or explain your actions—just do so with words that honor God.

But what about when we defend ourselves and the injustice continues—or worsens? In verse 17, we find an interesting turn of phrase: "It is better, *if it is God's will*, to suffer for doing good than for doing evil" (1 Peter 3:17, emphasis added). Sometimes, for reasons we may never fully grasp, it is God's will that we suffer injustice for a time. God allowed his own Son to endure injustice so that you and I might be saved from sin; God allowed Joseph to suffer unfairly so that countless lives might be spared from famine; perhaps God has redemptive purposes for your pain that you can't yet see.

Big picture? God blesses those who suffer unjustly, we need not fear others' threats, and the Lord knows how we feel. His friends betrayed him too.

When we consider all three passages together—Psalm 37, 1 Peter 2, and 1 Peter 3—we take away these powerful truths:

> God cares about justice.
> Your friend may fool other people, but she cannot fool God.
> God will not be mocked.
> God will hold your friend accountable for her behavior, and you for yours.
> God sees your suffering, hears your prayers, and cares about your pain.
> You may find unexpected blessings in suffering and mistreatment. We are never more like Jesus than when we suffer injustice with a righteous attitude.
> In the end, God himself will clear your name.

Cling to these truths, my friend. Let these Scriptures ease your fears, cool your anger, and comfort your pain. Let them give you hope, a North Star for your hurting heart. If you're the victim of ongoing gossip or lies, I encourage you to meditate on these passages daily—hourly, if needed. Let their truths wash over your wounds, diluting the pain and cleansing you from the would-be infection of bitterness. It won't be enough to read them once; you'll probably need to read them, journal them, memorize them, and pray through them many times. But one day you'll wake to find your heart settled, your mind at ease, your fears at rest. I pray that day comes soon.

One day God will set everything right.

One day the truth will come out.

One day you will be vindicated.

And one day you will receive God's blessing as one who has trusted him and suffered righteously, following in the noble steps of our Lord Jesus.

THOUGHT QUESTIONS

1. What are you most tempted to fret over when you suspect someone is talking about you behind your back? Do you worry about your reputation? Your job? Your other relationships? How might you hand those fears over to God?

2. How might meditating on God's faithfulness, fairness, and future justice help to settle your thoughts and calm your fears? What Scriptures can you cling to?

3. In what ways do you want to imitate Jesus' example in enduring unjust suffering? What most inspires or challenges you about his example?

4. If you need to defend your reputation or correct false information or lies, how can you do so in a way that preserves your integrity and honors God? (And if you need advice about your approach, who can give you godly counsel?)

14

MOURNING A LOST FRIENDSHIP

My heart still gives a little bittersweet throb
every time I see it resting there in its bowl.
It's still beautiful to me, precious to me,
broken wing and all.

"Have you heard from Carrie recently?" Amanda asks me over the phone.

"Not for ages," I say. With a sad squeeze of my heart, I find words for the truth I've been afraid to think even in the quiet of my own mind: "It's been so long that I think . . . it's time I let our friendship go."

And in speaking those words aloud, a sad sort of peace settles over me. *It's done. I'm not going to chase her down anymore. And now it's time to just . . . process and heal.*

If your efforts at reconciliation have hit dead ends, or a long drift has pushed the remnants of your friendship too far apart to be reunited, it may be time to accept that your friendship is over. If tossing the shattered remnants in the trash feels too extreme, it may be time to put that broken hummingbird high on a shelf, out of sight, giving yourself space to grieve.

We know to be gentle with ourselves if we go through a relational loss by way of death or divorce, but when it comes to friendship, we may expect ourselves to just "get over it." Move on. Pass by that broken hummingbird and feel nothing. Harden our hearts and say, "Good riddance." We may fight the sadness, or even feel guilty for the sadness, chastising ourselves with get-over-it thoughts like this:

> *You shouldn't be so upset about this.*
> *It's not like someone died.*
> *It was just a friendship—they weren't even family.*
> *You should be over this by now.*
> *Just move on.*

We can shout "shoulds" like this at ourselves all day, but they won't make the heartache of a lost friendship hurt any less. If anything, they add to the problem by heaping unnecessary guilt, shame, and self-accusation on top of an already painful pile of feelings. And if you haven't learned this truth in your life already, allow me to share an insight from personal experience: stuffing or ignoring your feelings, hoping they'll go away if you pretend they don't exist, always backfires.

You might get away with ignoring the pain of a broken friendship for a little while, but sooner or later something will hit that sensitive spot again and send those unresolved feelings rocketing back to the surface, stronger (and dare I say, maybe angrier or meaner) than ever:

> You may feel sideswiped by sadness.
> You may back away from a new friendship, suddenly afraid.
> You may distance yourself from your remaining friendships, trying
>   to protect yourself in case something goes wrong there too.
> You may snap someone's head off for a small offense because
>   it transported your feelings right back to That Awful Time
>   You Got Hurt—and now your feelings know better and are
>   prepared to defend themselves.

The loss of a friendship is a unique tragedy, one we may mourn for years. And loss needs to be grieved in order for healing to happen.

THE NEED TO MOURN

Scripture repeatedly acknowledges that broken friendships cause great pain—take a look at a passage from Psalm 55 that deals with this theme:

> My thoughts trouble me and I am distraught
>> because of what my enemy is saying,
>> because of the threats of the wicked;
> for they bring down suffering on me
>> and assail me in their anger.
>
> My heart is in anguish within me. . . .
>
> If an enemy were insulting me,
>> I could endure it;
> if a foe were rising against me,
>> I could hide.
> But it is you, a man like myself,
>> my companion, my close friend,
> with whom I once enjoyed sweet fellowship
>> at the house of God,
> as we walked about
>> among the worshipers.
>
> PSALM 55:2-4, 12-14

The psalmist, David, starts out lamenting a miserable situation: gossip, slander, vicious verbal attacks. As readers, we unconsciously assume these attacks must be the work of enemies who hate David and have always hated him. But as we read on, we get a shock: one of the people attacking David used to be his friend. Not just an acquaintance-level friend, or a get-coffee-once-every-few-months-type friend—no, this was a "close friend," someone with whom David "once enjoyed sweet fellowship at the house of God." They worshiped and sang together. Celebrated their love for God together. And that closeness makes the pain of betrayal infinitely worse: *If an enemy were insulting me, I could endure it . . .*

In Psalm 109 David writes again about being falsely accused by friends, and he says,

> In return for my friendship they accuse me,
>   but I am a man of prayer.
> They repay me evil for good,
>   and hatred for my friendship. . . .
> For I am poor and needy,
>   and my heart is wounded within me.
> I fade away like an evening shadow;
>   I am shaken off like a locust.
>
> PSALM 109:4-5, 22-23

David's heart was wounded; the sorrow was exhausting, leaching him of life, energy, and joy. David grappled with this loss for a long time; sorrow's radiation lingered with a long half-life. David did not name the friends who betrayed him in his psalms, but Scripture tells us that King Saul was one of the people who turned on David. Saul didn't just sling accusations and words; he threw spears as well. He soon forced David to live on the run, a hunted man. We have already explored how David eventually pressed Saul into an uneasy truce (chapter 9); now let's look back earlier in their relationship, when the conflict first began.

DAVID AND SAUL
Based on 1 Samuel 16–19

The tent is bathed in moon-silver. But David lies awake, sweating, heart galloping, mind roiling. Every time he closes his eyes, he hears the *whistle-thwack* of Saul's spear flying across the room and slamming into the wall, missing David's head by a fingertip.

What have I done but serve him? I killed Goliath, fought his battles, risked my life, led faithfully in his army. I've shared meals with him, sung and played to soothe his nerves more evenings than I can count . . . I thought Saul viewed me as a son. How could he try to kill me?

"My father is jealous of you," David's friend Jonathan had said that evening when he'd snuck out of the palace to check on him.

"How could a king be jealous of *me*? Not long ago I was watching my father's sheep in the fields while my brothers went off to war. I'm *nobody*!"

"And that's exactly why Father is jealous—your overnight rise from shepherd boy to giant killer and war hero makes the people adore you all the more," Jonathan said. "You are like them—and God smiles on everything you do."

"I wish he'd smiled a little harder today," David muttered. "Your father almost took my head off."

"His anger will pass," Jonathan said. "It always does. I'll talk to him. Help him see reason. He'll make things right with you, you'll see."

"I hope you are right. But something tells me your father and I will never be right again. I thought . . . at least I hoped . . ." He shakes his head, feeling a humiliated flush crawling up his neck. "I wanted to be a son to him. I thought . . . my friendship with you, all the ways I've shown my loyalty . . . I was foolish to think he'd love me back."

David's mind skips back to his father, Jesse, painful memories with jagged edges:

"Father, did you see my catch?" Little David proudly holds up a rabbit, killed with his slingshot after hours spent crawling through underbrush, hunting.

Jesse's eyes barely brush the rabbit, then shift out to the fields where David's older brothers are working. "Mmm," he says. "One day you'll be old enough to catch real game, like your brother Eliab."

Then a few years later:

"The prophet Samuel has come to anoint one of you king!" The servant girl skids to a stop outside the sheep pen where David is coaxing the last stragglers out with gentle prods from his staff.

David looks up to squint at her, confused. "One of who?"

"One of the sons of Jesse. Samuel just showed up, and now we're preparing a whole feast and everything, and then Samuel says he's going to anoint one of your father's sons the next king!"

David half steps toward her, then stops. "Wait, so did Father send you here to take my place? So I can join my brothers at the feast?"

"You?" The servant girl gives a scornful giggle, then tries—fails— to swallow it. "No. He sent me here to tell you to keep the sheep out all day. He doesn't want the sound of bleating to distract from the prophet's work. He wants your brothers to impress Samuel."

Shame heats David's face and fills his eyes. He turns back to the sheep so the girl won't see his tears. The prophet soon insists that Jesse invite David to the feast, but it's too late. David already knows his father didn't want him.

Back in the field with Jonathan, David tries to shake off the memories, but they cling like cobwebs. Even to Jonathan, he can't say what he feels: *When Saul took me in to his household, I thought I'd found a father-friend. A place where I belonged. A home where I was wanted. I thought so very wrong.*

Sadly, Saul's resentment of David only deepened over time, darkening into a twisted obsession; their friendship was never restored. David poured out his pain from this and other betrayals in psalms that minister to us even now.

As we have seen throughout this book, David wasn't the only person in Scripture to mourn hurts from trusted friends. The apostle Paul mentioned the pain of disloyalty and abandonment in a letter to his son in the faith, Timothy, a letter Paul penned shortly before his execution:

> Do your best to come to me quickly, for Demas, because he loved this world, has deserted me and has gone to Thessalonica. Crescens has gone to Galatia, and Titus to Dalmatia. Only Luke is with me. . . . At my first defense, no one came to my support, but everyone deserted me. May it not be held against them.
> 2 TIMOTHY 4:9-11, 16

You can hear the hurt in Paul's words as he describes being deserted by Demas—in fact, for a time, Paul says he was deserted by *all* of his friends. Paul stood trial without a single person by his side. Twice in these sentences, Paul chooses a word heavy-laden with emotional weight: *egkataleipo*, which means "totally abandoned, utterly forsaken."[1] It's a strong word, saturated with sorrow. We can imagine some tearful prayers in Paul's prison cell as he grappled with his hurts.

Jesus also mourned deeply personal betrayals, most directly from Judas Iscariot, but also from his other disciples. On the night of Jesus' arrest, we catch a glimpse of the pain Jesus felt knowing his friendship with Judas had already been broken: "Jesus was troubled in spirit and testified, 'Very truly I tell you, one of you is going to betray me.' His disciples stared at one another, at a loss to know which of them he meant" (John 13:21-22).

Jesus' grief over Judas's betrayal and his own impending suffering rolled off him in waves powerful enough to pull his disciples into the current. They didn't yet understand what Judas had done or why Jesus was so upset, but even so, they felt the Lord's anguish, and it overwhelmed them. Hours later, when Jesus asked Peter, James, and John to keep watch with him in prayer, they fell asleep, exhausted from sharing his sorrow (see Luke 22:45). We can only imagine the pain their failure added to Jesus' already hurting heart.

These examples of broken friendships did not find their way into Scripture accidentally (see 2 Timothy 3:16 and 2 Peter 1:20-21). By giving us these stories, God is intentionally recognizing the pain of broken friendships. He understands that this specific heartache *matters*. Grief over a lost friendship is not a time-wasting emotion we can easily shake off whenever we choose. God's Word depicts the pain of broken friendships as a heart-wrenching sorrow, a sorrow many of us—maybe even all of us—will endure.

MOURNING, PRACTICALLY SPEAKING

Taking time to mourn a lost friendship may sound like a good idea, an emotionally healthy practice, but it's easier said than done. It's the kind

---

1. Blue Letter Bible, s.v. "Egkataleipo," accessed December 7, 2022, https://www.blueletterbible.org/lexicon/g1459/niv/mgnt/0-1/.

of heart work we may want to just muscle through and check off our list, but you cannot rush grief. And maybe we aren't sure how to grieve this kind of loss, anyway. What might mourning a broken friendship look like?

It may look like crying.

It may look like praying through your feelings—not once, but many times. You may need to process new hurts or losses as they arise.

It may look like sharing your pain with spiritual mentors or fair-minded friends who can support you.

It may look like seeking professional counsel for advice in the situation or for help working through a struggle with depression.

It may look like acknowledging that you feel sad on certain days with significant meaning: birthdays, anniversaries, holidays, and other times you used to share with your friend. You may need to prepare yourself to feel those emotions ahead of time, making space for them so they don't catch you off guard or dominate your life for longer than necessary.

On days when I expect bad memories and rough feelings to show up, I find it helpful to set aside extra time to address my emotions. As a part-time introvert, I've found that extra prayer with God in the morning and extra downtime by myself at night often do the trick. A good book and some coffee and dark chocolate may play a prominent role in that downtime. If you're more of an extrovert who likes to process painful feelings with the help of other people, you may want to ask someone to keep you company—to meet with you to talk and pray. Figure out how you process best, and plan ahead. If we make space for tough feelings when we know they are coming, we may be able to resolve them more quickly.

GIVING YOURSELF CLOSURE

When most big things in life end, we get closure: Graduations. Goodbye parties. Funerals. But when friendships collapse, it's tough to find the closure we need. Perhaps the friendship ended in rough words that can't be unspoken. If you were ghosted or the friendship drifted, maybe there was no warning—just a sudden absence—and you never got to say goodbye . . . you didn't know you needed to.

A lack of closure makes it difficult to move forward. If the friendship fell apart in such a way that you didn't get the resolution you need, I'd encourage you to find a way to *give yourself* a sense of closure. Usually for me, this closure involves a specific prayer dedicated to finding peace: a prayer time in which I hash out the loss with God (even if it's for the millionth time) and intentionally release the relationship to him in a single prayer—or a season of prayers. I may say something like this:

Lord, I wish things were different. I still hope they can be. I still have hope for forgiveness and resolution, but I have done everything I know to do at this point, and the rest is in the other person's hands—and yours.

I ask you to heal our rift. To sew back together what feels irreparably torn.

But until that time, I give this relationship over to you. I ask you to heal my heart. To fill the hole left behind where that friendship used to be. I can't imagine it could ever be filled, but I know you are good and wise, and you know how to heal such wounds. I ask you to comfort me, to ease this ache, and to guard me from insecurity, self-protectiveness, cynicism, fear, and a hardened heart. Please help me to continue growing and changing the way you want me to.

Please bring other people—safe, trustworthy, reliable people— into my life. And please help my friend. I don't understand everything that's going on in her heart, but please do the work of healing and helping that she needs too. Where I have hurt her, please heal her. If she needs to change, please prompt her to change. If she needs to see herself more clearly, please give her that clarity. If she needs to forgive me and release bitterness, please help her to do so. Please bring love and friendship into both of our lives again, Father.

I surrender this relationship to you. Again, I ask for what feels like the impossible—healing and restoration—but until that time, with your help, I decide to move forward with my life. I decide to let go. I know that I am stronger with you than I am on my own, and that with your help, I will be okay. Thank you for helping me let go, move forward, and begin to heal. I don't expect the pain to vanish when I say amen, but I do ask you to bring a sense of peace and resolve into my heart. Thank you for hearing my prayer and caring about this with me, Father. I love you.

Usually, a prayer like this—or a season of prayers like this—will help me to pick myself back up again, let go, and move forward. To rest the shattered pieces of my hummingbird in the bowl of God's hands and leave them there. No, I don't walk away pain free, but I do have peace. Peace because I've done all I know to do, I trust that God loves me and my former friend, and I know he's working even when I can't see it. I know that we are both cradled in the best of hands. I know God wants healing and unity, and if they are possible, he will eventually bring them about. I know he is bigger than our misunderstanding, disagreement, and hurt. And I know that with his help, I'm going to be okay.

If you need more of a sense of closure, you could also try something more tangible:

Write your prayer like a letter to God.

Go to a place that reminds you of your friendship and pray there as a way of letting go.

Write a goodbye letter to your friend, even if you can't give it to her. Read the letter to God, then burn it.

Decide what to do with any mementos of your friendship that cause you pain: pictures, gifts, memorabilia. Perhaps you simply pack them away out of sight, or maybe it's time to find them a new home elsewhere. Of course, we don't get rid of mementos with a vengeful, angry spirit, but as a way of finding peace and moving forward.

Let's revisit the beautiful poem Solomon wrote:

There is a time for everything,
and a season for every activity under the heavens:
a time to be born and a time to die,
a time to plant and a time to uproot,
a time to kill and a time to heal,
a time to tear down and a time to build,
a time to weep and a time to laugh,
a time to mourn and a time to dance,
a time to scatter stones and a time to gather them,
a time to embrace and a time to refrain from embracing,
a time to search and a time to give up,
a time to keep and a time to throw away,
a time to tear and a time to mend,
a time to be silent and a time to speak,
a time to love and a time to hate,
a time for war and a time for peace.
ECCLESIASTES 3:1-8

Such wisdom for life—and broken friendships. When we can no longer embrace, when it's time to give up, when what is torn cannot be mended, when words fail and only silence remains . . . chances are, it's also time to mourn.

But one day, when time has softened the memories and the wound is no longer raw and easy-bleeding, we will be able to set the mourning aside. It will be time to reopen our hearts once more—carefully, carefully, baby steps, baby steps—to new people, new memories. One day we'll set foot onto a new path with a new friend.

Maybe at first we'll start walking side by side, but an arm's length apart, still shielding our wary heart, planning to turn around and say goodbye before we walk too far, get in too deep. But then we'll get swept up in the talking and laughing and story swapping, and we won't even notice how far we've gone—and how far we've come. Step-by-step, we'll leave our painful past behind, back there in the days of mourning.

Step-by-step, we'll ease into a new friendship—different than the one we lost, but a beautiful different. We may always miss that old hummingbird and all it represented, but with God nudging us forward, we'll rediscover all the beauty still out there for the finding. The finding and—with his help—the keeping.

THOUGHT QUESTIONS

1. What pain do you most need God to comfort and heal as you work through a lost friendship? What Scriptures speak to those hurts?
2. If it's time for you to mourn a lost friendship, what might give you a sense of closure?
3. Jesus experienced betrayal and abandonment from some of his closest friends. How does knowing that Jesus suffered relational hurts and losses affect the way you experience your own pain?

Part 4

LIVING MENDED

Shells

15

VULNERABILITY

She dropped to her knees,
the collection of friendship necklaces around her neck swinging wildly;
she scooped up another shell and handed it to me,
delight sparking in her eyes.

First week of freshman year, eighteen years old. I am wide-eyed and even wider openhearted. I'm on a mission for Jesus at my secular university: Find open hearts. Tell them about the Lord. Become besties in Christ forever and ever, amen.

The first three days in my dorm, I hardly sleep. The three-story building is crammed with 150 freshman girls, and I am determined to meet them all the first weekend, because right now, we're all the same: new, lonely, unsure and a bit insecure, eager to find our place, excited to find friends. The walls are down, smiles on full blast. But my old-soul self can already predict what will happen: in a week or so, all the "let's be friends" smiles and tell-your-life-story-to-random-groups-of-pajama-clad-girls-all-piled-in-one-room-eating-chips-all-night fests will come to an end. People will find their people, settle into friend groups, and close their doors—and hearts—again.

I go room to room, introducing myself and getting to know people. And I find there's room in my heart for every girl I meet. I have something in common with everyone (even if it's just "I'm new here too!"), and with every introduction, I leave thinking, *We could be friends.*

We could connect, share life, pull all-nighters, order warm cookies at midnight, eat cold pizza for breakfast . . . if only there was enough time. *We could be friends.*

I'm giddy-excited with the thrill of it, the joy of meeting new people, each with her own story, family, culture, all so different from mine. And I marvel at how God has brought us all together, from all over the country and even the world—India, Brazil, Germany, right here on my hall—and united us together under this one roof, in these tiny rooms. *We could be friends.*

But sure enough, two weeks later, the flood of meeting and greeting and info-swapping peters out to a slow trickle. A month later, hardly a drip of friendliness remains. Cliques have formed, breakfast circles closed. People have self-sorted into packs: sorority girls, studious girls, sporty girls, conquer-the-world girls . . . you name it, the group has formed, then closed. No room for a single new soul.

And watching the shutdown, my heart aches. Because my young heart is still singing its song: *We could be friends.*

LIKE LITTLE CHILDREN

Oh, to live young and unbroken forever! But life happens; hurt happens; friendships fall apart. In time, if we're not careful, a broken friendship can cast a shadow over all our other relationships, tainting them with mistrust and suspicion. It can even poison our happy memories. It can replace the joy of optimism, with its rose-colored glasses, with a new companion, one who views people, especially potential new friends, through the shadowed lenses of cynicism. We find ourselves on an endless perfect-shell hunt, rejecting shell after shell: *This one's too pink. That one's too flat. Too shiny. Not shiny enough. Too jagged. Missing a piece.* And we wonder why we always come home empty-handed.

Jesus once drew a child into his arms and said to the listening crowd, "Truly I tell you, unless you change and become like little children, you will never enter the kingdom of heaven. Therefore, whoever takes the lowly position of this child is the greatest in the kingdom of heaven. And whoever welcomes one such child in my name welcomes me" (Matthew 18:3-5).

We must change, Jesus says. We must strip away our adulthood, with its seriousness and selfishness and cynicism and too-busy-with-eyes-glued-to-our-phones-checking-this-work-thing-to-notice-people-around-us aloofness, and become playground playmates again.

Jesus can help us to remain hopeful, trusting, and optimistic about other people—even if life has taught us some tough lessons about people's frailties.

GOD'S EXAMPLE

Jesus isn't calling us to do anything he and the Father haven't already modeled for us. We don't often think of him this way, but God makes himself vulnerable. It's an astounding choice for the Creator of the Universe. He who is mighty and fearsome, all-knowing, all-owning; he who lacks nothing, needs nothing . . . he opens his heart and invites us in.

To fallible humans, we who imperfectly love him back and frequently let him down, he says,

> "I thought to myself,
>   'I would love to treat you as my own children!'
> I wanted nothing more than to give you this beautiful land—
>   the finest possession in the world.
> I looked forward to your calling me 'Father,'
>   and I wanted you never to turn from me.
> But you have been unfaithful to me, you people of Israel. . . .
>
> "My wayward children," says the LORD,
>   "come back to me, and I will heal your wayward hearts."
> JEREMIAH 3:19-20, 22, NLT

"I looked forward to your calling me 'Father,' and I wanted you never to turn from me." Those words gut me: plaintive, innocent, almost baffled by betrayal (even though he knew it would come). God spoke those words, through the prophet Jeremiah, to Israel. They had wandered from God and rejected his covenant, and the Father mourned.

How grateful I am—how amazed I am—that God shared those feelings with us. You and I know that feeling too: *I thought we'd be friends; I thought you'd never leave.*

But look how God puts his heart back out there, fully knowing our tendency to wander: "Come back to me, and I will heal your wayward hearts." God keeps loving us, even when we don't deserve it. He keeps loving, though few—so very few—respond to his love. How many times have humans let him down? And instead of guarding his heart, limiting his risk—*I'll keep loving them, but I'll offer less of myself; I'll keep loving them, but I won't give them everything*—he tries harder. His gestures become even more grand, culminating in the greatest offering he can possibly give to prove his love: he sacrifices his only Son in our place.

Our God is courageous and bold in his love.

Relentless in pursuing us.

Resilient in the face of rejection.

Our God is vulnerable, the most stubborn optimist there ever was.

When we are willing to remain vulnerable, we are being like God.

I'm not suggesting we knowingly set ourselves up to be hurt by unreliable, cruel people; only that we imitate God's heart of openness, his determination to keep believing the best in people, to keep hoping for a positive outcome, to keep offering love without a guarantee we'll receive it in return.

Why does God do this?

Because we are worth it.

Because relationship is worth it.

Even to God. (Wow. Let that sink in for a second.)

God doesn't *need* a relationship with us to be happy and complete. He's already fulfilled because (a) he's God, and (b) he always lives in perfect communion with Jesus and the Spirit. He doesn't need our friendship, but he wants it anyway. Fights for it anyway.

Perhaps we can draw some guidance from his example: when we

are deeply rooted and secure in our walk with God, his Son, and the Spirit—if they are our source of ultimate relationship, companionship, and peace—then putting our hearts out there with other fallible humans doesn't feel like such a terrifying risk. Security in God makes us bold enough to pick up a broken shell without fearing it might cut us. Confidence in God means we don't need another person's approval or friendship to be okay; we aren't looking to people for our confidence or identity . . . but hey, we still think friendships are enjoyable. They are a place to use our gifts, offer love, and enjoy connection. And so we open our hearts and ask new people to give friendship a try with us. We pick up those shells and take them home for a while. We know we'll be okay, even if the friendship doesn't work out.

JESUS' EXAMPLE

Like Father, like Son. God the Father was always putting his heart out there for people; Jesus the Son did the same.

As Jesus entered Jerusalem for the last time, bumping down a dusty road on a donkey's back, knowing he was marching toward his own death, his thoughts were not about himself. He did not retreat into silence, a prisoner of fear; nor did he succumb to resentment, a victim of anger. No, he openly wept—not for himself, but for the city and its future; he wept over the very people who would crucify him, mourning all they would soon suffer at the hands of their Roman oppressors:[1]

> As he approached Jerusalem and saw the city, he wept over it
> and said, "If you, even you, had only known on this day what
> would bring you peace—but now it is hidden from your eyes.
> The days will come upon you when your enemies will build
> an embankment against you and encircle you and hem you
> in on every side. They will dash you to the ground, you and
> the children within your walls. They will not leave one stone

---

1. Jerusalem was besieged and overtaken by Rome in AD 70. The city was burned and the Temple razed, its mighty stones toppled to the ground. Countless Jews lost their lives; many others fled, never to return. Jesus seemed to be looking ahead to that tragedy, mourning it.

222 | ELIZABETH LAING THOMPSON

on another, because you did not recognize the time of God's coming to you."

LUKE 19:41-44

Tears for his enemies. A heart torn open. Thinking not about his own future pain but theirs.

And Jesus' vulnerability continues: a day or so later, as he sits in the Temple, mere days before his death at the hands of the city's religious leaders, he cries out, "Jerusalem, Jerusalem, you who kill the prophets and stone those sent to you, how often I have longed to gather your children together, as a hen gathers her chicks under her wings, and you were not willing. Look, your house is left to you desolate" (Matthew 23:37-38).

Jesus reveals his true affection for his people, the intensity of his love, lamenting the relationship he has offered and they have refused: *How often have I longed to gather your children together, as a hen gathers her chicks under her wings.* But they push him away, rejecting his love. They meet his vulnerability with cynicism, his gifts with accusation. *You were not willing.*

BREAKING DOWN THE BROKENNESS

Vulnerability sounds lovely when we talk about it from a distance, doesn't it? Our hearts lean into it, whispering how they long to live open-hearted and unafraid, like Jesus did. But when it comes time to actually muster the courage to imitate Jesus and put our hearts out there, to do something, to say something vulnerable, reality checks us. Memories of past hurts revive, our pulse quickens, and our self-protective walls go up.

When we try to build a new friendship after we've been hurt—a process that requires some measure of vulnerability—a fear-dominated script starts to play in our minds. We talked about flipping scripts in chapter 4; let's revisit that idea in the context of being vulnerable with new people. If we don't learn to identify that script for what it is—fear in verbal form, a self-protective instinct desperately working to keep us safe—we may make the mistake of *automatically assuming the script is true.*

What's the script, you ask? It sounds something like this:

I bet she's not who she seems to be. She's just pretending.
She doesn't genuinely want to be friends. She's got an angle.
She doesn't like me or want to get close to me—she's just being polite.
If I tell her who I really am, she'll . . . judge me . . . back off . . . betray
    my confidence.
I could trust her with my real thoughts, but that would give her
    leverage to use against me if things fall apart one day.

All these scripts spring from different branches of the same root: fear. Sometimes that fear manifests as self-doubt and insecurity; other times it appears as dread of a negative outcome or bad plot twist; and other times it homes in on people's unreliability or dishonesty.

And you know what else these fears share in common? They all filter the present—and the future—through a past-tense lens. That lens saddles new relationships with old baggage. It makes assumptions about new friends based on what *former* friends have done. That lens says, *This relationship seems fine right now, but it's going to turn sour just like the last one did.* That lens fails to see a new friendship for what it is: a unique relationship with a different person.

If we want to move forward in new friendships, once more we have to take charge of the script in our minds. We have to tear it up and write a new one, a dialogue based on Scriptures like this one: "[Love] always protects, always trusts, always hopes, always perseveres" (1 Corinthians 13:7).

Love always trusts. Love always hopes.

Always trusts? *Always* hopes? Seriously? That sounds terrifying. Let's all take a moment to breathe into a paper bag.

But as we have said, God isn't asking us to do something he hasn't already done for us. God puts his heart out there, offers his love again and again, even knowing how much and how often people will fail him.

Love is brave. Love exposes its squishy underbelly to the world. It opens its arms even to people who might reject the hug. I'm not suggesting that we knowingly set ourselves up to be hurt or that we rush blindly into new relationships, inviting people in without finding out whether or not they are, indeed, trustworthy—I'm only suggesting that we be *willing* to open up to new people. That we take our armor down long enough to explore new friendships, and when we find worthy candidates, to gradually share more of our lives with one another. That we put a few imperfect shells in our pockets, take them home, and decide if they're shells worth keeping.

Here are a few strategies you might find helpful as you try to rewrite the scary script in your mind with a love-based script.

When you are getting to know someone new and the fear script says, *I bet she's not who she appears to be; I bet she's insincere or has an angle*, take a pause. Notice that thought. Take a few steps back so you can consider it more clearly. Now, decide to be fair to this new person. Remind yourself of a few things: *It's not fair to judge her based on people I've known in the past. She is her own person, and she deserves a fair chance from me as much as I deserve one from her. I'm going to give her the benefit of the doubt. I won't be naive, but I'm still going to hope for the best.*

When you find yourself thinking, *If I tell her who I really am, she'll . . . judge me . . . back off . . . betray my confidence*, call a time-out. Step away from that thought and remind yourself, *When I make an assumption like this, am I not also passing judgment? Am I not doing the very thing I don't want done to me?* Here's where Jesus' Golden Rule can guide our thoughts: "Do to others as you would have them do to you." Perhaps, by extension, we could say, "Think about others as you would have them think about you." If you want a potential new friend to believe the best about you, believe the best about her. If you want someone to give you a chance, give her a chance. If you want someone to take a small risk in sharing a piece of her honest heart with you, take a small risk yourself. And remember: you don't have to go all in right away. It's okay to take it slow and build trust over time. Just don't jump ship on the new potential friendship before you've given it a chance.

When you think, *I could trust her with my real thoughts, but that would give her leverage against me*, capture that thought before it goes any further (see 2 Corinthians 10:5). Of course, if you're not ready to share a vulnerable truth, you are not obligated to do so. But if fear and self-protectiveness are your primary reasons for holding back, remind yourself of these truths: *Not every friendship goes bad. Many friendships are positive and trustworthy. I refuse to assume the worst about this person's motives. Like my Father, I choose to be optimistic.* Again, you don't have to rush into vulnerability before you're ready or before the other person has been proven trustworthy, but in fairness to new friends, you can try to avoid making assumptions about others' motives based on past experiences.

Our internal dialogue wields powerful influence over our feelings and actions. If we don't take the time and energy to step back, pay attention to our thoughts and fears, and question whether or not those thoughts and fears are true and fair, we will end up stuck in a loop. Our brain will actually form neural pathways that reinforce our fears and insecurities—and then we'll wonder why we feel so stuck.

A bad experience with a past friendship does not mean we are doomed to have all negative experiences in our future. A betrayal in the past doesn't foretell a betrayal in the future. Yes, we've been hurt, but our friendship hurts need not limit our hearts forever.

We don't have to be ruled by fear. Thanks to the mighty Word of God, the power of the Holy Spirit, and some intentional thinking, we can write a new script, one that allows us to remain openhearted and vulnerable even after we've been hurt. With God's guidance, we can start fresh.

GROWN-UP, NOT CLOSED-UP

I've lived a lot of life since my starry-eyed days as a college freshman. I've made friends, lost friends, been ghosted, suffered drifts, and made a zillion mistakes. I've shed bucketfuls of tears over friendship issues. But in spite of it all, in spite of the fact that my heart wears a little more armor than it used to, I've never fully outgrown that bright-eyed inner teen with her "the glass isn't half-full of potential friends, it's totally overflowing" perspective—and I never want to. Every time I meet someone new, she still pops her eager head up and whispers, *We could be friends.* Sometimes her whisper is so quiet I hardly hear it; other times I want to place a gentle palm over her naive little mouth and squelch those words while I teach her a thing or two about Life in the Real World, but I don't. In my heart of hearts, I never want to silence her—I need her voice.

We could be friends.

I pray I can always hear—and always believe—those words. I pray God helps me keep my heart open, willing to be vulnerable. I pray he keeps me open to new friendships, no matter how full my "friend card" gets.

Maybe I'm naive. Maybe a little foolish. Because I'll definitely get hurt again. Definitely feel let down. Definitely face rejection. But . . . those are risks I'm willing to take, because the friends that stick are *so worth it.*

Having someone who can read your expression across the room and know something's wrong? That's priceless (and rare).

Having a friend who your kids can call to ask for advice? What a treasure.

Having a friend who'll listen to your woe-is-me story and gently, kindly tell you what you need to hear at the end? Such a gift. Such a need.

Having a friend who knows your coffee order (and her husband knows it too)? It makes you feel known.

Those friendships are precious, and I always want to leave room in my heart for more of them. As my daughter taught me that day on the beach, every shell holds bits of wonder; every shell could be worth taking home. The kindred-spirit, we-instinctively-understand-everything-about-each-other kind of friend doesn't come along all that often—maybe only a handful of times in a lifetime—but still, that doesn't mean we can't have friends. When we bring an openhearted attitude and a broader definition of friendship, we open ourselves up to having a jarful of joy—a shelfful[2] of jarfuls of joy! We allow the possibility of more daily-life friends who walk alongside us, sharing life and dating mishaps and work stress and marital woes and kid-raising struggles. To more burden-sharing friends and holding-us-up-in-prayer

---

2. Yep, "shelfful" is a real word. Who knew?

friends and checking-in-to-see-how-work-went-and-if-that-new-dinner-recipe-turned-out friends. Each shell is gorgeous in its own way: squeal worthy, take-home-as-a-treasure worthy.

Even if you've been hurt in the past.

Even knowing you could be hurt again.

However your heart has been battered or betrayed, I pray you don't let the brokenness win. I pray you fight to keep your heart open. To take a few risks. And maybe one day (maybe one day not as far off as you think), to share the big, the scary, the no-one-will-get-this-if-I-speak-it-out-loud feelings.

And . . . can I encourage you for a second? If you've made it this far in this book, you are already fighting, already showing tremendous courage and determination. You've done the heart-searching part of the work; now I pray you find the courage to keep that growth going. I pray—oh, how I pray—you are brave enough, resilient enough, grace-filled enough, to keep putting your precious, fragile, one-of-a-kind heart out there. To keep picking up shells until you find the keepers—the friends who make the risks worthwhile. The friends God has in store for you.

THOUGHT QUESTIONS

1. What aspects of God's and Jesus' vulnerability do you most admire? Why?

2. List two or three specific thoughts or fears that sometimes prevent you from being vulnerable. How can you rewrite those thoughts in a more godly way?

3. What makes your heart feel safe opening up to a new person? Talk to God about those things, asking him to bring people into your life who help you feel safe.

16

YOUR FRIENDSHIP FUTURE

Maybe if I weren't so careful, so picky,
I could see what my girl sees:
perfect imperfection, beauty in broken,
and endless possibilities—
a world filled to bursting with treasures worth taking home.

We love the God who breathes life into death and calls things that are not as though they were.

He wrings hope from despair.

Erects new buildings atop ruins.

Redeems all kinds of brokenness: Pain. Deceit. Betrayal. Division. Even death.

Where we see only heartache, God may see opportunity. Sometimes God reveals purposes for our suffering we never could have imagined. We know that "in all things God works for the good of those who love him, who have been called according to his purpose" (Romans 8:28). All things are not good, but in all things, God is working. All things are not good, but God can *bring about* good anyway. Friendship fallouts and fall-aparts and breaks and breakups are not good, but our God can redeem them all.

I don't know all the ways God might redeem the brokenness you've experienced.

Like Joseph, will you discover that God has been quietly working a redemptive plan all along, and now he's using your painful experience to help others?

Like Paul and Barnabas, will God teach you to trust his faithfulness even during a time when you're separated from a friend?

Like Ruth and Naomi, will years of bitterness be overtaken by years of joy?

Like Jan and Geri, will you eventually find reconciliation on the other side of your rift? Renewed friendship and hugs and laughter, plus a story, all shiny with golden grace, that spreads wonder-hearted hope to all who hear it?

Like my experience in losing my friendship with Carrie, will God's gentle kindness fill in the hole your friend left behind, helping you grow more empathetic, patient, and resilient—a better friend than you were before?

We've spent most of this book with our eyes trained on the past and present—grappling with hurts, working through complex situations and conversations, even looking back thousands of years to glean wisdom from biblical stories—but now let's look ahead. Let's cast our vision to the future, imagining what it might hold for our friendships.

In this chapter, let's consider some healthy ways to move forward in friendships. How might reexamining our definitions of friendship open us up to new friendships—or help us appreciate and deepen the ones we already have? If you could use some new friends in your future, what attitudes and steps might set you up to find them? And how can we nurture and strengthen our friendships with the hope that they last for a lifetime?

SURPRISE!

Don't you wish these pages could give you an actual sneak peek at your friendship future? Like, *In six months you're gonna meet a new bestie for the restie, and you'll meet in the greeting card aisle at Target, and you'll eventually discover you like all the same books but none of the same music, and* . . . I mean, that could be fun and all, but sometimes God's plans are so astounding, we would not believe them if we saw them played out on a screen. They're not just outside the box; they're practically intergalactic. God is the master of plot twists, the king of surprise endings (not to mention surprise beginnings and middles too).

Let's begin our look ahead by skipping back, back to a moment in the life of a teenager named Mary. A God-ordained surprise—a supernatural pregnancy!—had probably damaged most of Mary's relationships. (Can't you picture Mary's friends shaking their heads and saying, "You expect me to believe an angel appeared to you, and you're pregnant by the Holy Spirit? Uh-huh. Riiiiiiiight. Come find me when you're ready to tell the truth.") At a time in her life when Mary had probably never felt more alone, God provided the friendship she needed from a most unlikely source.

MARY AND ELIZABETH
Based on Luke 1

Mary's hand traces the curve of her belly, still surprised, amazed, by its changing shape. A few more weeks and there'll be no hiding it.

Unease ripples through her. *What will everyone say?* Her hand clutches the fabric atop her belly, making a fist as if to defend the little life growing inside.

A tap on the open doorframe startles her. Mother's face appears; her gaze lands on Mary's fist. Mary's other hand comes round to hug her abdomen, as if it needs two-armed protection. Most days Mary thinks Mother believes her story about the angel, the pregnancy by the Holy Spirit, but still some days, like today, Mary thinks she sees a sliver of doubt lurking in her eyes.

"It's settled," Mother says. "We're sending you to Elizabeth, my cousin. You'll be safe there from gossip and accusations."

Mary nods. She had expected to be sent away.

"Will Elizabeth believe me?" Mary asks. "Or will she treat me like, like a . . ." She does not finish; she does not need to.

Mother steps forward to rest her hands on Mary's shoulders. "Elizabeth herself is bearing a miracle babe—fathered by her husband, of course, but still, quite the story—so if anyone is going to believe you, it's Elizabeth."

"I hope so," Mary whispers, letting her head fall on her mother's chest, like the little girl she used to be, not so very long ago.

A few days later, after a long, dusty ride, Father helps Mary down from the donkey and escorts her up the winding lane to Zechariah and Elizabeth's home. He does not speak, but the warm hand he rests on her back says he loves her.

Even so, with every step, Mary's fear grows. Her tired feet pound out *what ifs*:

Uncle Zeke is a priest; what if he thinks I've sinned?

What if I spend all these months here in disgrace?

What if Mother and Father are wrong, and there is no safe place for me anywhere?

"I can feel your worry from here," Father says in his gravelly voice. "But it will be better for you here than at home, of that I am sure."

Mary gives a mute nod.

The front door bursts open and a plump woman comes running, her arms outstretched, her gray braid bursting free from its red shawl.

"Mary! At last you're here! I've been watching the lane for two days!"

Mary stops, too surprised to keep walking.

Elizabeth hurtles forward as if on the legs of a young girl and skids to a stop just before colliding with Mary. Her wrinkled cheeks are flushed, her dark eyes bright with joy. She flings her arms out, pulling Mary in for a hug, but an awkward one—they can't really reach, thanks to Elizabeth's swollen abdomen. Mary suppresses a giggle.

Elizabeth gives a squeak, bending over and rubbing her side. "The babe in my womb leaped for joy, knowing you are here! He's a feisty one, my John." She beams down at her belly. "I guess I should have known he would be, his birth being announced by an angel and all. Of course, you know all about that." Elizabeth reaches for Mary's hand and gives it a gentle squeeze. "Have you felt him move yet? Your little one?"

Mary can't help but smile. "I just felt him for the first time this week—like feathers tickling my insides."

"It is a wonder, is it not?" Elizabeth says, eyes sparkling, as if they share the most delightful of secret joys. *And so we do,* Mary realizes, grinning back at her.

Mary's father clears his throat.

"It's good to see you too, Cousin," Elizabeth says, with a sly, sideways glance at Mary's father.

"Don't mind me," he says. "Carry on with your . . . womanly talk. I'll go look for Zeke."

"Out back," Elizabeth says, jerking her head. "With the ewes."

Elizabeth places two warm hands on Mary's cheeks and draws her in to plant a kiss on her forehead. When they pull back, tears are tracing down the age lines on Elizabeth's cheeks. "Blessed is she who has believed that the Lord will fulfill his promise!"

"Blessed indeed," Mary says, through tears of her own. A song builds inside—a song of thanks, of wonder, of praise. *The Almighty has given me the gift, not just of this baby, but of a friend to walk beside me. To make me less alone. He has led me to the one woman on earth who knows how it feels to carry a holy child—the one woman on earth who can fully share my joy.*

Mary begins to sing.

No other woman had ever experienced what Mary did. No one could say, "I know what you're going through; I get how you feel. You know, the last time an angel told me I was going to have a baby, and the Holy Spirit descended upon me, and I had to tell my fiancé that I was pregnant but it was okay because it was God's baby, I remember I felt . . ." Um, no! No one could fathom, much less relate to, Mary's experience. Mary's faithfulness had prompted God to entrust her with the most astounding and privileged of tasks—to bear and raise his Son—and yet Mary's community, and even her friends, probably viewed the pregnancy as proof that she was sinful and lustful, dishonest and disloyal. How misunderstood Mary must have felt. How utterly alone.

But early in the pregnancy, God arranged for teenage Mary to spend a few months in the home of an aging relative, Elizabeth.[1] Like

---

1. Some theorize that when Scripture says Elizabeth and her husband were "well along in years," this indicates the couple was at least in their sixties. There was likely a fifty-year age difference between Mary and Elizabeth! (See Craig S. Keener, *The IVP Bible Background Commentary: New Testament,* 2nd ed. [Downers Grove, Illinois: IVP Academic, 2014], 179.)

Mary, Elizabeth was unexpectedly pregnant with a miracle child. Like Mary, Elizabeth's pregnancy had been announced by an angel. Like Mary, Elizabeth knew her son would have a special purpose in God's Kingdom. What a blessing it must have been to Mary to find understanding and companionship in Elizabeth, a most unlikely—but desperately needed—friend.

Like Mary, you may be wondering what's next. Like Mary, you may long for safe places—safe people—to share life's burdens with you. After all you've been through, do you dare to seek that safety in friendship once more? We've spent many pages discussing broken friendships, but as we look ahead, let's first consider what it takes to carry our fragile hearts out into the world again. How might we change our perspectives so we no longer see broken shells wherever we look, but rather a shore full of possibilities, beautifully imperfect shells worthy of a place in our hearts and homes?

OUT OF THE "BESTIE" BOX

A neighbor once shared with me, "I've looked and looked for a best friend, I've put myself out there with new people time and again, but I just can't find That Friend—you know the one I mean? The one who adores you and gets everything about you, and acts like an aunt for your kids, and walks through all the daily ups and downs with you?" She met my gaze with a shy half smile, but in her eyes I saw a chasm of sadness.

My heart ached for the loneliness and insecurity she felt. From the outside she appeared surrounded by a circle of devoted girlfriends, but inside, she still felt lonely. Still felt like something (or someone) was missing.

I think a lot of us can relate to that feeling—and having a friendship fall apart only magnifies it. We have acquaintances and friends, maybe even a lot of them, and yet we still long for something more. We have a picture in our mind of what a close friendship looks and feels like—*This is how we should feel about each other, relate to each other, show love to each other, spend time with each other*—and when our real-life friendships don't perfectly mirror that idealized picture, we wonder if something is lacking in us, or perhaps something is missing in the depth of our friendships.

But I suspect one reason we feel that way is we're unconsciously trying to force friendships into a one-size-fits-all box. Like my neighbor, we have an internal definition of close friendship, and if our existing friendships don't match that definition, we feel insecure or even disappointed. But as you look ahead to forging new friendships and strengthening existing ones, please remember that every friendship is unique, and many different types of friendships are meaningful, powerful, and precious.

Remember how my discriminating eyes examined scores of shells and found them wanting—none of them lived up to the "perfect shell" I had in mind? Sometimes we may scrutinize our friendships in a similar way and feel insecure or discouraged if they don't align with our mental picture. But when we embrace the concept of different types of friendships, we open ourselves up to new relationships—and to greater contentment in our existing relationships. It takes pressure off our friendships when we don't try to force them to become something they're not meant to be or can't be right away. The majority of our friendships may not be read-your-thoughts-across-the-room-and-be-an-aunt-to-your-kids-and-share-everything-in-common ones, but that doesn't mean the other friendships aren't valuable or worth investing in.

I also find it helpful to remember that we all have different friendship styles and preferences. Some of us are more private people who like having boundaries and structure to our friendships; others only feel close when they are all up in each other's business—and houses—at all times. To that I say, you do you! Don't evaluate your friendships based on someone else's definition! Build the kinds of friendships *you* want to build. If your friendships look or feel different from someone else's, that doesn't diminish the value of what you have.

Here are some of the life-giving types of friendships I've experienced and observed; I bet you could add a few of your own to the list:

Occasional Coffee Friends—You don't hang out all the time, but you check in every month or so, and you're always glad you did.

When you leave, your coffee cup is empty, but your connection cup is filled.

Grown-up Playdate Friends—You like doing the same things—tennis, yoga, art, painting, writing, gardening, concerts, sushi-eating—so you get together to do stuff. Your conversations may not be the deepest, but you have fun together.

Prayer Partners—You may not have a lot of interests in common, and you may be in different stages of life, but a small group or church setting has thrown you together. You know you can always send out a quick prayer-request text, and she'll be there. You pray each other through.

Major Life Event Friends—You don't talk all that often, but you're there for the big things, and somehow that's enough.

Girls' Trip Friends—Maybe you only get the gang together once a year or so, but when you do, it's epic.

Mom-Life Friends—Your kids are the same ages, so when the kids play, you hang out and enjoy each other's company, comparing notes on potty training, developmental milestones, and parenting strategies.

We Live in Different Places and Only Talk Every Few Months but Always Pick Right Back Up Where We Left Off Friends—Consistency is the name of your game. You don't demand a lot from each other, but you are committed to sustaining a relationship across the miles.

Each of these friendship types is a blessing. Like my daughter's kaleidoscopic collection of broken shells, each one is unique. Each one adds its own kind of joy to your life. Even if you don't see a potential new bestie in your life right now, I bet you've got some options for uplifting friendships you could pursue. Like Mary and Elizabeth, you may find a friendship you didn't know you needed in a place you'd never thought to look. And remember this: close friendships have to begin somewhere; every new relationship you invest in could one day deepen into a close friendship.

FINDING FRIENDS

As you start moving forward with some new perspectives, I hope you're beginning to feel a little sprout of courage unfurling inside: *Maybe it would be worth it to put my heart out there again—either by making a new friend or two, or by circling back to reinvest more deeply in some existing friendships.*

Let's start with what it might take to pursue some new friendships. Even if you're still a little nervous—you're not ready to run around town handing out friendship bracelets or anything—how might you begin to put yourself out there? How do you find potential friends, and once you find them, how do you take those first few steps?

Pray about your desire for friendship.

We were made for relationship. Created to crave intimacy. From the beginning, God said, "It is not good for the man to be alone" (Genesis 2:18). The longing to know and be known is knit into our very DNA. God himself exists in eternal relationship—Father, Son, Holy Spirit, and . . . us!—and he understands our deep longing for meaningful connection. If you've got room in your heart for some new people, a good place to start is to pray about your desire for friendship. Tell God about the kind of friendship you long to find, what would make you feel seen, known, and fulfilled. Tell him about your fears and insecurities. And then watch him work.

Put yourself in a position to make new friendships.

I recently attended a house-church service with friends in another city, and afterward, we stood around chatting. The hostess handed me a cup of coffee, then said, "How are your friendships going?"

I paused for a moment, surprised by the boldness of the question. But I always love it when small talk dives deeper, so I took a moment to evaluate, then gave as honest an answer as I could. They were going . . . better. I'd had several dear friends move away several years earlier, leaving me a bit lonely for a while, but I've been getting closer to some new friends I adore and enjoy.

"How are friendships going for you?" I asked. "It can't have been easy getting to know people, moving to a new city during the COVID-19 pandemic."

"It's been slower than I want it to be," she said. "So I've decided to just put myself out there. I've been going friend shopping."

"Friend shopping?" I laughed.

"Yes! I'm calling people from my church and asking if they'd like to be friends. And I'm telling them I want more than just an occasional coffee date—I'm looking for *friends*."

"That's so brave of you," I said, with feeling. "I love it."

This woman is putting herself out there, sharing her need with new people without apology or expectation. She's willing to be rejected, knowing that the people who do respond to her vulnerable request will be friends worth having. In fact, she has already taken a couple of girls' trips with a new group of ladies. They've shopped and shared Scriptures and sipped coffee and woven words on top of each other's—and somewhere in the middle of the coffee drinking and window shopping and story swapping, she found her heart swelling with joy, and she exclaimed, "You guys! I have a group of friends! I finally have a group!"

Even if you're not quite ready to go "friend shopping," don't you love the bold spirit this woman exudes? She reminds me that we don't have to sit around hoping new friends show up in our lives; we can take an active role in pursuing them.

And her example reinforces a lesson I learned while spending my entire girlhood moving up and down the Eastern Seaboard: you can't make new friends if you don't put yourself in the position to meet them. You can't collect shells if you never walk on the beach. Join a gym and chat with people in your classes. Become active in a small group at your church. Volunteer in your community and swap numbers with people you meet there. Join a book club, a quilting class, a Pilates class, a service organization—whatever floats your hobby boat. Just . . . put yourself in places where people are, and when you get there, be friendly. Initiate. Engage your courage for thirty heart-stopping seconds, and ask someone to meet up for coffee or a walk in the park or . . . whatever. Be a little bit brave, and watch what God does. Which leads us to our next point . . .

Be a little bit brave.

When we've been hurt, new relationships feel scary. Risky. Maybe not worth it. So when a new person comes along, someone who lights a little spark inside, that scary-hopeful, hey-we-could-be-friends feeling, fear steps in, splashing cold water on that poor spark before it can catch. A tempting color may be peeking out from beneath the sand, but it feels safer to leave that shell half buried. *What if it's not as beautiful as I thought? What if it's just a shard, too broken to enjoy?*

I've found it helps if I just take getting to know new people one step at a time. When I choose to be a little bit brave with my heart, I am able to dismantle some of the barriers my old fears keep trying to erect. Maybe I initiate with one not-too-scary overture ("Wanna grab coffee sometime?"), or I share one semi-vulnerable thing in a conversation, or I ask for prayer for something I'm going through, and then I just . . . wait to see how it goes. I don't have to spill my entire life story and figure out if a new person could be a bestie right away, but I can take small steps toward sharing my heart and getting to know theirs.

Good people are out there. People worth knowing. People worthy of trust. People who are a little bit broken just like you are, but whose cracks have only made them kinder, more interesting. Future friends who, if you'd let them in—cracking open your heart's door one inch at a time till a person can squeeze all the way inside—would enrich your life. They would fill your days with laughter and understanding and we're-in-this-togetherness.

We overcome fear one small victory at a time. And what a joy it is when all those little moments of courage add up to a big breakthrough, that heart-singing wonder of real connection. Elizabeth met Mary with open arms and tears of joy; Mary reciprocated her new friend's vulnerability with her own song of praise. Stay open, be a little bit brave, and watch what God does.

Be patient.

This planet is packed with eight billion people. Somewhere among those eight billion options, God has created people who would find your friendship a gift and delight—and they'll be a gift and delight to you. It may take some time, but you can find your people. Keep walking, keep searching the sand, and keep your eyes—and heart—open.

NURTURING NEW FRIENDSHIPS

So let's say you take some steps forward and you're beginning to cultivate a new friendship. First: yay! What a milestone! As Zechariah 4:10 says, "Do not despise these small beginnings, for the LORD rejoices to see the work begin" (NLT). However small your beginning, however cautious your overture, it is a victory worth celebrating, especially considering the pain in your past. The Lord celebrates your progress with you! Now, what are some ways to nurture and enjoy those new friendships as they grow?

Be the friend you'd like to have.
I always tell my kids (and myself!) that the best way to make (and keep) a friend is to *be* one. I always do best when I go into relationships planning to give rather than to receive. If I hope to find a thoughtful friend who checks on me when I'm going through a hard time, I try to be thoughtful and check on the people in my life. If I appreciate friends who make time for hanging out in person even when they're busy, I try to make myself available for them too.

As Jesus put it, "Do to others what you would have them do to you" (Matthew 7:12); perhaps we could also say, "Be the kind of friend you hope others will be to you." Be the friend you'd like to have, and watch what happens. Like attracts like. Some people won't respond to your overtures, but others will; in time, you may find your seeds of selflessness sprouting into true friendship.

Find joy in the not-super-close-yet friendships.
Ten years ago, I moved to a city where I knew no one and had to start building all new relationships from scratch. Periodically, my friend Emma (who still lives in my old hometown) has asked me, "Do you have good friends there?" (Apparently, people like asking me this question!) Every time she asks, my answer is different. I've walked through a variety of friendship seasons here, mostly because I live in a somewhat transient

town. Over the course of a decade, I've forged some deep friendships and enjoyed them for a while, only to have my friends move away, leaving me back where I started, needing to open my heart to new people.

I've learned not to obsess over whether or not I have an in-town, kindred-spirit, we-speak-the-same-heart-language BFF—sometimes I do, sometimes I don't. But I always have church-family friends, meet-for-coffee friends, work-out-at-the-gym friends, and meet-for-playdates-with-kids friends. I find joy and potential and blessing in all of those friendships. Will some of them blossom into something richer and deeper? Maybe! I hope so! But my heart has not been empty, even in the seasons when it's been holding space, and hope, for something more.

Don't compare your growing friendships to other people's.
Chances are, you're not as "behind" in the friendship game as social media makes you feel. Please resist the temptation to compare your friendships to what other people's look like from the outside, especially the incomplete snapshot we get from social media. People often write hyperbolic captions like, "I could never live without her" or "She's *always* there for me" or "She knows everything I'm thinking before I do." Maybe they are that close, and that's wonderful—you can celebrate that blessing with them. But even so, their friendship isn't perfect. Sometimes they hurt each other's feelings or miss a cue or let each other down. They're human and imperfect, sometimes even a little lonely, just like you are.

Your friendships are special because they are *yours*—and it's okay if they don't look exactly like anyone else's or if they are still in an early stage where you're trying to figure out where they're going.

STRENGTHENING FOREVER FRIENDSHIPS

Let's look ahead by faith to a day when all your baby steps of courage and vulnerability have begun to pay off. You're getting closer to someone, and the optimist in you keeps whispering, "One day we could be *really* close. This could go somewhere special." If you're an over-the-top big feeler like me, your imagination might toss you some scenarios where you spend your fifties and sixties throwing wedding and baby showers for each other's kids, your seventies and eighties taking river cruises around Europe, then spend your nineties living on the same hallway in an assisted-living home (which I like to think of as a dorm for little old ladies . . . I told you: over-the-top imagination).[2]

Anyway, you've started building a few close friendships. You want to deepen and preserve them, but your broken experience has you a little anxious and unsure: *How do I keep this going? How do we make this last?*

Best-friends-forever is something many of us dream about—and I truly believe it doesn't have to be a fantasy. Although I have lost some friendships along the way, I have a number of treasured friendships that have lasted for decades.

Melissa and I have been friends so long, I can't remember life without her. First we walked through childhood and college, then weddings and infertility and babies, and now we're navigating parenting-big-kids life (and parenting-kids-going-to-college life, I can't even) together.

Allison was my babysitter when I was little, and as I matured, so did our friendship. She is like a big sister to me, never forgetting a birthday or special event, always a step or two ahead of me in life, modeling what it means to love God and people at every stage.

Julie and I met at church when we were kids, reconnected a few times as teens and college students, but then landed in the same city as young moms. We were friends then, but as you're about to read, Julie came to visit me after I had my fourth child, and something new was born.

Karen and I were cross-country and track teammates who only hung out casually in high school, but somehow in college, we kept up and gradually deepened our friendship. We were in each other's weddings, and we keep in touch regularly.

Sara and I met a few weeks before I started my sophomore year of high school. My family's time in New Jersey didn't stick—we only lived there for eight months—but my friendship with Sara did. We have laughed-cried-prayed-and-everything-in-betweened each other through

---

2. If you like murder mysteries and love the idea of little old lady friends having adventures together from their assisted living home, check out the Thursday Murder Club mysteries by Richard Osman. It may be your new favorite series. I discovered this series thanks to Emma, who is not only my BFF but also my writing partner and the curator of my reading list. (Ahem—you could even read it with a new friend, wink wink?) You're ever so welcome (though really you should thank Emma).

multiple cross-country moves and life transitions, and now our children have become friends too.

Emma and I met as young moms (in a Barnes & Noble bathroom, of all places), and we soon became not only mom friends and writing partners, but the best of friends. I have always imagined that on the summer day when Emma was born in England, my guardian angel leaned over my crib in Florida to whisper in my six-month-old ear, "You don't know it yet, but your future bestie was just born all the way across the ocean. It'll be twenty years before she moves here, and then another ten years till you meet, but you just wait . . ."

Each of these friendships is precious to me in its own way, and how grateful I am that they've lasted for so long.[3] What does it take to keep friendships strong over the years, across the miles, and through life's changes? Here are a few principles I've found helpful.

Don't keep score.
I called her last; now it's her turn.
> *I went all out for her birthday; she needs to do the same for me.*
> *When she went through a hard time, I texted her every day. Why isn't she checking on me more often when she knows I'm struggling?*

The minute we start keeping score in our friendships is the minute our friendships begin to weaken. When we think this way, Satan gets a little foothold, a place where he can sow seeds of doubt, insecurity, and resentment.

Every long-term friendship has seasons where it's a bit lopsided. You'll have times where one friend is more available (physically or emotionally) than the other. You may give more for a while because your friend is hurting: she's going through a breakup, a divorce, a sickness, a mental health issue, a loss. One day it'll be your turn to hurt, and she'll kick in more than usual. This is the nature of life and friendship. Of course, if a friendship is *always* one-sided—if you're always giving and

---

3. How I wish I had room to talk about friends who are also family—my mom, sister, and sisters-in-law—and some friends God has brought into my life in the past five to ten years: Elva, Rachelle, Carmen, and all the amazing ladies in my small group and church family. I love and appreciate you all more than I can say. Here's to many more years of family and friendship!

never receiving—that's a sign of an unhealthy friendship that needs to grow. But even in the healthiest and most generous of friendships, we go through times of imbalance. Just as "love keeps no record of wrongs," so it keeps no records of texts sent, gifts given, Instagram birthday posts designed, and favors offered. Love simply gives, no strings attached.

Be there.

My friend Julie texted me:

> I want to come help you with the baby. Just tell me when, and I'll book a flight.

I sat there, holding a newborn in one arm and my phone in the other, and cried with relief and gratitude. I don't know how Julie knew how desperately I needed a friend to come see me, but somehow, she knew. And she came.

Julie and I had been good friends for a long time, but we'd never been *best* friends. We'd both had other people we relied on, plus six (now seven) kids between us, so . . . we'd just never taken our friendship to the next level.

But then Julie came to see me. To help me after I had my fourth child in a new town where I had no family and all my friendships were brand new. And just like that, our friendship went to the next level. Because she showed up. Because she was there.

———

I could feel the sorrow and stress oozing out of Emma's text message:

> The movers are coming next week, and I still have to teach, and the old house is a mess, and I'm afraid the new house will never feel like home, and I don't even know where to start packing, and I can't find my SOCKS!

And in those words I heard all the words she didn't say: "This is the house I came home to on my wedding night. This is the house I brought my baby home to. Leaving this house feels like losing my past. My heart is being ripped out of my chest. I am not okay."

I had a quick conversation with Kevin and my daughter Cassidy, then picked up my phone again, thumbs flying:

Cassidy and I are coming to help you pack and cry into your boxes and say goodbye to the old house and hello to the new one. We'll be there Friday.

I could practically hear Emma's grateful weeping all the way from two states away.

Cassidy and I drove six hours, and I'm not sure we packed as much as we intended to, but we made our friends laugh, we cried over the precious memories in the old house, and we gushed over the new house to try to help our friends feel at home in it. It was a wonderful weekend; at the end of it our friends felt a little better, and so did we.

Because we were there.

So much of friendship is *being there*. Seeing what the other person needs, dropping your plans if you can, and being there. For the graduation, the move, the breakup, the engagement, the miscarriage, the promotion, the goodbye. Even if you can't be there in person, you can be there through text messages, phone calls, and emergency cookie deliveries. Just be there the best way you can.

Don't be threatened by your friends' other friends.

This one's hard, right? We see our friends making other friends, and the third grader inside us feels jealous. Insecure. Threatened. Territorial. *She's mine! I saw her first! I don't want to share! I don't want anyone taking my place!*

When we open our heart to a new friend, it experiences something similar to what happens when a mother has a second baby: she doesn't cut her love for her first child in half and divide it between her two children; God grows a whole new chamber in her heart, doubling its capacity for love. Suddenly Mom has twice as much affection to go around. And if anything, she now loves her first child *even more* than she used to, because her heart has grown bigger. If one of your friends makes a new friend, she isn't taking the love she had reserved for you and giving it away to someone else; she's just opening her heart wider, adding a new chamber for a new person.

I've found that when my other friends make other friends, it only enriches who they are as people. They are happier and more confident; their lives are richer, and that makes them even more fun to be friends with. It also takes pressure off our relationship when I'm not their *only* person (and they're not mine). It's healthy for all of us to have a village of people to love and rely on. Because as much as I try to always be there for my friends, sometimes I can't be. I'm infinitely thankful that my besties have other friends—even other besties—who can support them when I can't.

Persevere through the hard seasons.

Every lifelong friendship goes through seasons, some of them blissful and deeply connected, others distant, confusing, and downright difficult. We all go through tough things in our lives, and those challenges affect our friendships. But hard seasons don't have to be friendship ending. They may push you a little farther apart for a time; they may confuse and confound you for a while; but with grace, prayer, and patience, you may be able to circle back to each other again. Maybe even closer than ever.

My friend Sara and I met when I was fifteen and she was one week past her fourteenth birthday. Ours was a magical, best-friendship-on-first-hang-out kind of connection. We laughed at the same jokes, spoke the same feelings language, even liked the same movies, music, and clothes. Her friendship was one of those rare friendship unicorns that comes along only a handful of times in a lifetime.

But ten years ago, I moved to a new state while having a miscarriage. In a ten-day span of dizzying misery, I was torn away from almost every anchor: family, friends, church, home. I was not okay, not myself, for a long time. Around the same time, Sara also made a dramatic cross-country move. A few months later, she lost her dad unexpectedly.

It was a strange season for us. For the first time, we were in different time zones, which was more challenging than we'd expected. When our schedules did align and we managed a phone call, we tried to support one another, but honestly? Neither of us had as much to give as usual. We were both running on empty. I wish I could have given more to Sara at the time, wish I could have been her go-to, cry-on-the-phone person like I'd always been, but I just couldn't. I'm sure she would have loved to do the same for me, but she couldn't.

The best we could do was stay in touch and pray for each other. We chose to love each other and believe the best about each other during the long, hard slog we were both going through, two thousand miles apart. We both built a few local friendships to fill in the emotional gaps we couldn't meet for each other.

And you know what? We hung in there. We didn't get hurt by each other's lack—we showed each other grace. We didn't even say these words aloud; we just . . . knew that even though we weren't as connected as we'd always been, we'd get there again. We weren't going anywhere. Our friendship was too seasoned, too precious, to lose.

We never did lose it. We wound our way back to each other bit by bit. Three years ago, Sara drove to Los Angeles from San Diego to hang out with me while I was in town on business. We crammed two years of talking into two days. Not long after that, Sara moved to Alaska, and even though the mileage between us doubled, the emotional distance felt cut in half. Last summer, I spent money I didn't really have to fly my entire family across the continent to spend time with Sara's family. The week we spent together was priceless. It not only allowed me and Sara to reconnect, but it also gave our now-teenage children the chance to bond. As I type these words, Sara's thirteen-year-old daughter, Zoe, is in my house hanging out with my thirteen-year-old daughter, Avery.

Don't get discouraged if your friend goes through something you don't understand or are unable to relate to and support the way you wish you could. Don't be threatened if she has to lean on a different friend because they have experiences or gifts you don't have. Just . . . stay. Hang in there. If the friendship is worth it to you, then it's worth wading through, and waiting through, the hard seasons. Lord willing, close friendship will be waiting for you again on the other side. Even if that side is in Alaska.

THE GOD WHO REPAIRS

We've spent most of this chapter talking about the future; let's ease back into the present. We began our book in a place of brokenness, standing over a mess, unsure how to proceed. Have you already begun the work of attempting repair, or are you still praying through your next steps, marshaling your courage? Have you already begun to line up the cracks and drizzle on the glue, but it's still a work in progress, so for now, you're still working with broken? Wherever your friendship is today, I pray God soon ushers you into a place where you're living mended—where even if your friendship isn't yet mended, *you* are.

Our God is the master mender, rebuilder, restorer, redeemer. Centuries ago, he made this promise to his people through the prophet Amos:

> In that day I will restore the fallen house of David.
>   I will repair its damaged walls.
> From the ruins I will rebuild it
>   and restore its former glory.
> AMOS 9:11, NLT

Amos foretold both a fall and a rise. He foresaw a day when God's people would mourn their lost home—a nation overrun, its mighty walls in ruins—but he also prophesied that God wouldn't let the story end that way.

When things fall apart, God shows up, tools in hand. It turns out God is in the repair business. The redemption business. The rebuilding-broken-walls business. The seventy-times-seven-chances business. But most importantly, he's in the hope business. He repairs, rebuilds, and redeems big things like kingdoms, and "small" (but ever-so-important) things like friendships, restoring hope brick by brick and heart by heart.

And astoundingly, when we do life God's way, he makes us like him; we step into the family business of repairing, rebuilding, and restoring:

> If you do away with the yoke of oppression,
>   with the pointing finger and malicious talk . . .
> then your light will rise in the darkness,

and your night will become like the noonday.
The LORD will guide you always;
    he will satisfy your needs in a sun-scorched land
    and will strengthen your frame.
You will be like a well-watered garden,
    like a spring whose waters never fail.
Your people will rebuild the ancient ruins
    and will raise up the age-old foundations;
you will be called Repairer of Broken Walls,
    Restorer of Streets with Dwellings.
ISAIAH 58:9-12

Brokenness was not the end of Israel's story, and it's not the end of yours. God can put you back together, piece by jagged piece. And when he's done his healing work on you, he'll help you share that healing with others.

———

I am cleaning my bedroom, moving junk mail and books off the dresser, and I pause, surprised into stillness. There sits my grandmother's bowl, fully mended, nearly restored to its original glory, happily enjoying[4] a safe home on my high-enough-to-escape-the-perils-of-a-nine-year-old's-cartwheels dresser. The bowl has been there a while, but the object inside the bowl has not. My broken hummingbird figurine is *resting in* my grandmother's bowl.

I'm not sure how the figurine got there, or when—maybe Kevin moved it? maybe one of the kids?—but there it is. And somehow, the bird and bowl look as though they were meant to be together. The bird's delicate body rests sideways inside the bowl, one chipped wing reaching for heaven, the bright eyes aiming high, as if the bird is just catching air, about to take wing. Its perch may be long gone, but thanks to Grandma's bowl, my hummingbird has found a way to fly again.

And as I stand there, it occurs to me: *Broken things can help each*

---

4. I like to think of inanimate objects, especially beloved heirlooms like Grandma's bowl, as having emotions, especially happy ones. Just go with me here. I'm on a metaphorical roll.

other. The repaired bowl needs a special place to do its holding-things work, a place outside the hustle and bustle of a busy household fraught with random acts of clumsy gymnastics. The hummingbird needs a protected place to rest where its remaining features can still soar—and still bring my heart comfort. And so these two imperfect objects have become the perfect pair.

As you head back out into the world of friendships, I pray that you, like my bowl and bird, find the perfect place—and people—to cradle your heart safely. To complement you, cracks and patches and hard-earned life lessons and all. As the Repairer and Restorer continues his good work in you, I pray he helps you to find purpose in your broken-ness. Perhaps the story behind your mended scars—and all the wisdom and compassion you gained along the way—will be exactly the story another broken heart needs to hear. The story it needs to heal, to rest, to test its wings once more. And maybe together, your two broken but mended hearts will be even more beautiful than they ever were apart.

If *broken* was the beginning of your story, let love be the end.

THOUGHT QUESTIONS

1. Take a look at the list of friendships described on pages 235–236. Which type(s) of friendship are easiest for you to cultivate? Which type(s) are more difficult?
2. If you are hoping to find some new friends, which step do you want to take next: praying about your hopes and needs, putting yourself in a position to meet potential new friends, being a little bit brave, or being patient?
3. What does close friendship look like to you?
4. What existing friendship would you like to invest in more? How might you take a step or two toward deepening that relationship?

Epilogue

UN-BROKEN

Let's imagine we're back at the café together, several months later. I'm shocking us both by trying a new drink today, a bulletproof coffee (google it; it's a thing), because I'm realizing that a little change—even if it's just a coffee change—can be good for me.

I ask, "So how are things with the difficult friendship?"

"Still complicated," you say, "but . . . moving in the right direction. In my heart if nothing else."

"That's great," I say. "And how about new friendships? I know it can be tough to put yourself back out there . . . any new prospects?"

You blow steam off the top of your drink and shrug. "I don't know. Maybe."

I take a sip of coconutty, buttery caffeine, pondering the strange joy of new. "I've got another story for you, if you care to hear it."

"Shoot," you say.

THE SOS

I'm lying in a hotel bed, so exhausted the room is spinning, but I am not fooled: sleep will tease and taunt, then run away, laughing. Every time I close my eyes, I relive this evening's conversation, the bizarre argument out of nowhere between people I love. An argument that slashed and drew blood, a wound I fear can never heal.

251

The room spins on, and maybe it's not exhaustion; maybe it's me. Maybe my anchor has been cut loose—all the people, the truths, that have always kept me tethered, safe at harbor, have been severed—and I am drifting, buffeted, lost.

Because it's not just tonight; short months ago, I'd sat through another out-of-nowhere conversation, a punch-in-the-gut disguised as a friendly get-together. And not long before that, others had said, "We love you and believe in you, but we don't want you, don't need you." Add it all together, and my world feels like a forest of thorns; everywhere I turn, I prick and bleed. No safe path, no safe people. Because people are paper—easily torn, easily burned, impermanent—and I am most fragile of all, just waiting for someone to crumple me, toss me aside. Tonight it feels like they already have.

The next morning, Kevin and I drive home from our trip in weighted silence, nothing to say, holding hands as together we drown.

Next day, I robot my way through a day at home, trying to lose myself—find myself—in laundrydishesmoppingparentingemailing-cooking, but as a new night falls, I am still stuck, spiraling down. I need intervention.

The Spirit urges, *Call someone, tell someone, ask for help*—but I can't pick up the phone.

I don't know who to call.

All my safe people are somehow connected to this conflict.

I am an island.

And maybe . . . maybe this past year, all the loss—miscarriage, move, rejection, hurt, depression—maybe it's damaged something inside me.

Maybe *I* am the broken thing.

Those six words, that choking fear, it sparks something inside. A desperate fight, a now-or-never need to kick toward the light, break the surface, find air, breathe; to push through, push past, un-break, survive.

I have to talk to someone. Give voice to this hurt, these fears. Not on the phone, face-to-face.

A new friend's face floats in my mind's eye, as if served up on a Holy Spirit platter, as if he is endorsing her, saying, *Call this one. I've vetted her for you; you can trust her.* I chew my lip. I don't know her all that well yet, not really. We're still learning each other, fumbling around in early I-like-you-do-you-like-me friendship. But she's deep waters like me, honest like me, deep in the Word like me. Those things I know.

Those things will have to be enough.

I pick up the phone.

I send an SOS text, the likes of which I have never sent.

Something happened, and I need to talk to someone. Can you meet me? Today?

Two hours later, we're sitting across from each other at Starbucks.

I'm shaking, holding my coffee two-handed (thank God it's a paper cup, no mug handles to negotiate, but still—two hands). She's looking at me with eyes filled with worry and . . . encouragement. Sympathy.

I take a deep breath and spill the story. I cry, with snot.

And when I finish, I start strapping on my armor, fearing she'll offer some kind of criticism or pasteurized, prepackaged platitude, but she simply says, "I'm so sorry." And somehow, she finds words that make me laugh. And more words that give me hope.

I leave the table with a burden ten thousand pounds lighter, a perspective a little less the-world-is-ending and a little more God-can-help-us-through-this, and a forever place in my heart for a new friend.

I drive home a little less broken.

———

We sit quiet for a moment, you and I, the air between us thick with thoughts once more.

"So . . . are you saying you think *friends* are the answer to broken friendships?" you ask.

I drum my fingers on the table, thinking hard. "I think they can be part of the answer," I say. "God and his grace are The Answer—but he also made us to crave intimacy with other humans. I can't believe I'm saying this, but I think some friends are worth the risks. Some friends—they un-break you."

You make a sound—part gargle, part sigh.

254 | ELIZABETH LAING THOMPSON

"That bad?" I raise an eyebrow.

You grin over your mug. "That scary. But . . . I'm willing to try. At least—I want to be willing to try."

"That's a start. I don't know that I was really ready to open my heart to a new friend that day at Starbucks, but . . . God kind of forced my hand. And that one victory was a breakthrough that set me on a path toward healing."

You blow air out of the corner of your mouth, thinking. "So let's say I was open to this idea . . . this semi-terrifying idea . . . of opening up to someone new. Where would I even start? Friendship feels so much harder at this age."

"Seems like this—right here, today—is a pretty good start. How does any friendship start, really? One conversation, one text, one coffee date at a time. Who can say when all the little moments—the small confessions, silly laughter, shared struggles—grow into something more?"

You nod; we both study our coffee.

After a while, I thread my fingers through my mug's handle and hold it up for a toast. "To friendship?"

You raise yours too, with a hopeful smile. "To friendship."

I lift my mug to my lips; the handle holds firm.

JESUS' PLAN FOR
CONFLICT RESOLUTION

Did you ever make a spit pact with a friend when you were a little kid? You know, you spit in your palm, and they spit in theirs, and you pressed them together, and somehow that meant *friends forever*? (I suspect all of this came to an end thanks to the COVID-19 pandemic, but hey—it was kinda fun if you got to live in the days before we were all germophobic.) Some of those spit pacts came with verbal promises too, promises that became a sort of Kid Code of Friendship Ethics: "I promise I won't tattle. I promise I won't call you names when I'm mad. I promise to pick you first on sports teams."

Spit pacts were serious business.

But you know, maybe our kid selves were on to something. Wouldn't it be nice if, somewhere early in our adult friendships, we made a few promises about how we would work out any conflicts or issues that came up? Because the truth is, even as adults, misunderstandings in friendships are deeply upsetting. We quickly jump to a place of panic, hurt, and disorientation. We're fumbling our way forward in the dark, with only our feelings as an ever-changing compass.

But the Bible has good news for Christians: *You don't have to make things up as you go.* You don't have to feel your way forward in the dark. Jesus knew his followers would have issues from time to time, so he laid out a plan to help us work out conflict!

MATTHEW 18: A STEP-BY-STEP PLAN

If I were to give Matthew 18 a title, it would be, "A Step-by-Step Plan for Working Out Conflict with Other Believers, Plus Some Bonus Material to Help You Understand God's Heart—and Check Your Own." (That's a pretty wordy title, which is probably why God didn't consult me.) Anyway, the point is, Matthew 18 is conflict-resolution *gold*. But many believers aren't familiar with it, so they have yet to benefit from its wisdom.

If you're still early in your friendship fracture, the Lord's practical wisdom in Matthew 18 might help save your friendship. And if you've been living with brokenness (or drifted-ness) for a while, Matthew 18 could help you identify some steps you may have overlooked—steps that might be worth trying even after all this time. Even if it's too late for these insights to help resolve your current situation, perhaps you'll gain some wisdom that will guide and protect you in future difficulties.

We won't reprint all of Matthew 18 in this book, but I highly recommend opening up your Bible and reading the entire chapter so you can grasp the bigger picture. I'd also suggest keeping your Bible open as you work your way through these strategies.

Let's start with Jesus' words in verses 15-17:

> If another believer sins against you, go privately and point
> out the offense. If the other person listens and confesses it,
> you have won that person back. But if you are unsuccessful,
> take one or two others with you and go back again, so that
> everything you say may be confirmed by two or three witnesses.
> If the person still refuses to listen, take your case to the church.
> Then if he or she won't accept the church's decision, treat that
> person as a pagan or a corrupt tax collector.
> MATTHEW 18:15-17, NLT

When we're feeling angry or hurt, it's astounding how quickly "Can I talk to you?" can mushroom to "If that's how you feel, this relationship is *over*!" We may be tempted to rocket from zero to Imminent Nuclear Fallout in a single conversation—but note that in these verses,

Jesus delineates a three-step process of gradual escalation in times of disagreement:

> First try this . . .
> If that doesn't help, do this . . .
> If that doesn't work, do this . . .

Jesus tries to help us avoid melodrama, keep our heads, and conduct ourselves with patience, righteousness, wisdom, and grace. So let's examine each step the Lord has given us one by one.

STEP ONE: GO TO THE PERSON

Verse 15 instructs us, "If another believer sins against you, go privately and point out the offense." We can extract powerful insights by breaking this step down and considering it one phrase and clause at a time:

"If another believer . . ."

In these first three words, we see that Jesus' plan is intended to guide our relationships with *other believers*. We aren't going to be able to apply them perfectly with people who aren't Christians. Non-Christians aren't trying to follow Jesus' ways, so it would be unfair to hold them to his standards. Jesus' directives can still serve as guiding principles in our relationships with unbelievers, but you're probably going to hit some roadblocks, especially once you get to step two.

". . . sins against you . . ."

Jesus seems to be talking specifically about times when people sin against us, not when they hurt our feelings or when we disagree with them on matters of opinion.[1] Admittedly, it can be difficult to tell the differ-

---

1. The Greek word used here is *hamartano*, which in English is usually translated as "sin." It means "to miss the mark; to err, be mistaken; to miss or wander from the path of uprightness and honour, to do or go wrong; to wander from the law of God, violate God's law, sin" (Blue Letter Bible, "Strong's G264 - *hamartano*," accessed May 2, 2022, https://www.blueletterbible.org/lexicon/g264/niv/mgnt/0-1/). It's instructive to note that multiple Bible versions translate this line, "If another believer sins," without including the phrase "against you." It is possible that Jesus' instructions are primarily intended to guide us when we notice sin in another believer's life, and not as a plan for conflict resolution. However, Jesus' principles are certainly helpful in providing godly parameters and steps when sin hurts our relationship with another believer.

ence between sin and hurt feelings—*They hurt my feelings, so isn't that unloving behavior, and isn't unloving behavior a sin?*—but when in doubt, I suggest we adopt the Lord's spirit—a spirit of generosity and grace.[2]

Why is it important to clarify that Jesus' advice here applies best to situations involving sin, not just hurt feelings? Some of us (*slowly raises hand*) are sensitive souls who tend to be easily wounded. A funny look, a sharp tone, a thoughtless word can gut us in an instant. We sensitives may have to learn how to discern which hurts are worth bringing up and which we need to work through (and let go of) on our own. I have learned the hard way that no one wants to be friends with a super-high-maintenance person who needs to discuss hurt feelings every 3.5 days—most people don't enjoy walking on eggshells. So I've had to work on myself and my thinking. When I feel hurt, I ask myself, *Is this a small matter I can cover with grace in the spirit of Proverbs 19:11: "A person's wisdom yields patience; it is to one's glory to overlook an offense"?* I've also learned to go back and mentally revise some of my responses, like so:

> *That off-kilter interaction between us wasn't a big deal.*
> *That comment wasn't directed at me.*
> *Everyone gets hangry and snippy sometimes.*
> *I took that joke the wrong way.*

Over time I've learned to view others—and myself—through a filter of grace and even a healthy sense of humor.

". . . go privately and point out the offense."
Let's finish up verse 15. Most likely, if you have a broken friendship, sin has happened on one or both sides, and one (or both) of you has a legitimate grievance against the other. That means the last part of verse 15 applies. If another believer sins against us, Jesus calls us to *talk to the person privately*. Directly. One-on-one.

In Jesus' day, conversations could only happen one way: in person.[3]

---

2. I suspect Paul and Barnabas's disagreement in Acts 15 landed in the realm of opinion. Scripture remains silent on who was right and who was wrong, which seems to hint that they both had valid points to make, and neither man was in sin. They just saw the situation differently.
3. I mean, I guess technically they might be able to send a letter, but . . . those could take a zillion years to be delivered, and they might not get there anyway.

Can we pause for a second to celebrate the beautiful simplicity and clarity of face-to-face conversations? The kind of conversation where we can read each other's facial expressions and body language, see the tears in a friend's eyes, hear the insecurity and kindness and regret in their voice (all things that help to soften our hearts and increase our empathy), and then hug it out at the end?

How many fights get worse, not better, when we try to text them out? *Why isn't there a period after that "no"? And—no emoji? Not even an upside-down smiley face? What does it all meeeeeeeeean? She sounds really mad.*

Um, did you notice the absurdity of that last sentence: "She sounds really mad"? How can someone "sound" mad in a text? *Texts have no vocal inflection!* Texting is a woefully inadequate form of communication, and can we please acknowledge that some people (ahem, Kevin, you are the love of my life, but I'm totally writing about you) are Texting Impaired? Some couples have adorable lovey-dovey text relationships that make me swoon, throw up a little in my mouth, and feel a little envious all at once: *Oh, Shmoopsy-Poo, my beautiful love, can you please pick up some milk on your way home from work? [Heart-eyes emoji.]* Me and Kevin? If I based our marriage on the expressiveness and passion in his text messages, we would need emergency marriage counseling at least twice a month. Our text exchanges work more like this:

Me: Hope you're having a great day! Would you mind picking up some milk on the way home, pretty please with a cherry on top? [Heart emoji.]

Kevin: Yes.

Me: Wait, yes you mind, or yes, you'll do it? [Squinty-eyed emoji.]

Kevin: Yes I'll get milk.

Me: Okay, thanks! You're the best! [Kissy-face emoji.]

Kevin: [Nothing.]

I have accepted this subpar aspect of our marriage; it seems digital aloofness is the price I pay for being married to in-person awesomeness, and I'm okay with that. It won't surprise you to learn that I never, ever try to work out a problem with Kevin via text message.

And that leads us to a potentially life-changing-and-relationship-saving Public Service Announcement: please don't attempt to communicate frustration, hurt feelings, or your thoughts about a conflict in a text message. Ever. Not one single time. *It will blow up in your face.*

"What about email?" you ask. I'm glad you asked. I suggest we apply similar rules to email. Email is not the ideal way to work out issues with people, though I will concede that if you struggle to express yourself clearly and fair-mindedly in person, sometimes it can be helpful to write out your thoughts, particularly in professional settings. However, please remember this: like texting, email doesn't provide the oh-so-important facial expressions and vocal inflections that help communicate our true emotions and intents. And as awful-cynical as this sounds, keep in mind that an email can easily be forwarded, copied, and shared without your permission. If you would be uncomfortable with anyone besides your intended recipient reading your words, don't put your words into an email.

Bottom line, when a friend sins against us, Jesus says that our first effort should be to arrange a private "Hey, can I talk to you?" moment— in person if possible. If speaking in person isn't possible, try the next best, most personal option: a video chat or phone call.

Can we also briefly pause to *amen* Jesus' wisdom in going directly to the person—not *around* the person? How many misunderstandings become worse because an upset person talks to other people—and suddenly a simple misunderstanding becomes a Big Thing, a he-said, she-said thing, in which people are taking sides. Jesus says to go *privately* to the person to discuss what happened.

Now, we have noted that some of us struggle to discern the difference between times when we are just being overly sensitive and times when another person has done something we need to address. If that's you, it might be wise to seek counsel from a neutral, godly party to say, "Hey, am I on the right track here, or do I need to drop this?" But please be careful whom you choose as your adviser, and be honest with yourself about your intentions. If your goal is just to gossip, vent, or feel validated in your position, then please pray through those feelings instead. Take a breath or ten, and when you have calmed down, go directly to the person who hurt you.

One other caveat: sometimes we know we need to talk to someone, but we truly don't know what to say or how to broach the issue wisely. If you have a godly, neutral person in your life who can advise you on your approach *without taking sides or complicating the issue*, such advice could be invaluable in helping your conversation go well. But ideally, your first step should be to go to the other person privately, without bringing another person into it.

HELPFUL MINDSETS FOR TRICKY CONVERSATIONS

Let's camp out on step one a bit longer, because if we can get step one right, we might never have to move on to step two, and we can stop conflicts from escalating into breakups. Here are a few principles you may find helpful if you need to approach a friend to discuss a wrong:

Ask questions instead of making accusations or assumptions.
Assume the best about your friend, and when you ask questions, choose language that gives them the benefit of the doubt. Instead of, "You left me hanging when you forgot about our plans," try asking, "Is everything okay with you? It's unlike you to miss things." Instead of, "You talked about me behind my back!" try asking, "I heard something that made me feel weird, but I wanted to ask you about it before I made any assumptions. Could you clarify what happened for me?"

Try saying, "The story I'm telling myself is . . ."
I learned this gem of a line from a college student I once mentored (proving yet again that mentoring is a gift to both parties!). Like me, when Hannah gets insecure or anxious, her imagination takes over, creating not-always-rational scenarios. But instead of assuming her imaginings to be true, Hannah has learned to go directly to the other person

and say, "Okay, I started feeling insecure after xyz happened. The story I'm telling myself is . . ."[4] This vulnerability lets your friends in on your internal dialogue, including your insecurities, and gives them a chance to clarify or even contradict the things your imagination is telling you. This phrasing prevents your friend from getting defensive because it puts the focus on *you* rather than *placing blame* on the other person.

Watch your pronouns when you have conflict.

Use *I* instead of *you*—focus on how you felt rather than what the person did, to avoid making accusations.

Instead of, "You didn't call me, which was really rude since you knew it was important to me, and you made me feel worthless," try saying, "I was waiting for your call, and I felt really sad when you didn't call. Did you know how important it was to me?"

Remember that most people are not intentionally vindictive or cruel. They are doing the best they can with the information they have.

My favorite part of the famous passage in 1 Corinthians 13 is two words in verse 7: love "always trusts." In my mind, "trusts" means that love assumes the best about others. Love gives people the benefit of the doubt. It doesn't jump to the worst-case-scenario conclusion but defers judgment (and hurt) until the other person has had a chance to clarify.

If we go into conversations expecting to encounter a friend with good intentions, integrity, and a kind heart, we will keep the temperature of the conversation down. We won't begin the conversation at DEFCON 1, aka imminent warfare. We won't start off by launching unfair accusations and leaving our friend feeling cornered and mistrusted.

Assume your friend wants to respond the right way.

Ever played out a conversation like this in your mind?

> Me to my friend (in my imagination): "You said this, and it hurt my feelings."

---

4. Although I heard this phrase from my friend Hannah, it was popularized by Brené Brown.

Friend to me: "Why don't you toughen up? You're way too sensitive. I hate it when you act like this."

Me to myself (trying not to cry in my imagination): *So I guess I shouldn't share the other thing that was bothering me, or she'll really think I'm too sensitive.*

Friend: "Speaking of sensitive, I've got a list of fifteen things you've done lately that I'm mad about. I'm not sure we can still be friends."

How tempting it is to hold phantom fights in our minds. We play out multiple versions of conversations with a person who has hurt us, filling in imaginary responses on their behalf. Most of the time, we fill in their part with unkindness, impatience, and defensiveness. These imaginary arguments do nothing to resolve the situation and everything to make us feel worse.

But this person is (or used to be) a friend, which suggests they have some positive qualities. So why not assume she is going to respond humbly and receptively? That way you won't go into the conversation pre-angry—that is, preemptively angry for things you're afraid they *might* say (but haven't actually said). You won't go into the conversation with your defenses up, your snippy comebacks preloaded and ready to launch. Here's where 1 Corinthians 13:7 can guide us once more: "Love never gives up, never loses faith, is always hopeful, and endures through every circumstance" (NLT).

Pray for the Spirit to bring unity.

A few years ago, I started praying something like this before I went into complicated conversations with other Christians: "Dear God, I know the Spirit wants us to be united even more than I do, and he lives in me and in this other person as well. Please let him speak to us both, calling our hearts in the right direction so we can work this out in a way that pleases you. I invite him to teach us, guide us, and change us. Please bring us closer to unity in him through this conversation." What a difference that prayer has made! The Spirit wants unity above all else, and he is eager to help us attain it. The more we invite him to participate in our conversations, the more active he becomes.

Trust that God is working on both of your hearts.

You may not come to perfect agreement at the end of your initial conversation, but that's okay. You can still be unified in Christ and at peace with one another, respecting your differences of opinion. You are both a work in progress, and God will continue to reveal new insights and reshape you both over time. I draw comfort from Paul's words in Philippians 3:

> All of us, then, who are mature should take such a view of things. And if on some point you think differently, that too God will make clear to you. Only let us live up to what we have already attained.
> PHILIPPIANS 3:15-16

Some Christians thought differently than the apostle Paul, but Paul was at peace with that. He didn't try to hammer his perspective into other people's hearts; he stepped back and allowed God to work.

STEP TWO: TAKE ONE OR TWO OTHERS

So let's say you've tried step one—you went directly to your friend, but the conversation didn't go well. You're still stuck. You still disagree. Someone's still hurt or mad (or both). What now? Again, it may be too late for these thoughts to apply to the friendship breakup you are grappling with, in which case you may want to file this study under the "helpful guidelines for future conflict" in your heart. But if you are still figuring things out, still in a place where resolution or reconciliation might be possible, I pray you'll find help from Jesus' words. We find step two of Jesus' plan for conflict resolution in verse 16 of our Matthew passage:

> But if you are unsuccessful, take one or two others with you and go back again, so that everything you say may be confirmed by two or three witnesses.
> MATTHEW 18:16, NLT

At this point, Jesus says it's time to bring in help. It's time to sit down and have a conversation with one or two people you both trust.

Jesus is *not* saying, "It's time to go talk to one or two other people in order to vent to them. It's time to gossip and recruit some people to your side." We don't bring other people into the conversation just to feel validated; we bring them in to listen to *both* sides and arbitrate.

We get a glimpse of step two in action in the early church through a comment the apostle Paul made in his letter to the church in Philippi:

> Now I appeal to Euodia and Syntyche. Please, because you
> belong to the Lord, settle your disagreement. And I ask you,
> my true partner, to help these two women, for they worked
> hard with me in telling others the Good News. They worked
> along with Clement and the rest of my co-workers, whose
> names are written in the Book of Life.
>
> PHILIPPIANS 4:2-3, NLT

Imagine how it must have felt to be Euodia or Syntyche, unexpectedly finding your name called out in Paul's letter: blazing ears, flaming cheeks, that stomach-twisting *please-can-I-melt-into-the-floor* feeling . . . Theirs must have been a doozy of a disagreement to make it through the "church news pipeline" all the way to Paul's ears.

Paul pleads with the two women to work things out—in the NIV, his plea is translated, "Be of the same mind in the Lord." When we serve Christ, we invite Christ to direct our thoughts, opinions, and goals, which should usually lead us to a place of peace and unity. But note that Paul also asks a spiritual friend to help these women work out their conflict. He calls on a church leader to sit down with these women to help them talk through their issues—to exercise step two of Jesus' guidelines.

If you and your friend are members of the same church fellowship, perhaps you can seek support from a mature Christian friend, small-group leader, godly mentor, pastor, or Christian counselor. Ask them to sit down with you together, hear out your disagreement, and help you come to a place of better understanding and forgiveness. If you aren't in the same church family, perhaps you share a mutual relationship with a believer you both trust, and you can invite them to arbitrate your conversation.

STEP THREE: BRING IT TO THE CHURCH

So what do we do if a person has sinned but will not listen to anyone? Jesus allows one last step:

> If they still refuse to listen, tell it to the church; and if they refuse to listen even to the church, treat them as you would a pagan or a tax collector.
> MATTHEW 18:17

I'll be honest: I have rarely seen this step applied as Jesus described it—only a handful of times. Public church discipline is complicated, particularly with the way most modern people "do church." Again, let's remember that Jesus is not referring to situations where opinions differ or feelings have been hurt; he is referring to situations where sin is involved. Step three is an extreme measure that Jesus applies specifically to situations where a person is engaging in some sinful behavior and refusing to repent—hence the need to explain to the church, "This person has claimed to be a follower of Christ but is refusing to follow the Lord's ways in this area, and so we need to take note of their behavior."

Perhaps we can find clarification in observing how the apostle Paul applied these principles in the church in Corinth:

> I wrote to you in my letter not to associate with sexually immoral people—not at all meaning the people of this world who are immoral, or the greedy and swindlers, or idolaters. In that case you would have to leave this world. But now I am writing to you that you must not associate with anyone who claims to be a brother or sister but is sexually immoral

or greedy, an idolater or slanderer, a drunkard or swindler. Do not even eat with such people.

What business is it of mine to judge those outside the church? Are you not to judge those inside? God will judge those outside. "Expel the wicked person from among you."
1 CORINTHIANS 5:9-13

Paul encourages the church to confront, expose, and remove fellowship from any brothers and sisters who engage in serious sin and an unwillingness to repent. If people want to be members of the body of Christ, they must live by Christ's rules. They cannot claim to be members of Christ while continuing to live in hypocrisy and deliberate sin. (It's also important to note that while Paul preached a hard line about righteousness and fellowship, he also showed a lot of grace in practice. In a later letter to the same church, 2 Corinthians, Paul urges the church to welcome a repentant brother back into the church family after a period of separation, and "to forgive and comfort him, so that he will not be overwhelmed by excessive sorrow" [see 2 Corinthians 2:5-11]).

Paul makes it clear that these rules do not apply to those outside the church. We are not necessarily called to remove fellowship from someone who is outside Christ and does not live as a Christian—that would be an unfair expectation. Remember that Jesus frequently ate with tax collectors and sinners—"I have not come to call the righteous, but sinners," he said, when religious leaders criticized him for hanging out with sinful people (Matthew 9:13).

How Jesus' instructions apply to your broken friendship I could not say, but I pray they give you food for thought. I pray they help you discern the difference in the kinds of fellowship and friendship we can expect from believers as opposed to unbelievers. If your friendship has reached a point where some kind of break may be necessary, I encourage you to weigh your decision in prayer and with counsel from church leadership or a godly adviser. (See also chapter 12, "When You Need a Break," for more thoughts on separation.)

PETER'S RESPONSE

I love that halfway through Matthew 18, the author takes a little break from Jesus' instructions to show us Peter's response to Jesus' words. Peter asks about forgiveness: "Lord, how many times shall I forgive my brother or sister who sins against me? Up to seven times?" (Matthew 18:21). We touched on this story in chapter 7, "The Path to Healing"; let's dig in a little deeper here.

The rule follower in me adores Peter for trying to commit Jesus to a precise number. Isn't that what we try to do with the Lord too—"Hey, she's already hurt me six times, so . . . that's enough, right? She's used up all her chances, and I'm allowed to be done with this relationship after the next time, right, Lord? *Right?*"

You can feel Peter trying to wrap his heart around what Jesus said, just as you and I have been wrestling with his words. It seems that Peter was trying to be generous and noble in his response. Seven times was a *lot* of times even if we take the number at face value, but as we have already observed, seven is also a symbolic number in Jewish thought, representing perfection or completion. (Admittedly, it's possible Peter was also showing off for the other disciples, trying to one-up them in his "righteousness.")

But Jesus one-ups Peter . . . or maybe we should say he seventy-seven-times-ups Peter: "I tell you, not seven times, but seventy-seven times" (Matthew 18:22). Jesus is basically saying, "Whatever you think is complete and perfect, multiply it by *God's* version of perfection. God calls you to waaaaaay more forgiveness than you think you can handle." And then, as Jesus so often did when trying to make a point, he tells Peter a story, the parable of the unmerciful servant.

THE PARABLE OF THE UNMERCIFUL SERVANT

Matthew 18 closes with the story of a servant whose master forgave him a debt of an astronomical amount of money (think millions of dollars). A staggering act of you-have-your-life-back-again grace. What did the servant do? You'd think he would run home and hug the whole world, trying his best to pay forward the astounding grace and kindness he had received.

Nope.

When the servant went home, he found a man who owed him a pittance (think lunch money) and threw the man into jail until he could pay back the few dollars he owed.

When the master heard about the servant's greed and lack of mercy, he raged, "You evil servant! I forgave you that tremendous debt because you pleaded with me. Shouldn't you have mercy on your fellow servant, just as I had mercy on you?" (Matthew 18:32-33, NLT). Then the king sent the servant to prison to be tortured until he had paid his entire debt.

Jesus concludes the story with this sobering warning: "That's what my heavenly Father will do to you if you refuse to forgive your brothers and sisters from your heart" (Matthew 18:35, NLT).

Deep breaths. It's a lot to swallow—and it's meant to be. In this story, let us remember that *we* are the servant who has had a devastating debt lifted. We never could have forgiven ourselves, never wiped our own sin-slate clean. We were doomed to wander this world shouldering the crushing weight of shame from our pride, lust, greed, selfishness, and rebellion. Our own hearts were bleeding from self-inflicted wounds that never could heal. But God stepped in to pay the price for us. To bleed and die in our place. He didn't just erase our sins, leaving the ghost of the marks on the page; he snatched the page out of our hands and burned it to ash. "As far as the east is from the west," he took our sins away. "As high as the heavens are above the earth," he lifted the guilt from our shoulders (Psalm 103:11-12).

We could never apologize enough.

We could never thank him enough.

We could never work off this debt.

We didn't deserve it, yet here we stand, forgiven and free.

We are called to do the same for others.

Whether or not they apologize or deserve it.

Let's remember this when we are tempted to withhold forgiveness from others.

After Jesus laid out his plan for conflict resolution, he went on to say,

> I also tell you this: If two of you agree here on earth concerning anything you ask, my Father in heaven will do it for you. For where two or three gather together as my followers, I am there among them.
>
> MATTHEW 18:19-20, NLT

Where two or three gather, I am there among them. When we come together in Jesus' name—even when we come together to attempt to resolve a misunderstanding—he is there in the room with us. Even if the only thing we can agree on is that we long to *find a way to agree* with one another, the Father is with us, and he is working to bring about what we ask. In faith, let us leave room for God to work—and people to change.

Let's close our study by remembering Jesus' prayer the night before he died. His suffering was impending, his heart overwhelmed with anguish and dread, but Jesus took time to pray about future believers (that's us)—specifically, to beg God to help us get along:

> My prayer is not for [my disciples] alone. I pray also for those who will believe in me through their message, that all of them may be one, Father, just as you are in me and I am in you. May they also be in us so that the world may believe that you have sent me. I have given them the glory that you gave me, that they may be one as we are one—I in them and you in me— so that they may be brought to complete unity. Then the world will know that you sent me and have loved them even as you have loved me.
>
> JOHN 17:20-23

I quote this prayer not to shame us but to remind us how precious, how difficult, unity is. When we fight for it and attain it, what a testimony we are to this divided world, so splintered by hatred and fear.

When we forge unity, what does Jesus say happens? "*Then* the world will know that you sent me and have loved them even as you have loved me" (verse 23, emphasis added). When people see us loving each other through our differences, in spite of our differences, to the other side of our differences, they can't help but exclaim, "God is in these people!" Our hard-fought unity testifies that Jesus is real and God is love. There is no greater miracle.

ACKNOWLEDGMENTS

Every book you write takes you on a different emotional journey, and this journey was . . . well, I'm not gonna lie—it was kind of intense. What a sobering privilege it was to be entrusted with other people's difficult friendship stories. I am thankful to each person who shared their experiences with me. May God honor your generosity, humility, and courage, and may he use your pain to comfort and help others.

I am grateful to God for helping me hold the weight of these stories and visit some challenging places in my memory, heart, and in his Word. Thank you, Father, for your strength, guiding hand, and faithful presence.

My family has been a tremendous source of support. I can't thank Kevin enough for all the times he spoke confidence and courage into me, for fully embracing all the time and energy it took to write and revise this book, and for understanding why this work mattered, even when it brought up tough memories. Kevin, thank you for all the times you cook, clean, chauffeur kids, and [insert a thousand other acts of service and kindness here] to give me the time and space I need to do my work. What a blessing it is to have you as my friend and partner in life. And thank you to my kids for understanding and supporting the demands of my job—for not complaining when I have to write, for praying for me and asking me how it's going, and for celebrating the milestones along the way.

I couldn't juggle the demands of writing and family life without the unflagging support of my gracious in-laws, Bill and Glenda. Thank you so much for shuttling kids around town, having us over for dinner, and helping me and Kevin have date nights even when life gets hectic.

My parents, siblings, and siblings-in-law were so supportive. Huge thanks to Mom and Alexandra for hearing me out day after day as I processed all the ideas and feelings. Thank you for so generously offering your wisdom, perspective, and experiences.

My writing partner and best friend, Emma, gave me desperately needed guidance at crucial moments along the way. Thank you for lending me your unique blend of compassion, integrity, grace, biblical wisdom, and real-life practicality, coupled with your unparalleled talent as a writer.

I love doing life with my local church, especially my small group. Thank you for checking on me often, overlooking my hat-head-meets-sweatpants phases, and faithfully praying me through this book. Your encouragement and prayers meant more than I can say.

I am deeply thankful to the Whitaker family for allowing me to stay at your beautiful home for several writing getaways. Those stays allowed me to detach from daily responsibility and immerse myself in prayer, the Word, and these words, and this book wouldn't have come together without those times.

Thank you to my agent, Ingrid Beck, for being a compassionate sounding board and expert guide. I'm so grateful for all the ways you look out for all your authors—you truly have our best interests at heart, and I always feel safe and well cared for in your capable hands.

It is such a privilege to work with the amazing team at Tyndale. Jillian Schlossberg, thank you for seeing the need for this book and fighting to make it happen. Thank you for allowing me to collaborate with you throughout the entire process—you excel at respecting authors' opinions and feelings, and you invite us to have meaningful involvement in every aspect of the publishing process. Thank you for giving me the freedom to tell stories and write outside the box, and thank you for wholly offering the full force of your compassionate and insightful heart to all you do.

Ginormous thanks to my developmental editor, Debbie King—you had your work cut out for you! Thank you for the patient, expert guidance, especially as we reverse engineered my Big Last-Minute Ideas. (Please remind me not to have late-in-the-game ideas again, ha!) I don't know that I've ever needed more help figuring out how to structure a book and its themes—thank you for having the vision and skill to help me untangle a big pile of creative ideas and knit them into a cohesive and coherent whole. And thank you for always adding an emoji or two to your emails. ;-)

Many thanks to Alyssa Clements for all the support you provided along the way; it is a joy working with you, and I so appreciate your heart and hard work.

Ron Kaufmann, the cover is stunning. Thank you for somehow hearing and understanding what I love in design even when I didn't know how to describe it. Thank you for capturing the gentleness, compassion, and *hope* I want readers to feel from the moment they pick up this book.

Thank you to Laura Cruise for the beautiful interior design—it is elegant and classic. Many thanks to Kimberly Hutson for your outstanding work typesetting, and to Claire Lloyd for catching all the errors that would have driven my perfectionist self to utter insanity had they escaped notice. Thank you to Brianna Coyle and Megan Alexander for all you have done to help this message get out there—I'd be lost without the gift of your gifts.

I am always astounded by the skill and heart the Tyndale marketing team pours into helping books find their way into the hands of the readers who need them. Cassidy Gage, thank you for the hours and skill you have devoted to helping this book find its place in the world.

Amanda Woods, thank you for making the work of publicity an adventure and joy. You make every little step, even the parts where work is involved, feel like fun in disguise. I adore working with you!

And if you've read all the way to the end of this book, including the acknowledgments—you've just made my writer's heart beyond happy. Thank you for taking a moment to celebrate and appreciate all these worthy people with me. It's been a privilege sharing all the talent they have poured into these pages with you.

ABOUT THE AUTHOR

Elizabeth Laing Thompson is a speaker, a novelist, and the author of many inspirational books for women and teens, including *All the Feels*, *All the Feels for Teens*, and the When God Says series. She writes to help others find hope when they're waiting, help when they're hurting, and humor in holiness. Her work has appeared in numerous outlets, including Proverbs 31, *Power for Living*, *Focus on the Family* magazine, and *Brio* magazine.

After a long struggle with infertility, Elizabeth and her husband, Kevin, became the always exhausted but totally grateful parents of four children, three of whom are now teenagers. When she's not inhaling Starbucks mochas and plotting her next book, Elizabeth works from home as an editor and church volunteer (that's code for "pastor's wife"), and as a snack maker, couch snuggler, laundry slayer, floor mopper, not-so-gourmet chef, and interpreter-slash-counselor of teenage feelings. She prays the lessons she is learning, trying to wrestle Christ into the chaos of daily life, will give others hope, practical help, and a lot of good laughs.

BY ELIZABETH LAING THOMPSON

All the Feels

All the Feels for Teens

When God Says No

When God Says Go

When God Says Go: A Devotional Thought Journal

When God Says Wait

When God Says Wait: A Devotional Thought Journal

The Thirteenth Summer

The Tender Years: Parenting Preschoolers